Relational Ethics in Practice

CW01510527

Relational Ethics in Practice presents a new collection of narratives on ethics in day-to-day therapeutic practice. Highly experienced professionals from a range of roles in the therapeutic professions explore ways of developing ethical and effective relationships. The contributors provide the reader with engaging and informative narratives that indicate how ethics can inform and influence practice in a variety of clinical contexts across the helping professions. These personal and professional narratives will encourage people to think more proactively about ethics and the impact that they have on both therapeutic practice and life in general.

Throughout this book, Lynne Gabriel, Roger Casemore and their contributors emphasise that the consideration of the ethical dimension is of paramount importance to successful processes and outcomes in every therapeutic relationship. Chapters cover a number of topics including:

- how theoretical approaches can inform ethical decision making and practice
- practical difficulties and ethical challenges
- innovative and unconventional approaches
- informed consent across various contexts
- pointers for good practice
- the notion of the 'wounded healer'.

Relational Ethics in Practice: Narratives from Counselling and Psychotherapy will appeal to a wide range of readers involved in the helping professions including counsellors, psychotherapists, researchers, supervisors and trainees.

Lynne Gabriel is a Reader in Counselling and Relational Ethics at York St John University, York and is Head of Postgraduate and Post-Experience Counselling Studies at the University. Lynne is former Chair of the British Association for Counselling and Psychotherapy's (BACP) Professional Conduct Committee and was elected as Chair of BACP from October 2008.

Roger Casemore is a Senior Teaching Fellow and Director of Counselling and Psychotherapy Courses at Warwick University.

Relational Ethics in Practice

Narratives from Counselling
and Psychotherapy

Edited by Lynne Gabriel and
Roger Casemore

Routledge
Taylor & Francis Group

LONDON AND NEW YORK

First published 2009
by Routledge
27 Church Road, Hove, East Sussex BN3 2FA

Simultaneously published in the USA and Canada
by Routledge
270 Madison Avenue, New York NY 10016

*Routledge is an imprint of the Taylor & Francis Group,
an Informa business*

Typeset in Times by
RefineCatch Limited, Bungay, Suffolk
Printed and bound in Great Britain by
TJ International Ltd, Padstow, Cornwall
Paperback cover design by Jim Wilkie

This publication has been produced with paper manufactured to
strict environmental standards and with pulp derived from
sustainable forests.

British Library Cataloguing in Publication Data
A catalogue record for this book is available from the British Library

Library of Congress Cataloging-in-Publication Data
Relational ethics in practice : narratives from counselling and
psychotherapy / edited by Lynne Gabriel and Roger Casemore.
    p. cm.
  Includes bibliographical references and index.
  1. Counselling–Moral and ethical aspects. 2. Psychotherapy–
Moral and ethical aspects. I. Gabriel, Lynne. II. Casemore, Roger.
  BF636.67.R45 2009
  174′.91583–dc22

                             2008027871

ISBN: 978–0–415–42591–9 (hbk)
ISBN: 978–0–415–42592–6 (pbk)

For Pat

For Ruth

Contents

Figures, tables and boxes

FIGURES

TABLES

BOXES

Contributors

Dr Aaron Balick is a UKCP registered integrative psychotherapist working in private practice. In addition to his clinical work he is a trainer and lecturer in several higher education settings in London. Aaron also works as a mental health writer and media contributor through various platforms including BBC online, radio and television alongside his role as a media spokesperson for the UKCP. He has a special interest in relational psychoanalysis and psychotherapy and is a founding member of The Relational School UK.

Roger Casemore is a Senior Teaching Fellow and Director of Counselling and Psychotherapy Courses at Warwick University. He has been an active member of the British Association for Counselling and Psychotherapy since its inception and was Chair of the Association from 1982 to 1985. He is currently a member of the Professional and Ethical Practice Committee. Roger has maintained a private psychotherapy practice for over 40 years and runs his own consultancy company specialising in organisational development and the management of change. He is a Fellow of BACP and a Chartered Fellow of the Chartered Institute of Personnel and Development and his work has been published widely, with his most recent publication being *Person-Centred Counselling in a Nutshell*.

Dr Subodh Dave is a Consultant Psychiatrist in General Adult Psychiatry, working with the Derbyshire Mental Health NHS Trust. He is also a Clinical Teaching Fellow at Derby Medical School, University of Nottingham. He did his basic medical training in Mumbai, India and has been in the UK since 1995. After achieving the membership of the Royal College of Psychiatrists, he worked as a Clinical Research Fellow at the University of Birmingham studying the genetics of depression. He has a keen interest in neuropsychiatry and consultation-liaison psychiatry which is complemented by his involvement with the philosophy of psychiatry.

Dr Alan Dunnett is Head of Counselling Studies at York St John University. He chaired the national consortium which defined the core curriculum in counsellor education for the British Association for Counselling and Psychotherapy. His research interests lie in the areas of constructs of mental and emotional health, and in exploring characteristics of healthy communities. A counsellor educator for over two decades, he is currently co-editing a text bringing together perspectives on professional education within a rapidly changing social, political and regulatory context.

Kim Etherington is a Professor of Narrative and Life Story Research, Fellow of BACP and BACP senior accredited counsellor and supervisor. Alongside her private practice she co-ordinates, tutors and supervises dissertations on the MSc in Counselling (Research Unit) and undertakes doctoral supervision and research at the University of Bristol, UK. She has published seven books and many journal articles based on research interest ideas drawn from her teaching at the university and practice as a counsellor, supervisor, consultant and trainer in voluntary and statutory organisations, especially in the field of trauma, abuse and health. She is particularly interested in using collaborative and reflexive methodologies and in using narratives as a means of understanding human experiences and lives.

Dr Lynne Gabriel is a Reader in Counselling and Relational Ethics at York St John University, York, UK. At York St John University, Lynne is Head of Postgraduate Counselling Studies Programmes, leads the MA Counselling Studies programme and supervises PhD counselling students. Lynne is a Fellow of BACP and has been an active member of BACP since 1998, through committee membership and chair roles. Lynne has presented at national and international conferences and published practice guidelines and papers on ethical practice. Her textbook on dual and multiple role relationships in therapy, *Speaking the Unspeakable: The Ethics of Dual Relationships in Counselling and Psychotherapy*, is published by Routledge. Her research interests include relational and practice ethics, research and researcher ethics, qualitative research methods, client perspectives on therapy and therapists, supervision and spirituality.

Dr Peter Jenkins is a Senior Lecturer at Salford University, consultant and trainer. Peter has published widely in the field of counselling and the law. He also co-authored a best-selling textbook on counselling children and young people. Peter regularly presents at UK and international conferences.

Nic Neath is an integrative counsellor working for the Baobab Centre in York and in a university student counselling service. Nic has an interest in creative techniques, power dynamics, and difference and diversity. She has a background in retail management, business and community project administration and voluntary sector training. A developing existential and phenomenological aspect of Nic's therapeutic practice arises from her academic studies in literature and philosophy.

Dr Jeremy Tudway is a chartered clinical and forensic psychologist and cognitive behavioural practitioner with an independent practice, Phoenix Psychological Services. He specialises in work with clients presenting with long-standing personality and severe mental health problems and with clients who have a history of offending behaviour both in the community and in secure settings. Dr Tudway has taught post-graduate level Clinical Psychology as a tutor on the Coventry and Warwick Universities Doctoral Programme in Clinical Psychology; Forensic Psychology at the University of Birmingham, and as an external examiner in clinical psychology at the University of Exeter. He teaches the CBT module on the Diploma in Person-centred Counselling and Psychotherapy and teaches on the Advanced Diploma in Cognitive Behavioural Practice for Person-centred Counsellors, at the University of Warwick.

Dr Moira Walker is a registered psychotherapist and Fellow of BACP. She lives in Dorset and practises as a psychotherapist, trainer and supervisor. She has worked in universities, the voluntary sector and in health and social services settings. She has worked with survivors of abuse for many years and written widely, particularly on the subject of abuse, but has also co-edited two major series of books on counselling and therapy. Her publications include 'Supervising practitioners working with survivors of childhood abuse: counter transference, secondary traumatization and terror' (*Psychodynamic Practice*, May 2004); *Questions of Abuse* (Wiley); *Hidden Selves: An Exploration of Multiple Personality* and *Surviving Secrets: The Experience of Abuse for the Child, the Adult and the Helper* (Open University Press).

Dr William West, PhD is a Reader in Counselling Studies at the University of Manchester, UK where he is Director of the Counselling Studies Programme and delights in supervising doctoral students. He is a Fellow and accredited practitioner member of the British Association for Counselling and Psychotherapy. William's key areas of research and publication include: counselling and spirituality, culture, traditional healing, supervision and qualitative research methods.

Dr Val Wosket was formerly a Senior Lecturer in Counselling at York St John University and now works in private practice as a psychotherapist and supervisor at the York Clinic for Complementary Medicine. Her publications include: *Egan's Skilled Helper Model: Developments and Applications in Counselling*; *The Therapeutic Use of Self: Counselling Practice, Research and Supervision* and *Supervising the Counsellor: A Cyclical Model* (with Steve Page). Val is a UKRCP Registered Independent Counsellor and is BACP Senior Accredited as a counsellor/psychotherapist, supervisor and trainer. She has particular interest and experience in working with complex trauma and dissociation and is a member of the teaching faculty of the UK section of the European Society for Trauma and Dissociation (ESTD-UK).

Acknowledgements

Both authors wish to thank the chapter contributors for their inspiring and informative chapters and for delivering their work to us on time.

We recognise and cherish the myriad ways in which our students, clients, supervisees and colleagues inform our thinking and work – as well as the many people we meet in workshop and conference settings. We thank you all for your influence and generous contributions to our thinking.

We also wish to acknowledge the cherished love and support of family and friends, as well as the valued support of colleagues in our respective workplaces.

In particular, Roger wants to say: thank you to Lynne for the experience of a new and very collaborative partnership. Thanks to my wife, Ruth, for her constant support and for giving me the space and time to do this. Extra thanks to Mary Sutton at Warwick and Jean Aaron-Walker and David Morgan in Shetland for their advice, guidance and encouragement.

In particular, Lynne would like to thank Roger for his support and collaborative work on the book. A special thank you goes to Pat for her love, support and encouragement. Thank you to parents, Jean and Syd Pearson and brother, Paul Pearson; to Elaine Parker, Avril Gornall, Jill and Ian Overfield. Lynne valued the support of colleagues in the Faculty of Business and Communication at York St John University: in particular, Diana Wetherell-Terry, Jackie Mathers, Alan Dunnett and Lindsay Smith. Lynne would also like to thank Latilla Woodburn and Betty Harrison – two truly amazing women.

We would both like to acknowledge and thank David Britten for his contribution. Finally, we wish to thank the staff at Routledge, in particular Joanne Forshaw, Senior Editor and Jane Harris, Senior Editorial Assistant – thank you for your support.

Lynne Gabriel and Roger Casemore
October 2008

Chapter 1

Introduction

Lynne Gabriel and Roger Casemore

Relational ethics in practice

A selection of narratives on ethical and unethical relationships from counselling, psychotherapy, psychology, psychiatry, training, research and supervision

The ethical dimensions of helping relationships are receiving increasing focus in the social and healthcare professions, not least because of the continuing rise in complaints against therapists and increasing interest in the nature of the client–practitioner relationship. Within the counselling and psychotherapy field, there is a recognition (both implicit and research-based) that the ethics of this relationship are of paramount importance to successful processes and outcomes. The quality of the client–practitioner encounter and practitioners' ways of being in the lived reality of the therapeutic relationship is difficult to access. Hence this text, which invites experienced practitioners from diverse theoretical and practice positions to share their thoughts on and experiences of forming relational ethics in various relationship types and contexts.

Prior to outlining the chapter contents, it is important to offer a definition of what is meant here by *relational ethic*. The *Oxford Reference Dictionary* (1986) defines 'ethic' as 'a set of moral principles' and 'relation' as 'narration, a narrative'. In the context of a helping relationship we can construe relational ethic as a co-constructed ethical and moral encounter, with associated relationship experiences and processes, that both influences and in turn is influenced by the complex multidimensional context in which the relationship occurs. The term relational ethic represents the complex medium through which decisions and interactions associated with the processes and progress of a relationship are mindfully and ethically engaged with (Gabriel, 2001a, 2002, 2005).

The process of translating philosophical theory and ethical thinking into practical application can feel far removed from the lived experience of intra- and interpersonal relating. Devising our own approach to relationship ethics can be challenging, despite the existence of ethical frameworks or codes of ethics. As the day-to-day reality of therapy practice can feel conflicted and chaotic at times, so there is significant value in hearing from the different chapter authors – each of whom provides an accessible narrative that can inform ethical thinking about and being in relationships. Some of the chapter authors offer theoretical context and concepts, while others draw more on personal and practice experiences. This rich variety serves to provide readers with a host of different approaches to relational ethics and we present a collection of works that illuminate and inform relational ethics in helping practice. The chapters cover a range of topics including:

- exploration of how a practitioner's theoretical approach informs their ethical decision making and practice in helping work and relationships
- examples of practical difficulties and ethical challenges, along with pointers for good practice
- examples from practice and some innovative or unconventional attitudes and approaches
- informed consent across a range of approaches and contexts
- the notion of the 'wounded healer' and practitioner self-care
- examples from personal and professional experience.

This book makes an unusual and special contribution to the developing body of knowledge on practice ethics. It covers a wide spectrum of helping approaches and explores topics that reflect the diversity of theory and practice in the field including: counselling, psychotherapy, forensic psychology, psychology, psychiatry, supervision, training and research. We do not claim to offer an exhaustive approach to ethical thinking and practice – that is impossible in the world of applied ethics. What we do provide is a thoughtful and engaging collection, invaluable to today's practitioners across the psychological therapies.

Underpinning the authors' work are several ethics codes and guidelines, including: the British Association for Counselling and Psychotherapy's (BACP) Ethical Framework, the United Kingdom Council for Psychotherapy's (UKCP) Code of Ethics; those who work in psychology or psychiatry draw upon other guiding frameworks, including the British Psychological Society's (BPS) Code of Ethics.

In *Chapter 2*, Lynne Gabriel explores the therapeutic relationship, with a focus on the intriguing concept of the role of the practitioner as a *boundary rider*, *process sentinel* and *ethics warrior*. She sets out a model through which practitioners can develop a personal–professional relational ethic for their therapeutic relationships with clients. Her work is based on qualitative inquiry into complex dual and multiple role relationships and draws on keynotes, papers and workshops at UK and international conferences. Gabriel explores findings from research into clients' and practitioners' experiences of overlapping role relationships. She proposes a model for relational ethics that facilitates a multidimensional perspective covering: relational context; intentionality; assessment; relational capacity and skills; relational responsibility, role fluency and spatial capacity – all of which are situated within the context of a collaborative client–practitioner narrative. Gabriel highlights the importance of understanding the link between therapist intentionality and relational integrity, showing how a therapist's intent in a dual or multiple role relationship becomes central to its process and progress and influences whether the relationship or overlapping roles are beneficial or detrimental.

In *Chapter 3*, Roger Casemore offers a view that practitioners should be more concerned with developing ethics as a way of being which permeates their whole life, rather than a set of rules which govern their working practices. He suggests that our ethical values and principles should form part of our way of being that informs how we are and what we do in all aspects of our lives, rather than being a set of rules which we put into operation in the counselling room. Casemore explores the ways in which the relational work of therapy should be firmly contained within a commitment to relational ethics. He draws a parallel with the person-centred approach as 'a way of being' based on the integration of the three central conditions for therapeutic growth–congruence, positive regard and a non-judgemental stance – as deeply held aspects of the self of the therapist, rather than a set of techniques to be used with clients. He strongly questions whether it is possible to be an ethical practitioner in relationships with clients, if one is unethical in everyday life. Integrity in relationships with self and others is central to Casemore's premise.

Aaron Balick, in *Chapter 4*, investigates relational ethics when working with lesbian, gay, bisexual and transgendered individuals. He explores how meanings of sexual identity are made within a complicated dialectic of difference, where gender and sexual identity are experienced in ways that are both multiple and relational, rather than from a perspective of conventional binary thinking. Balick focuses on the implicit conditions that create an ethical relational space and challenges therapists to be in touch with the multiple and relational aspects of their own gender and sexuality and risk engaging directly in relational dynamics that are likely to provoke uncomfortable aspects of their own sexuality.

In *Chapter 5*, Val Wosket draws on her personal-professional experience of relational ethics in supervision to explore the notion that the supervisory relationship is central to the process of effective supervision and that the full and effective exploration of ethical issues in supervision is always rooted in the quality of the relationship between supervisor and supervisee. She bravely uses examples from her own practice where she made mistakes by using her own ethical agenda as a supervisor, in order to emphasise the important learning that can come from mistakes and omissions. She also reminds us of how we may be wounded healers, offering us a challenge to consider the ways in which each of us brings experiences from past relationships into present relating and experiencing. With her supervisee's consent, Wosket uses a casework example from her supervision practice that demonstrates how ethical concerns that are out of conscious awareness can surface and become available for exploration in supervision. She also explores issues of supervisor power and authority and shows how relational ethics in supervision are largely about using the relationship with supervisees to mediate and work with issues of uniqueness and difference. At the end of her chapter, Wosket echoes a view held by most of the writers in this book, that relational ethics at its best can and must allow for creative, spontaneous and even unorthodox practice that privileges the needs of individual clients and supervisees over the limits and constraints of externally imposed professional protocols. Unorthodox does not mean unethical and the relational ethic espoused here denounces personal or professional abuse.

Kim Etherington, in *Chapter 6*, explores the ethical requirements for those involved in undertaking narrative, reflexive research. A reflexive relational ethic is central to her research thinking and practice. She suggests that in such research it is important to make transparent the researcher's values and beliefs as these almost certainly influence the research process and its outcomes. Etherington shows how interactions in the relationship between researcher and researched give rise to ethical, moral and methodological issues. Illuminating this by using case material from research involving gathering life stories from past drug users, she advocates developing the research relationship as one of consultancy and collaboration and identifies the ethical issues arising from the various ways in which power issues permeate every aspect of research relationships. Etherington also strongly challenges the continuing influence of psychodynamic research which discourages practitioners from any form of self-disclosure and suggests the need for researchers to be more transparent and more present in their writing.

In *Chapter 7*, Nic Neath writes from a personal perspective, as a graduate from a diploma in counselling course, describing her experiences of relational ethics as a student, exploring her views on relational ethics in training, post training and the early stages of her counselling practice. She describes how, as a student, the landscape of her training seemed littered with a range of ethical dilemmas, each with potentiality for perilous adventure or shortfall in relational engagement, largely as a result of 'not knowing what she did not know'. She explores some of the questions she had after training ended and identifies some of the philosophical, theoretical and relational issues that may not be given enough time in training. The chapter raises questions about whether we can ever be fully informed as trainees, when consenting to training or therapeutic processes. Her work also causes us to question the use of visualisation techniques that generate potent psychological and emotional material. It generates questions about consent and reminds us that it is a process that unfolds over time.

In *Chapter 8*, Subodh Dave, a consultant psychiatrist, explores relational ethics in psychiatric settings, sharing the richness of his learning from the experience of the transition from working in India, his country of origin, to working here in the UK. He strongly advocates a relational approach in psychiatry, particularly in developing relational ethics to inform processes of assessment and the formulation of treatment plans. He describes how his shared experience and relationships with patients helped him to adapt to working in a foreign land. Using case material he underlines the importance of taking account of the patient's values and preferences and criticises the lack of guidance on relating to patients who fail to engage or on the ethical or moral imperatives of the clinician in such a common clinical scenario. He suggests that relational ethics is an action-oriented approach based on nurturing positive and healing relationships, in direct contrast to a competing rights perspective, which seems to prevail in the NHS. Dave challenges strongly with his individual view that evidence based medicine alone does not lead to improved patient outcomes but needs the addition of relational, value based medicine. He concludes with a strongly held view of the need for training for psychiatrists to create a new wave of *ethical governance* – a framework of learning and working that will enable individuals and organisations to achieve and maintain highly ethical practice; a framework which will facilitate and encourage diverse individuals and organisations to work in partnership and respectful relationships, with mutual respect for each other as diverse moral beings.

Chapter 9 brings legal issues into counselling and therapy's relational domains. Peter Jenkins writes about key legal aspects of the relationship between practitioner and client. This includes legal definitions of the boundaries of safe practice and the legal responses to perceived breaches of such boundaries. He explores the theme of 'therapy as evidence', with personal reflections on his approach to ethical practice in his work as a counsellor trainer. Jenkins offers legal perspectives on the relationship between therapist and client and how therapy is not only a helping relationship and a therapeutic activity, but also one which is framed by powerful ethical considerations and, ultimately, one which is constrained by the law. He offers a personal dimension, describing the growth of his own personal-professional ethical stance, and clearly outlines the ethical and legal responsibilities of therapists and trainers and how these can often be in conflict.

In *Chapter 10*, Alan Dunnett writes about the role of practitioner self-care, stating clearly his view that counsellors should ensure that they do not use their work with clients to meet their own emotional and psychological needs. A practitioner's capacity for self-care is central to their ability to provide an appropriate relational and ethical environment for their clients. Dunnett explores the power of the impact of a client's stories on the therapist and the role of the organisation in increasing or ameliorating this impact. He questions the validity of the current promotion of the cognitive behavioural therapies which suits the philosophy and talents of some practitioners far better than others. He suggests that counsellors required to retrain in these approaches to therapy should question the ethics of working with clients from a theoretical position about which they have serious misgivings. He questions whether such individuals are likely to practise effectively if they experience psychological dissonance between their value system and the values of the organisation. Crucially, he states the nature of the counsellor's relationship with himself or herself and with the organisation that the counsellor works in represents as much an ethical concern as the management of direct interaction with the client.

In *Chapter 11*, William West writes provocatively, drawing on his experiences and the experiences of others as counselling trainers, describing some of the ethical relationship challenges he has faced. He explores the notion that therapist training is based on faith in the chosen modality, rather than research on its efficacy, and that this might help us to understand the dynamics of training, the training team and the professional bodies. He uses a case study to highlight potential relational and ethical problems within therapy training teams. He acknowledges that therapist training is difficult and demanding and needs proper resourcing to be carried out effectively and comments on the existence of 'self-exploitation' of staff involved arising from their personal commitment to deliver quality training with inadequate resources. West advocates the need for a more robust scheme of accreditation of trainers and comments that if there are concerns about the quality of practice by therapists then the issue of the quality and delivery of training becomes even more important. With statutory regulation of counselling and psychotherapy imminent, this is a key issue for practitioner educators.

In *Chapter 12*, Roger Casemore identifies how his ethical stance on the strict application of some aspects of the British Association for Counselling and Psychotherapy's Ethical Framework for Good Practice in relation to dual and multiple relationships has changed over recent years, as a result of his work in remote rural communities and small organisations. Casemore draws on case material and personal and professional experiences to show that there are significant differences in the ways that ethical principles need to be applied to relationships in different geographical and organisational contexts. From his own experience of inadvertent breaches of confidentiality, he declares the need to be clear and explicit and to seek agreement about the ways in which boundaries, relationships and aspects of confidentiality need to be varied within different cultural and organisational relational contexts. He emphasises the importance of living with the spirit and the ethos of the Ethical Framework in relational ethics, rather than being hidebound by the rules.

In *Chapter 13*, Lynne Gabriel considers the *researcher–contributor research alliance*. Gabriel draws on the concept of the *working alliance* to explore the significance of developing an ethical relationship which closely parallels the therapeutic alliance between therapist and client, which she describes as the *research alliance*. She examines role and relationship conflict and ethical dilemmas that can arise for counselling practitioners when taking up the role of researcher. Gabriel identifies from her own experience as a researcher how conflict and stress arising from researcher–practitioner role duality can be made more manageable by careful ethical thought and action. Gabriel argues that qualitative research interviewing demands a great deal of the researcher's knowledge, skills, abilities and ethical literacy. Hence the need to develop conceptual and practical 'tools' that are researcher, contributor and context specific and offer a practical model for developing ethical research alliances.

In *Chapter 14*, Jeremy Tudway writes as a clinical forensic psychologist and draws on cognitive behavioural therapy (CBT) and rational emotive behavioural therapy (REBT) to consider ethics from a relational perspective, which is essentially intuitive in nature, rather than rule bound. He identifies a number of relationship dilemmas for the CBT and REBT therapist and illuminates these with examples from his work with high-risk clients. He explores some aspects of the power of the therapist and the importance of establishing an ethical relationship in which this power is not abusive. He makes some helpful suggestions for working ethically and lawfully with clients who present with highly challenging beliefs and behaviours.

In *Chapter 15*, Moira Walker offers an in-depth narrative on developing an ethically safe relationship when working with adult survivors of abuse. She explores feminist therapy and considers this in the context of psychodynamic models and its significance in working with adult survivors. Drawing on her practitioner experience, she powerfully explores the complexities and challenges of her work. She argues that in the client–therapist relationship the practitioner must offer genuine responses to carefully considered therapeutic needs, not dangerous knee-jerk responses to unrecognised or unprocessed countertransferences. Walker's work provides invaluable theoretical concepts for those who work with adult survivors of abuse.

In *Chapter 16*, Lynne Gabriel offers a moving account of how the experience of personal trauma can impact on one's capacity for ethical relations with oneself and with others. She describes how her experience of significant loss had a major impact on her self-concept and severely limited her capacity to sustain meaningful, reciprocal and intimate relating, temporarily causing her to withdraw and lose relational contact with herself and other people. Gabriel notes the concept of the wounded healer, raising questions about perceptions of well-being and the flawed therapist. Drawing on her experiences of research into relationships and her work as a practitioner, Gabriel advocates the importance of each therapist, trainer and supervisor being able to form their own personal and professional relational ethic. She suggests that in a therapy context this should be a collaborative and reciprocal venture, involving both therapist and client in developing the relational ethic. While Gabriel recognises that not all therapy modalities will uphold this approach, she argues that a collaborative stance proactively engages the client in key relationship processes such as facilitating the negotiation of process consent.

Relational Ethics in Practice provides the reader with a wide range of engaging and informative narratives on how ethics inform and influence the chapter authors. It also offers sustained narratives on personal and professional challenges and difficulties that can undermine ethical practice. The book shows how ethics is an exciting area of practice development – ethics can be seen as dull or dry when, in reality, it is a vibrant, diverse and exciting field that crosses all areas of work and life, not just therapy.

We offer this selection of chapters as prompts for practice and exemplars for evolving ethical relationships. We encourage readers to extract what is relevant for them and informs their own approach to relational ethics. The book gives access to rich personal and professional narratives on ethical thinking. It shows personal and professional relational ethics in practice and provokes people to think more proactively about ethics and the impact of ethics on work and life. An innovative collection of narratives on relational ethics, we hope that you will find them informing, challenging and inspirational.

Chapter 2

Relational ethics, boundary riders and process sentinels

Allies for ethical practice

Lynne Gabriel

Introduction

This chapter[1] draws on aspects of research, theory and practice to set out concepts and metaphors that are allies for effective and ethical practice. With the ethical dimensions of client–practitioner relationships receiving increased attention in the helping professions and associated literature, practitioners need to identify ways of mediating the tensions and challenges inherent in client and therapy work.

The *relational ethic*, *boundary rider* and *process sentinel* concepts are allies for ethical practice. They evolved from research into boundaries and inquiry into client and therapist experiences of complex dual and multiple role relationships and will be of interest and practical value to a range of practitioners involved in counselling and therapy, including: counsellors, psychotherapists, trainee practitioners, supervisors, trainers, psychologists, allied health professionals and service providers.

The origins of a relational ethic, boundary rider and process sentinel

Researching dual and multiple role relationships

The inevitable complexity of therapy means that we need to develop our ability to form, facilitate and mediate effective helping relationships and relational boundaries. When researching boundaries in therapy relationships (Gabriel, 1996) and client/therapist experiences of dual and multiple role relationships (Gabriel, 2002, 2005) the data offered rich material out of which the ideas for the concepts *relational ethic*, *boundary rider* and *process sentinel* arose and suggested ways of managing relational dynamics and boundaries. Interview data from over 50 clients and therapists (not 'matched pairs') showed that dual and multiple role relating can be both beneficial and harmful (Gabriel, 2002, 2005). A summary of key findings is shown in Box 2.1 (for comprehensive details, see Gabriel 2002, 2005).

Box 2.1 *A summary of key findings from research into clients' and practitioners' experiences and perceptions of non-sexual dual and multiple role relationships*

→ A dual or multiple role relationship can have powerful beneficial and/or detrimental outcomes.

→ A non-sexual dual relationship can be as damaging as the reported effects of sexually abusive dual relationships.

→ Not only can a dual relationship harm the client, but it can also harm the therapist.

→ Finding a 'way of being' in dual or multiple role relationships can generate conflict and distress.

→ Some individuals appear able to more easily mediate between dual or multiple role relationships.

→ Conflicts can arise from the contexts in which the relationship roles occur.

→ Difficulty in managing role boundaries, role transitions, role identities and role conflicts was common.

→ Successful dual relationships appeared to be predicated on a positive emotional bond.

→ The presence of this bond during the life of the therapy relationship appeared to influence decisions about whether or not to engage in further contact beyond or outside a therapy context.

→ Concurrent dual relationships appeared to be more difficult to deal with than sequential relationships.

An important fact to note is that all contributors were themselves therapists at the time of their research interview. Additionally, at the time of their dual or multiple role relationship, many of the client contributors were either trained or trainee therapists. These are significant points, indicating that the emotional potency and stress generated in some relational situations can override prior knowledge and understanding of the therapy process for clients who themselves are trained or trainee therapists. Chillingly, it might suggest that those therapy clients who have no therapeutic knowledge and no (or limited) understanding of the process of therapy are especially vulnerable.

Therapy practitioners may be making unexamined assumptions about the capacity of clients to be responsible in the therapy relationship or to support themselves emotionally and psychologically in a dual relationship. Not all clients are able to do so. Even when a client is an experienced therapist at the time of the dual or multiple role relationship, it does not offer 'protection'. While we might assume that an experienced therapist in the role of 'client' could be self-supporting in a dual relationship, research suggests otherwise (Gabriel, 2002, 2005).

If therapist 'clients' find it difficult to discuss or disclose abusive non-sexual dual relationships with their therapist or others, what are the implications for clients with no therapy knowledge? Given that a client's relational responses may not only be transference based, but might also relate to the 'real' relationship between the client and therapist (Greenson, 1967; Rennie, 2000), then the therapist in a dual or multiple role relationship situation needs to be especially alert to the client's communication in the relationship and to create opportunities for *meta-communication* (communicating about our communication) whereby the individuals reflect on and evaluate the relationship, in the process informing subsequent communication. This informed and reflexive practice underpins the notion of *relational ethic*.

Defining relational ethic

Relational ethic was defined in Chapter 1 (p. 1) and I use the term here to denote a medium through which decisions, actions and interactions associated with a relationship are mindfully approached (Gabriel, 2001a, 2002, 2005). The term combines the notions of 'ethic' and 'relation' to form an ethical narrative thread that weaves through all aspects of a relationship. Of course, the ethics or morals underpinning an individual's relational ethic will be informed by their philosophy and world view. For example, my approach has been influenced by feminist, social care and social constructionist concepts of relationships (see, for example, Gergen and Kaye, 1992; Gergen 1994a, 1994b, 1997, 1999; Noddings, 2002; Jordan *et al.*, 2004). In addition, I am interested in how our individual, collective and social identities influence our relational ability (see, for example, Appiah's, 2005, *The Ethics of Identity*, for an interesting approach to the ethics of identity and diversity). Viewing the relationship through multidimensional lenses offers a deeper, richer view of relational complexity. Figure 2.1 illustrates the multidimensional nature of this approach to practice ethics.

The relational dimensions

Figure 2.1 depicts relational ethics in practice and shows a multidimensional perspective that covers: relationship context; assessment; intentionality; relational capacity; spatial ability; relational responsibility; collaborative narrative and pragmatic skills. These dimensions are briefly outlined below. Although set out here in linear fashion, in the lived experience of engaging with relational ethics, the dimensions interweave.

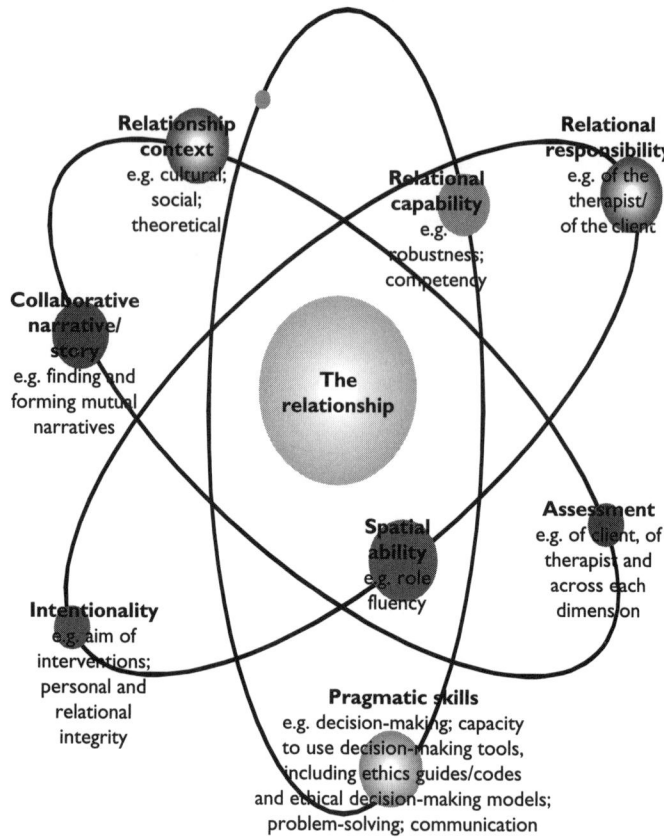

Figure 2.1 Allies for ethical practice: developing a relational ethic.

Relationship context

It is self-evident to state that the contextual dimension(s) of the relationship will play a significant part. In the model here, context denotes the wider environment of the dual or multiple role relationship and will include theory and concepts that underpin the therapist's thinking and practice, as well as the social, cultural, professional and political contexts in which the relationship occurs. The theoretical approach that informs the therapist's practice is a key contextual feature and will influence how the dual or multiple role relationship is perceived, experienced and responded to. Review and collaborative consideration of the different relationship contexts are important. This can happen in a number of ways, including mutual reviews and client–therapist/ dual relationship partner conversations that reflect on the relationship contexts and how they influence, impinge on, or complicate the relationship. Here, the term *dual relationship partner* refers to the client and therapist involved in the dual or multiple role relationship.

Assessment

Research into dual and multiple role relationships (Gabriel, 2002, 2005) found that few practitioners were assessing relational competence or capacity to sustain self in an overlapping role situation. That said, these relationship situations can be circumstantial or unexpected, leaving no opportunity for planned assessment or risk analysis. With the move towards statutory regulation of helping professions and the development of a core curriculum for counselling and psychotherapy training, assessment is likely to feature far more prominently. This assumes, of course, a particular theoretical and clinical stance and not all therapies or therapists will advocate assessment. Within the frame of the relational ethic presented here, assessment implies a practitioner capacity and willingness to consider their own and their client's ability to enter and sustain oneself in a dual or multiple role relationship.

Leigh (1998) has argued that where a dual relationship is likely, then the client must be referred to another clinician. Of course, referral to a different therapist, electing not to pursue a dual relationship, or ending a particular role or relationship might well be the appropriate option, although in situations of unavoidable or intended overlap, it might be possible to assess an individual's intentionality and relational capacity (see Gabriel, 2002, for further information). Exactly how this might work in practice is not straightforward. However, knowledge of relational style might be a useful way to predict the possible progression or outcome of a dual relationship. For example, where an individual manifests what in *DSM-IV-TR* (APA, 2000) criteria might be classified as 'borderline' symptoms, we might need to question whether they could manage being in a dual or multiple role relationship.

The process of assessment imagined here is about client *protection* and therapist *preparedness*. Essentially, this would assess the client and therapist for their capacity to sustain self in a complex relationship situation. An assessment could identify skills or qualities that are likely to help or hinder the relationship. For example, if an individual has a history of violent childhood sexual abuse, there is likely to be a need for clearly defined, compassionate boundary holding in the relationship and complex overlapping roles would be contraindicated. An element of assessment can also occur in a supervision context, where relational dynamics and choices can be considered.

Intentionality

While the notion of intentionality might appear to be the therapist's responsibility, a client's intentions will also play a crucial part in the process and outcome of any client–therapist relationship (not just dual and multiple role relationships). The idea of therapist intentionality has been noted in the therapy literature (see, for example, Russell, 1993, 1999; Gabriel and Davies, 2000). Russell (1999) regards the concept as associated with therapeutic technique and I use it similarly here, to signify the intentions and subsequent actions/interventions of the individuals in the relationship. There is an important link between intentionality and relational integrity. Thus an individual's intent in a dual or multiple role relationship becomes central to its process and progress – all the more reason why it is important that the individuals (as far as is possible) are aware of their motives.

Arguably, an individual's intentionality in a dual relationship corresponds with the role they are enacting and its associated responsibilities. If this is the case, dual relationship partners, for example, would identify and agree role obligations and, in most cases, the therapist would need to initiate this process. So, the therapist takes on relational responsibility to instigate communication, gradually relinquishing their facilitation as the client increasingly collaborates in the processes and progress of the relationship. We might expect this, yet a significant feature of many client stories of dual relationships was that their therapist did not appear to 'check things out' with them (Gabriel, 2002, 2005). Explicit discussion of the relationship situation is crucial (Casemore, 2008). Surely, identifying a client's understanding and awareness of the relationship constitutes a relational responsibility the therapist cannot ignore?

Relational capacity and spatial ability

Although relational capacity and spatial ability are shown separately in Figure 2.1, they are discussed in tandem here, as they are intimately and inextricably connected in the lived experience of a relationship. Essentially, *relational capacity* refers to an individual's degree or emotional and psychological robustness and competency in relating with self and others. *Spatial ability* denotes an individual's ability to deal with role changes and conflicts within the wider context of the dual or multiple role relationship.

Possessing skills, knowledge and ability to deal with relational conflict and stress is clearly an advantage in any dual or multiple role relationship situation. A therapist's training and post-graduate practicum period will ideally develop their understanding and practical experience of managing duality phenomena and specific dual relationship situations – essentially, the practitioner develops 'role fluency' (Clarkson, 1994, 2000). This might involve learning how to deal with the challenges of, say, assuring and maintaining confidentiality across various roles. Additionally, for the therapist, it inevitably involves the challenge of developing ethical and moral awareness and the ability to work and problem solve from within an ethically minded, morally aware relational ethic.

An individual's agency in a given role will shift over time and context.

Thus, ideally, there would be a constant conversation between the dual relationship partners. In certain relational contexts a capacity for role fluency and the ability to sustain oneself in situations of conflict and dissonance is critical to the success of a dual or multiple role relationship (Gabriel, 2002, 2005). Change, dissonance, conflict, uncertainty and role anxiety – all of these are everyday relational experiences and all are intensified when working in a complex relationship situation. For example, where therapists work in multiple role jobs and in a combination of private practice, voluntary sector and organisational practice, it is not uncommon to encounter clients in a range of non-therapy situations. Some overlapping role connections cannot be avoided and associated anxieties and relational tensions have to be dealt with.

Unlike some interpretations of role theory, where an individual's role in an event or situation is fixed, from a symbolic interaction perspective 'role' is regarded as fluid with the potential to change over time and context (Stryker and Statham, 1985). This view of role is fitting when considering complexities of a dual or multiple role relationship. It does mean, however, that we need to develop a capacity for role fluency and ethical literacy (Gabriel, 2001b), with the therapist carrying the responsibility for generating conversations and reviews about relational issues.

Whilst a capacity for role fluency is useful for the therapist, the same could be said for the client. It helps to view role fluency as *shapeshifting*. That is, it is the capacity to move into and between various relational shapes or roles. An individual's capacity to move between roles could be assessed and we could consider how the individual can develop their ability to deal with the role shifts. While developing role fluency, role boundaries are crucial and ways of 'marking and minding' them become a significant part of the process, with practitioner supervision playing a pivotal role here. In addition, explicit and collaborative boundary and role monitoring is essential. However, all of this is contingent on the client's and therapist's psychological robustness.

We probably assume too much about client and therapist capacity to both sustain self in and to move between, relational roles. Notions of the 'sussed therapist' are not uncommon and limit the capacity for transparent and congruent discourse on our limitations, or realistic fears and anxieties in relational situations. Therapist self-awareness and a robust self-concept may be important indicators of capacity to be in a dual relationship, so cannot be ignored. None of us might want to be viewed as a 'wounded healer' or 'flawed therapist', but that said, are we not all 'wounded' to some degree (Kiddle-Bailey, 2007)? Perhaps what is important is that we are aware of our wounds and that they do not undermine our relational decisions and interactions.

Relational responsibility

Few would disagree that practitioners are morally, ethically and professionally responsible to their clients. Competent and respectful service is expected and assumed by clients, alongside the profession's concomitant expectation that practitioners will attend to maintaining their personal and professional skill, resourcefulness and robustness. With the increasing likelihood that counselling and psychotherapy will be statutorily regulated, there are significant implications for the training and development of practitioners.

In complex situations relational responsibility is ideally negotiated and shared between the relationship partners. This moves away from perceiving relational responsibility as a task or function residing with one or other (usually the person in the position of 'expert' or figure of authority; in the case of a helping relationship, it might be perceived as the therapist) of the people involved in the relationship. While the therapist role traditionally attracts particular notions of responsibility and obligation, it should not assume greater status, purpose or authority in the relationship. I am suggesting it is a collaborative venture, with the person in the role of current or past therapist ethically and professionally obligated to raise relational issues and to encourage and facilitate client capacity for mutual decision making (Gabriel, 2002, 2005). Playing a pivotal role in this premise is the therapist. They occupy a central role, facilitating development of conjoint responsibility until such time that the client can mobilise their own ability and responsibility. Thus, relationship partners become *conjointly responsible* (McNamee and Gergen, 1999). Obviously, an individual's capacity for conjoint responsibility might vary as, for instance, there could be clients for whom complex overlapping roles are contraindicated. Assessment or risk analysis must come into play in such cases.

Helping approaches and practitioners who balk at the prospect of negotiating a dual relationship with a patient or client, because of the complications of the client–therapist transference relationship, will avoid the complexities of overlapping role relationships. While this is a reasonable decision, the reality is that in our social, professional and cultural contexts, overlap is unavoidable. Therapists who most successfully manage overlapping role situations communicate an image of a skilled, experienced and compassionate dual relationship partner who involves the person in the role of 'client' in deciding relational matters across the various roles they share (Gabriel, 2002). Disturbingly, some client stories suggest that therapists do not recognise their relational responsibility in their client relationships (Gabriel, 2002).

Complex relational territory is testing. Of course, in our daily lives multiplicity and overlapping connections are commonplace and we are probably accustomed to filling numerous roles across a range of work-life-home settings. Yet when we bring this into a professional or contracted helping territory, conditions immediately change. To renege on our relational responsibility is not a valid option.

A collaborative narrative

As a means of bringing the dimensions into a coherent picture of relational experiences, the parties to the relationship form a mutually relevant and collaborative narrative or story. The relationship's dual or multiple roles can be understood and mediated through the interaction of the partners and the construction of shared meanings. Role identities and interactions need some framework or shared understanding. This can be brought about through regular mutual reviews of the relationship processes and progression.

Of course, the story will change as each of the relational dimensions shifts. Therefore, regular reflection and review will form an essential part of constructing a collaborative narrative. To sustain self in a complex dual relationship situation involves developing an ability to speak out and express opinions on, as well as responses to, situations that arise out of the relationship. The notion of speaking out applies to both clients and therapists, although differs for each group. For clients, it is largely about empowering self, as well as being supported and challenged to do this by the 'therapist' dual relationship partner.

It is likely, as Gabriel's (2002) research suggests, that many clients are unable to speak out in the relationship. Thus, the implications for the individual and the relationship are of immense proportions. Additionally, where the client is unable to challenge the therapist/dual relationship partner's perceived 'inconsistencies' and 'mistakes', or is unable to contribute more equally and mutually to the development or directions of the relationship, there exist conditions that allow for exploitation or harm (intentional or unintentional) to occur.

Pragmatic skills

Central to the competent use of the relational ethics model presented here is the capacity to develop one's decision-making and problem-solving ability. Tools for ethical thinking are constantly evolving (see Gabriel, 2005 and Gabriel and Casemore, 2005, for useful references) and readers will find models that best fit their own approach to ethics in practice.

Also important for managing and working through day-to-day ethical challenges is the capacity to communicate well—both with oneself and with others. The importance of skills for effectively managing the interaction and communication between aspects of an ethical challenge (or the people involved in it), or for engaging with the multidimensional relational ethics model shown here, cannot be underestimated. Such 'ethical literacy' (Gabriel, 2001a) accrues over time and requires not only a comprehensive understanding of the bases upon which decisions and actions are taken, but also a knowledge of the philosophical premises that underpin them. Arguably, all ethical frameworks are imbued with social, cultural and professional mores.

To acknowledge and fully understand what informs our thinking and practice is to recognise and respect the diverse communities in which we live and work. The development of ethical literacy and communication skills for effective ethical decision-making will occur in a number of contexts; not least practice, but importantly, a practitioner's training should provide them with ample opportunity to develop their knowledge of and skills in relational ethics.

The relational ethics model shown here suggests a dialectical approach to decision-making. In dialectical thinking, regular engagement with the contradictions and discrepancies between the general and the particular features of ethical situations or challenges will facilitate a practitioner's development. Through ongoing use of reasoning and relational skills, the practitioner's capacity for ethical thinking and practice in a wide range of contexts will gradually extend. Practitioner training and Continuing Professional Development (CPD) need to provide opportunities to accrue these important skills.

Constructing a relational ethic

A practitioner's relational ethic will encompass a combination of theory and knowledge drawn from years of therapy, training, supervision and research experience. While all of the dimensions outlined in Figure 2.1 and the above sections are important, an understanding of intentionality (both practitioner and client) and relational capacity (assessment of both practitioner and client capacity) is crucial. In addition, used in conjunction with a decision-making framework for dealing with ethical issues (such as those suggested by Gabriel, 1996, 2005; Bond, 2000; Gabriel and Davies, 2000; Gabriel and Casemore, 2005), as well as the concepts of *boundary rider* and *process sentinel*, they collectively provide valuable allies for thinking about, or being in, dual or multiple role relationships, although can be used in any relational situation. What may be regarded as a dilemma or ethical matter in a relationship might vary between different theoretical or philosophical perspectives (MacKay and O'Neill, 1992), but a feminist practitioner might argue that all relational interactions should be regarded as ethical actions or endeavours (Brown, 1991). To enable a practitioner to add the boundary rider and process sentinel concepts to their 'toolkit', they are defined and described in the following sections – it is for the practitioner to 'flesh out' the concepts in relation to their own practice.

Further allies for ethical practice

Boundary riders and process sentinels

Defining *boundary*

A boundary is . . . a limit line, with inherent fluidity and permeability, as well as safety and security. It is a limit line that requires the thoughtful actions of the boundary rider, the counsellor, to monitor and repair where necessary in order, as far as is possible, to ensure security and safety.

(Gabriel and Davies, 2000: 17–19)

Defining *boundary rider*

The boundary rider monitors and maintains the limit . . . and extent of a given relationship.

(Gabriel, 2005: 59–60)

The practitioner as *boundary rider* forms, facilitates and holds appropriate and ethically mindful relational boundaries in their client relationships. A practitioner can invoke boundary rider in her or his unique way. Essentially, it provides a 'short-hand' concept for tracking the limits and ethical edges of the relationship. The practitioner as boundary rider is a useful metaphor for the way in which we form, facilitate and hold relationship boundaries in our work with clients – this applies not only to dual and multiple role relationships but also to relational dynamics in all helping work. The metaphor can be brought alive in a unique way by each practitioner as they bring their theories and practice preferences to bear on the notion of boundary rider. Essentially, it offers a creative solution to facing and engaging with the inevitable challenges of helping work and relationships.

Box 2.2 *Boundary rider*

The boundary rider:

➜ tracks relational extent and limits
➜ identifies relational ruptures
➜ responds swiftly and mindfully to breach ruptures

> → facilitates relational boundaries with courage and tenacity
> → can adapt in and to difficult relational terrain
> → collaborates with clients and others to hold and facilitate the therapy work and relationship
> → appropriately sustains self and supports others in chaotic and conflicted situations
> → is robust and can survive difficult relational situations.

The process sentinel

The *process sentinel* concept is invoked to trace and track ongoing relational processes and situations. It facilitates reflexive practice and ethical literacy through a constant attendance to relational processes. As a creative means to ethical ends, it offers the practitioner a tool that can be honed to suit their theoretical and practice approach.

Defining *process sentinel*

The process sentinel is the guardian of the relationship and relational processes. They work in collaboration with relational partners to maintain and develop relational content, process and progress.

(Gabriel, 2006)

Box 2.3 *Process sentinel*

The process sentinel:

→ develops comprehensive relational skills and capacity
→ can work with complex ethical issues
→ maintains a capacity for reasoned and ethical responding in chaotic and conflicted relational situations
→ has a capacity for an 'eagle eye' perspective on relational processes as well as the ability to focus in on the minutiae of situations
→ embodies and epitomises reflexive relating.

Through ongoing development of relationship knowledge and ability, the practitioner is constantly honing and refining their skills, thus enhancing their capacity as a process sentinel. Reflexivity is embedded and embodied in the notion of process sentinel, with the practitioner bringing experience, reflection and development to an ongoing iterative cycle of development.

Concluding comment

Duality, multiplicity, complexity and conflict are universal and ever-present features of human existence. This chapter has offered relational concepts to support ethical thinking and practice. The *boundary rider* and *process sentinel* concepts were introduced and a model through which practitioners can develop their own personal-professional relational ethic was presented. The concepts discussed here serve as an ethical practice portfolio for helping practitioners. They are offered in a creative spirit, to prompt ethical 'play' and thoughtful development of relational ethics in practice.

Note

1 Based on an abridged program presented at the American Counseling Association's (ACA) Annual Conference and Exhibition, 26–30 March 2008, Honolulu, Hawaii, and materials published in ACA's VISTAS 2008.

Acknowledgements

The author wishes to acknowledge the contributions to her thinking made by workshop delegates at a range of UK and international conferences, regional consultations and workshops. She also wants to thank her York St John University counselling studies and leadership students for their keen interest in and contribution to her thinking on ethics.

References

American Psychiatric Association (APA, 2000) *Diagnostic and Statistical Manual of Mental Disorders: DSM-IV-TR*. Washington, DC: American Psychiatric Association.

Appiah, K.A. (2005) *The Ethics of Identity*. New Jersey: Princeton University Press.

Bond, T. (2000) *Standards and Ethics for Counselling in Action*, 2nd edn. London: Sage.

Brown, L.S. (1991) Antiracism as an ethical imperative: an example for feminist therapy. *Ethics and Behavior* 1, 2, 69–86.

Clarkson, P. (1994) In recognition of dual relationships. *Transactional Analysis Journal* 24, 1, 32–38.

Clarkson, P. (2000) *Ethics: Working with Ethical and Moral Dilemmas in Psychotherapy*. London: Whurr.

Gabriel, L. (1996) *Boundaries in lesbian counsellor–lesbian client relationships*. Unpublished MEd manuscript. York St John University, UK.

Gabriel, L. (2000). Dual relationships in organizational contexts. *Counselling* 11, 1, 17–19.

Gabriel, L. (2001a) A matter of ethical literacy. *Counselling and Psychotherapy Journal* 12, 14–15.

Gabriel, L. (2001b) *Working in a Multitask Job*. Rugby: BACP.

Gabriel, L. (2002) *Dual relationships in counselling and psychotherapy*. Unpublished doctoral thesis. University of Leeds, UK.

Gabriel, L. (2005) *Speaking the Unspeakable: The Ethics of Dual Relationships in Counselling and Psychotherapy*. London: Brunner-Routledge.

Gabriel, L. (2006) *Boundary riders, process sentinels and ethics warriors: allies for ethical practice*. Paper presented at a workshop at the British Association for Counselling Annual Training Conference, October.

Gabriel, L. and Casemore, R. (2005) The ethical decision making process: a suggested model for practitioners. In BACP *Talking Therapies: An Essential Anthology*. Rugby: BACP.

Gabriel, L. and Davies, D. (2000) The management of ethical dilemmas associated with dual relationships. In C. Neal and D. Davies (eds) *Pink Therapy, Vol. 3: Issues in Therapy with Lesbian, Gay, Bisexual and Transgendered Clients*. Maidenhead: Open University Press.

Gergen, K.J. (1994a) Exploring the postmodern. *American Psychologist* 49, 412–416.

Gergen, K.J. (1994b) *Realities and Relationships*. Cambridge, MA: Harvard University Press.

Gergen, K.J. (1997) The place of the psyche in a constructed world. *Theory and Psychology* 7, 6, 724–745.

Gergen, K.J. (1999). *An Invitation to Social Constructionism*. Thousand Oaks, CA: Sage.

Gergen, K.J. and Kaye, J. (1992). Beyond narrative in the negotiation of therapeutic meaning. In S. McNamee and K.J. Gergen (eds) *Therapy as Social Construction*. Thousand Oaks, CA: Sage.

Greenson, R.R. (1967). *The Technique and Practice of Psychoanalysis*, Vol 1. New York: International Universities Press.

Jordan, J.V., Walker, M. and Hartling, L.M. (2004) *The Complexity of Connection*. New York: Guilford Press.

Kiddle-Bailey, K. (2007) *The wounded healer*. Unpublished MA dissertation. York St John University, UK.

Leigh, A. (1998). *Referral and Termination Issues for Counsellors*. London: Sage.

MacKay, E. and O'Neill, P. (1992) What creates the dilemma in ethical dilemmas? Examples from psychological practice. *Ethics and Behavior* 2, 4, 227–244.

McNamee, S. and Gergen, K.J. (eds) (1999) *Relational Responsibility: Resources for Sustainable Dialogue*. Thousand Oaks, CA: Sage.

Noddings, N. (2002) *Starting at Home: Caring and Social Policy*. Berkeley, CA: University of California Press.

Rennie, D.L. (2000) Aspects of the client's conscious control of the psychotherapeutic process. *Journal of Psychotherapy Integration* 10, 2, 151–167.

Russell, J. (1993) *Out of Bounds: Sexual Exploitation in Counselling and Therapy*. London: Sage.

Russell, J. (1999) Professional and socio-cultural aspects of the counselling relationship. In C. Feltham (ed.) *Understanding the Counselling Relationship*. London: Sage.

Stryker, S. and Statham, A. (1985) Symbolic interaction and role theory. In G. Lindzey and E. Aronson (eds) *Handbook of Social Psychology*. New York: Random House.

Chapter 3

Ethics as a way of being

Roger Casemore

Introduction

The British Association for Counselling and Psychotherapy (BACP) Ethical Framework (2002) was written to enable practitioners to develop appropriate moral and ethical qualities and not to be reliant on a set of rules of behaviour. The framework was written specifically to move away from the approach of the previous codes of ethics which had developed as very prescriptive sets of rules of what therapists should do or not do. In my experience as a supervisor and trainer, I find that many therapists are still looking for the rules they should abide by and as a consequence may be struggling with developing confidence in the Ethical Framework. In this chapter I want to reformulate the view that the ethical principles enshrined in the BACP Ethical Framework (2002) cannot be effective if they are treated as a set of rules of behaviour which are switched on when the therapist sits down with a client in the counselling relationship. It is my view that each of us as therapists needs to hold ethical values and principles as an integrated aspect of our self-construct. I wish to suggest that for each of us our ethical values and principles should form part of our way of being that informs how we are and what we do in all aspects of our lives. I will then explore an example of an ethical conflict I have been faced with in my work as a person-centred supervisor.

Background

I take the most commonly accepted definition of the word 'ethics' from Wikipedia, the online encyclopedia (2008):

> **Ethics** (via Latin *ethica* from the Ancient Greek [ἠθικὴ φιλοσοφία] 'moral philosophy', from the adjective of ἦθος *ēthos* 'custom, habit'), a major branch of philosophy, encompasses right conduct and good life. It is significantly broader than the common conception of analyzing right and wrong. A central aspect of ethics is 'the good life', the life worth

living or life that is satisfying, which is held by many philosophers to be more important than moral conduct. The major problem is the discovery of the 'summum buonum', the greatest good. The right act can be identified as the one causing the greatest good and the immoral act as the one impeding it.

Aristotle believed that we should study ethics in order to improve our lives, and therefore its principal concern is the nature of human well-being. Aristotle follows Socrates and Plato in taking the ethical virtues or principles to be central to a well-lived life. Therefore practical wisdom, as Aristotle conceived it, cannot be acquired solely by learning general rules. We must also acquire, through practice, those thinking, emotional and social skills that enable us to put our general understanding of well-being into practice in ways that are suitable to each occasion (*Stanford Encyclopedia of Philosophy*, 2006).

The development of human values

The very nature of human development through imitation and assimilation predicates that we will acquire opinions and biases from those with whom we are in contact while we grow up. As we develop through childhood and adolescence into adulthood, we acquire values and beliefs about ourselves and about other people. We develop these values in order to help us to determine the kind of person we should be and what we should or should not do. Many of these values are introjected into us at an unconscious level by our parents, families, teachers, religious leaders and by society in general, through education and through the various forms of the media. These introjected values produce attitudes in us including preconceived opinions or biased views, in favour of or against almost anything you can think of, but most particularly in relation to other people who are in some way different from us. Rooted in our primitive atavistic memory is the knowledge that in order for each of us to survive and succeed in our own individual small world, we have to strive to be as alike as possible to the significant other people who also populate our small world. Through that process we acquire beliefs, views and opinions that are not based on evidence and can quite often be completely irrational or illogical, ill informed and rooted in ignorance As we mature and grow older, we also deliberately choose to acquire other values on the basis of our experience of people and of life. These values are most often (but not always) acquired unconsciously and are more likely to be based on the evidence of our experience and knowledge arising from our interactions with other people.

In early life, these attitudes and values are largely absorbed unconsciously as we grow and develop. They become an integrated part of ourselves, a part of our way of being. As we mature and develop we also acquire both consciously and unconsciously further attitudes and values. As we acquire these, our personalities and ways of interacting with the world and others in it can be seen to change. Our early values and those we acquire in later life shape who and how we are in the world. They form the basis of our way of being.

A parallel process

Understanding this aspect of human development has led me to consider that perhaps this should also happen with developing my beliefs in a set of ethical principles and values in counselling. The BACP Ethical Framework clearly describes the values which should underpin the relationship between counsellor and client, between supervisor and supervisee and between counselling tutor and counselling student. It identifies the fundamental principles of those relationships and clearly predicates how we should be in each of those relationships. The framework does not attempt to offer a set of rules for behaviour, but rather a set of principles, establishing an ethos for ethical relationships. This, for me, parallels Carl Rogers' belief in the person-centred approach to therapy being about a way of being, rather than a set of techniques. Rogers developed the theory that there were six 'core conditions' which were both necessary and sufficient for therapeutic growth (Rogers, 1957). He described these six conditions as:

1   Two persons are in *psychological contact*.
2   The first, whom we shall term the client, is in a state of *incongruence*, being vulnerable or anxious.
3   The second person, whom we shall term the therapist, is *congruent* or *integrated* in the relationship.
4   The therapist experiences *unconditional positive regard* for the client.
5   The therapist experiences an *empathic understanding* of the client's internal frame of reference and endeavours to communicate this experience to the client.
6   The communication to the client of the therapist's empathic understanding and unconditional positive regard is to a minimal degree achieved.

Of these six conditions he viewed conditions (3), (4) and (5) as being attributes or characteristics of the counsellor. He held the view that these three conditions, which I have termed the 'central conditions' (Casemore, 2006), could not and should not be used as a kind of technique but that they need to be developed as an integrated aspect of the counsellor's personality. Rogers took this further to develop the most significant of the differences between the person-centred approach to counselling and other approaches. This lies in the belief that the experiencing of the three central conditions is important in every relationship and in every aspect of life. He strongly held that the person-centred approach is more than a way of developing a therapeutic relationship with clients. Rogers described it as 'a life affirming way of being' (Rogers, 1980). He suggested that these conditions were not a technique to be switched on when the therapist sits down with a client and that any attempt to do so would be experienced by the client as inauthentic and would prevent a therapeutic relationship from occurring.

It strikes me that this must also be true for the principles of the Ethical Framework. These fundamental principles need to be espoused as an integrated aspect of my way of being in all areas of my life. How can it be possible to ascribe to and choose to use those ethical principles to govern my work, and then choose not to allow them to govern how I am in the rest of my life? Surely the ethical therapist, determined to be ethical in their therapeutic relationships, must also do their utmost to be ethical in all their other relationships? It falls to all of us working in the field of counselling and psychotherapy to be ethically aware and ethically mindful in all aspects of our lives, not just in our work.

The Ethical Framework

Values

The BACP Ethical Framework identifies a set of fundamental values that all counsellors should commit themselves to:

- respecting human rights and dignity
- ensuring the integrity of practitioner–client relationships
- enhancing the quality of professional knowledge and its application
- alleviating personal distress and suffering
- fostering a sense of self that is meaningful to the person(s) concerned
- increasing personal effectiveness
- enhancing the quality of relationships between people
- appreciating the variety of human experience and culture
- striving for the fair and adequate provision of counselling and psychotherapy services.

Most of these values seem to me to be those which I should hold across all aspects of my life. They are clearly essential as values to underpin my work as a therapist and it seems inequitable that I should ascribe to different values in other aspects of my life. This is no less true of the ethical principles which arise from these values.

Ethical principles

The BACP Ethical Framework identifies these as follows:

- *Fidelity* – honouring the trust placed in the practitioner.
- *Autonomy* – respect for the client's right to be self-governing.

- *Beneficence* – a commitment to promoting the client's well-being.
- *Non-maleficence* – a commitment to avoiding harm to the client.
- *Justice* – the fair and impartial treatment of all clients and the provision of adequate services.
- *Self-respect* – fostering the practitioner's self-knowledge and care for self.

It seems to me that these principles need little alteration to enable me to apply them to all aspects of my life:

- *Fidelity* – honouring the trust placed in me.
- *Autonomy* – respecting my own and other people's rights to be self-governing.
- *Beneficence* – a commitment to promoting other people's well-being.
- *Non-maleficence* – a commitment to avoiding harm to other people.
- *Justice* – the fair and impartial treatment of other people.
- *Self-respect* – fostering my own self-awareness and self-knowledge and taking respectful care of myself.

The Ethical Framework then goes on to list the personal moral qualities that therapists are strongly encouraged to aspire to. Again, these seem to need little revision to enable them to be applied as a set of qualities to aspire to in everyday life.

Moral qualities

- *Empathy* – the ability to communicate understanding of another person's experience from that person's perspective.
- *Sincerity* – a personal commitment to consistency between what is professed and what is done.
- *Integrity* – commitment to being moral in dealings with others, personal straightforwardness, honesty and coherence.
- *Resilience* – the capacity to work with other people's concerns without being personally diminished.
- *Respect* – showing appropriate esteem to others and their understanding of themselves.
- *Humility* – the ability to assess accurately and acknowledge one's own strengths and weaknesses.
- *Competence* – the effective deployment of the skills and knowledge needed to do what is required.
- *Fairness* – the consistent application of appropriate criteria to inform decisions and actions.
- *Wisdom* – possession of sound judgement that informs practice.
- *Courage* – the capacity to act in spite of known fears, risks and uncertainty.

Being ethical and being human

In the Ethical Framework, it is suggested that it would be inappropriate to prescribe that all practitioners should possess all of these qualities, since it is fundamental that these personal qualities are deeply rooted in the person concerned and developed out of personal commitment rather than the requirement of an external authority. It seems to me important to remember that while as human beings we have huge potential and will always strive to be the best we can, at the same time our very humanity gives us an innate capacity to be flawed in some way and never to be able to achieve perfection. That means that we can only ever strive to be ethically mindful in our work, where determined self-discipline and the effective use of supervision may enable us to be more successful. To be ethically mindful across all other aspects of our lives must be innately more difficult to achieve and yet I believe that it is something that we should strive for. It also seems to me that the more ethically mindful I can be in everyday life, the easier or more natural it will be for me to be ethically mindful in my work as a therapist.

Some examples from work and from life

In my work, over more than 40 years as a therapist and over 30 years as a supervisor and trainer, there have been countless ethical relationship dilemmas which have arisen. I would like to explore just one of these from supervision in which the dilemma could be seen to be as much about how the supervisee was in everyday life as it was about how they were in their counselling working relationships.

The principle of autonomy

The principle of autonomy is, for me, encapsulated in the dictat 'Never do anything for your client that they can do for themselves'. This is perhaps the simplest exemplar of the principle of never behaving in a way that will undermine the autonomy of the client. As a trainer and as a supervisor, I have used these words many, many times over the years. I recall numerous times in supervision hearing different supervisees struggling with how best to help their client deal with practical issues in their life. Time and again I have heard supervisees report that they had decided to write a letter on the client's behalf and as they talked they seemed to be seeking my approval of them for doing that. Somehow the counsellor seemed to be determined to 'help' the client by doing it for them and failed to see how this undermines the client's autonomy.

When I have explored this further with the supervisee, it has often become apparent that they have a strongly altruistic approach to life. (I might even say an excessively altruistic approach, though this might be construed as judgemental on my part!) Their whole life seems to be centred on helping other people, taking responsibility for other people, responding to other people's needs and demands. Often this can be seen to be rooted in strong parental introjections from childhood, with the injunction that others must always be put first. Introjections rooted in position in the family, gender, class and other cultural and social values may serve to trap the individual in a firmly held belief that they always have to do things to help other people and that they must not let others struggle to do things for themselves.

I would suggest that as therapists we need to be aware of this tendency in ourselves in our everyday lives and to work towards holding an ethically mindful position in which we look after ourselves and take the risk of allowing others to struggle and to do things for themselves when they are clearly capable of doing so. It does seem to me that the person who is a continual helper, who is always helping and doing things for everyone else, is actually subtly placing themselves in a position of enormous power. They put themselves in the powerful position of being 'the giver' and hold everyone else in the subjugated position of 'the receiver'.

Carl Rogers saw therapy as a process of stages by which the individual, experiencing being received by the counsellor, changes over a period of time from a static, unfeeling, fixed, impersonal type of functioning to a more 'in-motion' position, which is marked by a fluid, changing, acceptant experiencing of differentiated personal feelings (Rogers, 1969). In this process, Rogers saw the function of the therapist as enabling the client to move towards becoming more resourceful and more fully functioning. Therapists who take action on behalf of their clients, which clients are capable of doing for themselves, actively prevent their clients from becoming more fully functioning.

Paulo Freire, a contemporary of Rogers writing in the field of education (Freire, 1972), suggested that there is a culture of silence in society which oppresses us all. In our work with people, we need to recognise that real learning only takes place in us when we take ownership of it through the struggle to learn how to be different. As therapists we must learn to be alongside our clients, supporting them as they struggle and enabling them to learn through doing things for themselves. Taking action for them, even just the simple writing of a letter for the client, contributes further to their being stuck in not functioning fully and may negate all the other valuable things we and they have done in working together. If we feel pleased at having done something to help a client, by taking action on their behalf, then we need to look at whose introjections of worth we are responding to in us and which of our needs we are meeting, with the pretence that we are meeting the needs of the client.

If we have a tendency to be a 'rescuer' in everyday life and a belief that we 'must' always help everyone else, we should be working to become more aware of this tendency and its unethical nature. We should be working hard to modify this tendency to rescue others, to a position where we more naturally check if someone can do something for themselves, before leaping to their aid. If we can become more mindful of this in our everyday life, it will I am sure enable us to be more mindful of our clients' autonomy and their need to do things for themselves and we will more naturally avoid rescuing them.

I have chosen just one example of an ethical principle which I feel needs to be more fully applied in everyday life as a part of our way of being in life, in order that we can apply it in a more integrated and natural way in our work as therapists, supervisors and trainers. I am aware of a tendency in me, at this moment, to want to explain all the other ethical principles in the same manner using other examples from my experience. It strikes me that this would be an example of me wanting to 'help' you to understand. It seems to me more appropriate to take the view that you are capable of doing this for yourself and I do not want to undermine your autonomy in any way. You can choose to explore this concept further using examples from your own life and work experience, in order to create your own learning.

Conclusion

In conclusion I would like to quote from the Ethical Framework (BACP, 2002: 4):

> The challenge of working ethically means that practitioners will inevitably encounter situations where there are competing obligations. In such situations it is tempting to retreat from all ethical analysis in order to escape a sense of what may appear to be un-resolvable ethical tension. These ethics are intended to be of assistance in such circumstances by directing attention to the variety of ethical factors that may need to be taken into consideration and to alternative ways of approaching ethics that may prove more useful. No statement of ethics can totally alleviate the difficulty of making professional judgements in circumstances that may be constantly changing and full of uncertainties. By accepting this statement of ethics, members of the British Association for Counselling and Psychotherapy are committing themselves to engaging with the challenge of striving to be ethical, even when doing so involves making difficult decisions or acting courageously.

I would suggest that we should all be engaging with the challenge of striving to be ethical in all aspects of our lives, not just in our work. We need to work towards having an ethical way of being, rather than not doing things that are unethical.

References

British Association for Counselling and Psychotherapy (BACP, 2002) *Ethical Framework for Good Practice in Counselling and Psychotherapy*. Rugby: BACP.

Casemore, R. (2006) *Person-Centred Counselling in a Nutshell*. London: Sage.

Freire, P. (1972) *Cultural Action for Freedom*. Harmondsworth: Penguin.

Rogers, C. R. (1957) The necessary and sufficient conditions of psychological personality change. *Journal of Consulting Psychology* 21, 95–103.

Rogers, C. R. (1969) *On Becoming a Person*. London: Constable.

Rogers, C. R. (1980) *A Way of Being*. New York: Houghton Mifflin.

Stanford Encyclopedia of Philosophy (2006) http://plato.stanford.edu/entries/aristotle-ethics/ (accessed 10 September 2008).

Wikipedia Online Encyclopedia (2008) http://en.wikipedia.org/wiki/Ethics (accessed 10 September 2008).

Chapter 4

Relational ethics beyond the sex and gender binary

An integrative relational approach

Aaron Balick

> Self revelation is not an option; it is an inevitability.
>
> Lewis Aron (1999)

Introduction

Several provocative questions need to be asked in order to position this chapter in a way that I hope is not inherently self-evident. That is, to wonder aloud why space would be made in this book to approach relational ethics with regard to a client group that can broadly be described as being sexually non-conventional. We can start by asking whether it is even necessary to have a separate chapter investigating relational ethics when working with lesbian, gay, bisexual, transgendered (LGBT) individuals? Are the issues not the same with heterosexuals as they are with LGBT individuals? Is hiving off another section to address these issues simply another representation of the way in which matters such as gender and sexual identity, sexual behaviours and sexual orientation are continually set aside as something 'other'? Is the process of asking these questions itself making the task more complicated than it needs to be? After all, people are different, and difference matters. Identities that exist outside the dominant paradigm do come with their own sets of dynamics: dynamics that affect those both inside and outside that paradigm. While working with marginal sexual identity individuals may throw this paradigm into sharp relief, I would argue that it is also present, limiting and marginalising within individuals of 'conventional' identities too.

In this chapter I will be focusing attention on how such dynamics work within LGBT client groups, while continually acknowledging that such dynamics are universal in all psychotherapeutic work. My underlying position, as I will discuss further below in this chapter, is that all gender and sexual identities are relationally constituted and not at all straightforward. For this reason, the concept of LGBT becomes limiting whereas 'queer' is inappropriate for other reasons that will be discussed. For the sake of brevity I will continue to use LGBT along with other phrases (sexual minority individuals, sexually marginal clients, etc.) but will request that the reader understand these as terms used for convenience.

Marginal identities are provocative. Diana Fuss (1991) understands the challenging dynamic of marginality in terms of 'inside' and 'outside' constructions. According to Fuss, inside/outside works by enabling meanings to be made from the tension of boundaries within binary oppositions such as homo/hetero or masculine/feminine. These very boundaries form the skeleton of how individuals situate themselves within meaning, as Fuss describes it:

> Inside/outside functions as the very figure for signification and the mechanisms of meaning production. It has everything to do with the structures of alienation, splitting, and identification, which together produce a self and an other, a subject and an object, an unconscious and a conscious, an interiority and an exteriority. Indeed, one of the fundamental insights of Lacanian psychoanalysis . . . is the notion that any identity is founded relationally, constituted in reference to an exterior or outside that defines the subject's own interior boundaries and corporeal surfaces.
>
> (Fuss, 1991: 1–2)

Meanings of sexual identity, then, are made within a dialectic of difference. While this difference has conventionally been seen as a binary one, I would suggest that it is more complicated than that: gender and sexual identity is experienced multiply and relationally. I use the terms 'multiple' and 'relational' to draw a distinction between the specific perspectives of both conventional binary thinking, which aims to categorise and pathologise marginal sexualities, and contemporary queer theory which, in an attempt to undermine the binary, envisions gender to be essentially fluid, performative and socially constructed (e.g. Butler, 1999). I take an integrative view of gender identity that includes influences from psychoanalytic and developmental perspectives (Freud, 1905; Fast, 1984; Stoller, 1984), deconstructive perspectives from the tradition of Foucault (1998) and developed by such thinkers as Butler (1991, 1999, 2002), Sedgwick (1990) and Weeks (2003) in line with a relational perspective in clinical practice and contemporary psychoanalytic theory advocated by Benjamin (1988), Corbett (2002), Dimen (2003), Goldner (1991), and Harris (2005), to name but a few.

The balance between such models is precarious and not always straightforward. Developmental models hold that there is a constant tension between biological sex, gender identity, gender role, etc. Within this model, identities emerge through a combination of genetics and biology that blend with culture and are developed relationally, first between infant and parent and later through wider social interaction (Stoller, 1984: ix). Contrary to this, queer theorists challenge the notion of identity altogether, wishing to undermine and deconstruct them as repositories of social power (Seidman, 1993). Relational psychoanalytic theory works within the tensions of these two divergent models. There is not room in this chapter to explore the nuanced differences between the divergent social, political and clinical aims of such theories but it is important to acknowledge that the aims of the different discourses are distinct. For a start, much queer theory is grounded in continental philosophy and is politically oriented and aclinical in its conception. The clinical position of affirmative psychotherapy, a transtheoretical perspective developed to work with LGB clients, will be reassessed in the light of the theoretical bodies mentioned above. The overall aim will be to assess what makes an ethical relationship with clients of all sexual and gender identities.

Beyond affirmative therapy

Much has been written with regard to the shifting perception of homosexuality from within the mental health field (Lewes, 1995; Davies, 1996; Dean and Lane, 2001; to name a fraction). Clearly, things have changed a great deal since homosexuality was removed as a mental illness from the *Diagnostic and Statistical Manual* in 1973 (Lewes, 1995). Most mainstream mental health practitioners now perceive homosexuality, bisexuality and lesbianism as a normal variant of sexual behaviour. Unfortunately, this growth of 'normal variant' theory has not completely extended to transgender and transsexual experience. Many individuals who experience themselves as transgendered today feel as if their identities are underrepresented and largely misunderstood.

Despite these changes, many practitioners, and perhaps more importantly ordinary members of the public, have continued to pathologise and stigmatise homosexuality, homosexuals and the myriad of non-straight identities and sexual practices that exist in our varied species. While I would argue that the binary nature of our social matrix in which we exist limits and impedes everyone within it, the dominant model of 'compulsory heterosexuality' (Rich, 1993) is particularly damaging to individuals who experience themselves as far outside this dominant paradigm. As Jack Drescher has aptly pointed out:

> All gay men have been raised with family and friends' expectations that they become heterosexuals. Many report feeling different from heterosexual peers and understand that their same-sex attractions presented obstacles in complying with desires and aspirations of their heterosexual parents . . . gay men . . . often recall childhood experiences that symbolised, to them, the cultural biases against their homoerotic longings.
>
> (Drescher, 1998: 13)

While Drescher may be accurately describing the experience of many gay men brought up in the West, the paradigm can be expanded to include any sexual or gendered identity or behaviour that runs contrary to family and social expectations. For example, something as benign as a little boy who wishes to play with dolls rather than trucks, or the little girl who wants to grow up to be a Formula One mechanic, may encounter both implicit and explicit shame-based imperatives intended to bring them into line with the expected gender role. Such inducements to shame would surely affect the development of coping strategies deployed to hide authentic gender expression in exchange for more acceptable modes of expression. Winnicott (1965), though not referring specifically to gender, coined the term 'false self' in an effort to describe the process used by the infant to satisfy the mother's needs, but only at great expense to his or her 'real' self. Such a false self would conceivably develop in response to suppressed expression of authentic gender by family and larger social networks.

Further light can be shed on this dynamic from a Jungian perspective. Like Winnicott, Jung's conception of the term 'persona' is not gendered. Yet, as I have pointed out previously, 'if we gender concepts like individuation and persona, we can see that the authentically gendered individuating force is subsumed under the social expectations played out by the persona' (Balick, 2006). Theoretical insights from across the spectrum can only further elucidate the complex machinations of human experience. Whether these insights come from object relations (as with Winnicott) or from analytical psychology (in the case of Jung), a thoughtful and cohesive integration from the margins to the orthodoxies of psychotherapeutic theory can only add to a more inclusive understanding of both the 'margins' and 'orthodoxy' of lived human experience.

Many individuals coming to psychotherapists are looking for ways to rehabilitate whatever it is that has been subsumed under the earlier need for parental acceptance. Whether one chooses to understand this as a struggle between the real and false self, or the desire for individuation waylaid by the prerogatives of the persona, the aims are identical – enabling the client to reacquaint themselves with the uninhibited (and in this case gendered) experience of themselves which may have been stunted or left behind in their younger years.

Gay affirmative therapy (GAT) has largely been developed to account for and create a clinical strategy for healing the essentially sociological effects of growing up LGBT in a largely straight world. Davies (1996) has written a comprehensive discussion of the GAT model, based primarily on Clark's (1987) 'twelve guidelines for retraining' and 'ground rules for helping'. Additionally, Davies (1996: 26–27) advocates 'the core condition of respect' into which he includes respect for the client's 'sexual orientation', 'personal integrity', and 'lifestyle and culture'. Further, Davies advocates an active role in educating the client with regard to coming to terms with their sexuality, advising on books and/or videos, HIV awareness, and local gay/lesbian resources in the community (pp. 35–36). More recently, Langdridge (2007: 5) has distinguished two 'forms' of GAT which he terms 'weak' or 'ethically affirmative' and 'strong' or 'LGB affirmative' therapy. In Langdridge's model, ethically affirmative therapy is part and parcel of humanistic/integrative work because it would be unethical to work without core conditions of respect or without knowledge of LGB needs with LGB clients, in any case. Furthermore, Langdridge states that 'within this form of practice [ethically affirmative therapy], a gay identity may be valued equally with a heterosexual identity but it is not affirmed in the sense of being *strengthened, supported* or *made firm*' (2007: 6). Conversely, LGB affirmative therapy is described as being more radical in its explicit affirmations, which are made 'to reduce feelings of shame and guilt amongst their clients . . . the therapist uses their authority to try and counter the internalised homonegative values of society' (p. 7). Langdridge goes on to critique both strands through an engaging and challenging phenomenological perspective. I wish to engage GAT, along with the frameworks mentioned above, within a debate on relational ethics with LGBT clients.

In the clinical setting, we must consider the relational co-constructions of gender and sexual identities that are worked through between therapist and client: relational co-constructions that will echo and re-work earlier constructions around sexual identities. Where marginalised identities are concerned, we must be particularly careful that the therapist does not unconsciously foreclose the possibility for the multiple experiencing of gender and sexual identity either for their client or for themselves.

While GAT was constructed to bolster and affirm identities that may have been undermined through family and social interactions which were then internalised, it runs the risk of encouraging an affirmed identity that is not quite right on the experiential level. Langdridge (2007: 8), describing previous criticism to GAT, notes that GAT 'might limit and prematurely foreclose the sexual identity work of an LGB client'. This is an area where 'strong' LGB affirmative therapy could run into problems; it could encourage the adoption of a strong attachment to an identity that may in itself be illusory or premature. It is here that the postmodern (and arguably a-therapeutic) queer perspective may shed light: queer theory's suspicion of identity categories comes into use. It forces us to ask ourselves where these notions of identity come from, and whether they are in fact liberating. However, queer theory's answer, which is generally an idea of gender and sexual fluidity, is not an adequate response to this problem. As Seidman (1993: 133) has warned:

> [The] very refusal to anchor experience in identifications ends up, ironically, denying differences by either submerging them in an undifferentiated oppositional mass or by blocking the development of individual and social differences through the disciplining compulsory imperative to remain undifferentiated.

The consulting room is the very arena where clients (and therapists) will find themselves attracted to identities, and then working out together whether or not they fit. While affirming an identity prematurely would be counter-productive, advocating a queer informed 'fluid' or ungrounded identity might be equally unhelpful. To make this mix even more complex, GAT as described above, only accounts for *conscious events* in the therapeutic encounter, not the *unconscious* ones.

Whatever code of respect or core conditions a therapist brings into the consulting room, there will always be an unconscious component. Though an integrative practitioner, my perspective on these dynamics is broadly psycho-analytic in nature, though I hope to work across theoretical perspectives. For example, while existential theory may not conceive of the unconscious in the way that psychoanalysis does, there is sufficient overlap. Borrowing Sartre's term 'unreflected consciousness', Spinelli (1997: 140) describes an event where 'the opposing elements of one's position are available to reflec-tion, or open to one's awareness, they remain at an implicit rather than explicit level so that they appear to be concealed from conscious thought and action'. However one chooses to acknowledge the 'implicit', this is indeed the mode in which I believe many gender and sexual identities express themselves.

As I have mentioned elsewhere (Balick, 2007), it is crucial that the therapists themselves become aware of their blind spots with regard to their own internalised imperatives, values, judgements and internal object relational world, lest they obliterate possible contact or discovery with their clients of whatever sexuality. Davies (1996: 28) demonstrates that this position is not neglected in GAT when he states that 'therapists have a duty to explore their own values for attitudes which may cause them difficulties *prior* to working with lesbian, gay and bisexual clients'. However, I would push this one level further and ask how therapists' attitudes, values and unconscious states oper-ate in the psychotherapeutic encounter. Furthermore, we must ask ourselves if it is a reasonable expectation that we can truly be 'clear' of some of our less than savoury judgements and values – conscious or unconscious.

The personal state of the therapist is critical if you take the perspective, as advocated by Aron (1999: 248) that 'the patient–analyst relationship is con-tinually established and reestablished through ongoing mutual influence in which both patient and analyst systematically affect, and are affected by each other'. Sexual and gender identities are one of the key elements that are systematically affected by each other. Approval and disapproval, judgement and moral condemnation are all likely to be perceived by the client, regardless of the explicit comments of the therapist. Some of these feelings may be projections of the client's own fears, but some are bound to be accurate. What does the therapist do with his or her reactions to the client's being?

Working relationally, working ethically

As demonstrated in the epigraph to this chapter, it is my position that thera-pist disclosure is consistently occurring regardless of what may or may not be said in the consultation room. The client consistently picks up subtle cues from the therapist; these cues are composed of transferences, countertransferences, projective identifications and real dynamics between the person of the therapist and the client. Dominant social constructs inhabit the consulting room as much as they do in the outside world, and for this reason, it is crucial that therapists do not make assumptions about their patients which reflect dominant modes. Richard Isay (1993), an out gay analyst, argues that in the absence of any further information, the basic implication within the psychoanalytic setting is that the analyst is going to be heterosexual. The case of a gay therapist withholding information about their sexual orientation from a gay client would be colluding with the heterocentric position. Furthermore, the resistance to acknowledge and name the marginal position is likely to harden the feeling of marginality in both client and therapist. Isay (1993: 199) advocates therapist self-disclosure in such a circumstance 'in the service of the collaborative work', a radical position for a psychoanalyst, though recognisably and commendably typical of humanistic/integrative practice.

In order to work ethically with individuals of any sexual or gender identity, therapists must be in a position to consider their own responses within the relational matrix that is co-created there. Goldner describes the co-evolving nature of a subject's gender development in the following way:

> Gender can be used as a vehicle to establish, maintain, or deny, crucial attachments. Thus, gender can be said to provide a deus ex machina for the relational dilemmas of development. Conceptualising gender in these terms highlights the ways in which personhood, gender identity, and relationship structures develop together, coevolving and codetermining each other. From such a relational perspective, it is not useful to think of gender as being 'acquired' by the child at all; rather, the symbolic structure of gender shapes and organizes the conflict-laden layering of internalized self-representations and object ties that become the child.
>
> (Goldner, 1991: 261–262)

It is within the therapy room that such 'self-representations and object ties' can be accessed, loosened, and in many cases, healed. The intersubjective nature of this work is subtle, but requires the therapist and client to remain open to how they experience their gender and sexual identities and feelings in vivo.

I will illustrate this difficult concept with a case vignette. A young gay man, who I will call 'Tim', had been coming to see me for private psychotherapy to resolve some issues about his relationships with men, which were in general fraught with difficulty. I wish to thank Tim for his consenting to my using material from his session here. While his name and other identifying information have been disguised, I have as accurately as possible, from memory, reconstructed the session material.

Though in a long-term relationship with a man, Tim often felt himself lacking power and agency in relationships with men in general. In contrast to women, men were an unknown quantity, difficult to read and, from Tim's point of view, routinely capable of negative judgement and destructive thoughts. Tim's relationship with men was causing him difficulty in life via the inevitable relationships that would occur in work and social situations; not to mention the potential for such a dynamic to impinge on loving relationships with men as a gay man. Throughout our therapy together, I became aware how *our* relationship was developing, since I was one of the men in Tim's life; one who's role was to provide care, understanding, insight and validation. Achieving this role, as the 'good' psychotherapist, was difficult and not always achievable as my position as a man was frequently figure (rather than ground) in the room.

On one occasion Tim was reporting to me about how he was required to meet with two 'gruff' men through work, men who had a history of domestic violence. While Tim was expressing his anxiety and concern about this upcoming meeting, I noticed my own sense of anxiety as I put myself in Tim's shoes. As Tim carried on, I noticed the anxiety in my stomach along with the thought, 'Yes, I'd be anxious too in that position'.

As I was coming to terms with my thoughts, and trying to make space to contain Tim's anxieties, Tim said, 'But that wouldn't bother *you*. You could just sit there all masculine and neutral like that, no problem'.

Tim's comment was surprising to me. He was constructing me as 'neutral and masculine' while I was experiencing myself as identifying with his worry and concern. In an effort to normalise the situation and bring attention to what I would describe as an idealising transference (enhanced with a projection of solid masculinity), I chose to share my initial feelings with Tim, disclosing to him that I too would feel anxious in the given situation. Rather than normalising the situation, however, Tim felt that I was 'just saying that' to make him feel better. Tim went on to say that he was concerned that these men at work would intuit that he was gay, and that this could be a problem. In the same circumstances, thought Tim, his therapist would have been protected from such insinuations through his 'masculinity' and 'neutrality'.

At this moment an odd thing began to happen to me. I started to *feel* masculine and neutral, just as he'd described it to me. This feeling took me by surprise and shocked me, as I usually do not experience myself in such a way, especially in my role as an integrative psychotherapist. What was occurring here is a process clearly delineated by Orbach (1999):

> Patients bring selective aspects of themselves to the therapy relationship and both consciously and unconsciously stimulate responses in the therapist – responses often at odds with the usual idiom of the therapist. So the therapist can find herself, at particular moments within the therapy, inhabiting a role, a stance, a set of responses not quite of her making . . . By deconstructing and analysing these personal dramas the therapist

finds a route into understanding the difficulties and dilemmas which beset her patient.

(Orbach, 1999: 192)

This is precisely what began to happen in this case. As Tim explained his fantasy of how I'd react in the given situation, I actually began to *feel* masculine and neutral: a feeling at odds with my usual idiom, to borrow Orbach's phrase. Here was a profound opportunity to work relationally with Tim, to bring the dynamics to the surface and work with them *in the room*.

I disclosed to Tim my mystification at feeling masculine and neutral. I mentioned that my own 'poofiness' felt miles away, and had been replaced by this feeling of masculine neutrality. Tim expressed surprise at my disclosure that there were times when I could be 'poofy', but then remarked that sometimes he could see the edges of my poofiness when I made jokes or laughed during a session (i.e. when I became human). I wondered aloud if something happened in our relationship where he got stuck with all the poofiness, and I got stuck with all the masculine power: something that was indicative of Tim's relationship with other men. By bringing my personal experience of Tim into the foreground, we gave these phenomena a voice and could work more consciously with the material. While this did not provide us with immediate answers or solutions to the deeply engrained dynamic, it did start to reveal the relational dynamics in a real and accessible way. These complex dynamics were brought to the surface, lived in the room, and through identifying co-created transferential phenomena, they were made conscious.

What occurred in the room between Tim and myself was more than a transference that needed interpretation, or a sexualised position that required affirmation; it was a co-created dynamic that was being lived in the room. In order for a therapist to work effectively with such material, he or she must be prepared to work with aspects of their own sexual or gendered identities that may be provoked in the session – phenomena of sexual identity that may indeed feel uncomfortable. Tim was courageous enough to speak about his difficulty in sitting in the room with me (and the ghosts of these neutral masculine men). It would only be fair that I acknowledge those aspects of myself that may have been colluding in such a dynamic: that is, the security of leaving my soft 'poofy' nature outside and residing in the masculine neutrality of a transference interpretation. This second position would heap all of the responsibility on to Tim, rather than acknowledge the co-creation of the situation between the two of us. The capacity to bring such elusive dynamics into the room is essential for effecting change of both intra and interpsychic relationships.

Conclusion

While each member organisation of the United Kingdom Council for Psychotherapy (UKCP) has its own set of ethical principles, the UKCP code of ethics provides general principles and statements. With regard to relationships, the UKCP code states that therapists must maintain appropriate boundaries with clients (past and present) and desist from exploiting them in any way, sexually, financially or emotionally (UKCP, 2006). In this chapter I have chosen not to address explicit infractions of such standards; some work has already been done in this area by Gabriel and Davies (2000). While I would concur that more thinking should be done about such issues, as there are distinct differences that need to be considered, I chose instead to focus on the implicit conditions that create an ethical relational space. Therapists working within all aspects of the sexuality spectrum must ask themselves if they are providing a comprehensive therapeutic opportunity for their clients. Can therapists be in touch with the multiple and relational aspects of their own gender and sexuality in a way that does not foreclose opportunity for full exploration on the side of their clients? Are therapists prepared to take the risk, to plunge directly into relational dynamics that are likely to provoke uncomfortable aspects of their own sexuality? If this is not the case, then I would suggest that it is perhaps not ethical to work with sexual minority individuals: not to mention how such positioning may foreclose some possibilities with sexually 'conventional' clients as well. Knowing the cultural world of the client is not enough. Affirming is not enough. Perhaps what makes the therapeutic endeavour enough is the potential to enter a space where one does *not know*. Arrival at that place of knowledge is something that arises in the relational matrix between therapist and client.

There are myriad concepts and theoretical positions that can help enable therapists to work better with clients both within and outside the mainstream. In this chapter I reviewed the input of developmental theories, queer theories, relational theories and the affirmative model of working with LGB clients. My approach advocates that the most ethical position one can take is to acknowledge, as much as possible, the felt dynamics of the therapist in relationship with his or her client. This positioning has no requirement that the therapist identifies in any way with a particular sexual or gender identity. Only that they make room for any sexual or gendered experience that they may have in the room with their client, and then make use of that in a way that they identify as most useful for the client. The ethically responsible position is to use as much of the self as possible to encounter as much of the client as they choose to bring into the therapeutic encounter.

References

Aron, L. (1999) The patient's experience of the analyst's subjectivity. In S. A. Mitchell and L. Aron (eds) *Relational Psychoanalysis: The Emergence of a Tradition*. Hillsdale, NJ: Lawrence Erlbaum Associates, Inc.

Balick, A. (2006) *Liberating sexual identity and gendering sexual desire: rethinking gender and psychoanalysis in the face of queer theory*. Paper presented at the International Association of Jungian Studies Conference: Psyche and Imagination. Greenwich, London, UK.

Balick, A. (2007) Gay subjects relating: object relations between gay therapist and gay client. In E. Peel, V. Clarke and J. Drescher (eds) *British Gay and Lesbian Psychologies: Theory, Research, and Practice*. Binghampton, NY: Hayworth Press.

Benjamin, J. (1988) *The Bonds of Love*. New York: Pantheon Books.

Butler, J. (1991) Imitation and gender insubordination. In D. Fuss (ed.) *Inside/Out: Lesbian Theories, Gay Theories*. New York and London: Routledge.

Butler, J. (1999) *Gender Trouble: Feminism and the Subversion of Identity*. London: Routledge.

Butler, J. (2002) Melancholy gender-refused identification. In M. Dimen and V. Goldner (eds) *Gender in Psychoanalytic Space: Between Clinic and Culture*. New York: Other Press.

Clark, D. (1987) *The New Loving Someone Gay*. Berkeley, CA: Celestial Arts.

Corbett, K. (2002) The mystery of homosexuality. In M. Dimen and V. Goldner (eds) *Gender in Psychoanalytic Space: Between Clinic and Culture*. New York: Other Press.

Davies, D. (1996) Towards a model of gay affirmative therapy. In D. Davies and C. Neal (eds) *Pink Therapy: A Guide for Counsellors and Therapists Working with Lesbian, Gay and Bisexual Clients*. Maidenhead: Open University Press.

Davies, D. and Neal, C. (1996) An historical overview of homosexuality and therapy. In D. Davies and C. Neal *Pink Therapy: A Guide for Counsellors and Therapists Working with Lesbian, Gay and Bisexual Clients*. Maidenhead: Open University Press.

Dean, T. and Lane, C. (2001) Homosexuality and psychoanalysis: an introduction. In T. Dean and C. Lane (eds) *Homosexuality and Psychoanalysis*. Chicago: University of Chicago Press.

Dimen, M. (2003) *Sexuality, Intimacy, Power*. Hillsdale, NJ: Analytic Press.

Drescher, J. (1998) *Psychoanalytic Therapy and the Gay Man*. Hillsdale, NJ: Analytic Press.

Fast, I. (1984) *Gender Identity: A Differentiation Model*. Hillsdale, NJ: Analytic Press.

Foucault, M. (1998) *The Will to Knowledge: The History of Sexuality 1*. Trans. R. Hurley. Harmondsworth: Penguin.

Freud, S. (1905/1953) Three essays on the theory of sexuality. *SE* 7: 123–245. London: Hogarth Press.

Fuss, D. (1991) Inside/out. In D. Fuss (ed.) *Inside/Out: Lesbian Theories, Gay Theories*. New York and London: Routledge.

Gabriel, L. and Davies, D. (2000) The management of ethical dilemmas associated with dual relationships. In C. Neal and D. Davies (eds) *Issues in Therapy with Gay, Lesbian, Bisexual and Transgender Clients*. Maidenhead: Open University Press.

Goldner, V. (1991) Toward a critical relational theory of gender. *Psychoanalytic Dialogues* 1, 249–272.

Harris, A. (2005) *Gender as Soft Assembly*. Hillsdale, NJ: Analytic Press.

Isay, R. (1993) On the analytic treatment of homosexual men. In C. Cornett (ed.) *Affirmative Dynamic Psychotherapy with Gay Men*. Northvale, NJ: Jason Aronson.

Langdridge, D. (2007) Gay affirmative therapy: a theoretical framework and defence. *Journal of Gay and Lesbian Psychotherapy* 11, 1/2.

Lewes, K. (1995) *Psychoanalysis and Male Homosexuality*. Northvale, NJ: Jason Aronson.

Orbach, S. (1999) *The Impossibility of Sex*. Harmondsworth: Penguin.

Rich, A. (1993) Compulsory heterosexuality and lesbian experience. In H. Abelove, M. A. Barale and D. M. Halperin (eds) *The Lesbian and Gay Studies Reader*. New York and London: Routledge.

Sedgwick, E. (1990) *Epistemology of the Closet*. London: Harvester Wheatsheaf.

Seidman, S. (1993) Identity and politics in a 'postmodern' gay culture. In M. Warner (ed.) *Fear of a Queer Planet: Queer Politics and Social Theory*. Minneapolis and London: University of Minnesota Press.

Spinelli, E. (1997) *Tales of Un-Knowing: Therapeutic Encounters from an Existential Perspective*. London: Duckworth.

Stoller, R. (1984) *Sex and Gender, Vol. 1: The Development of Masculinity and Femininity*. London: Maresfield.

UKCP (2006) *Code of Ethics*. www.psychotherapy.org.uk (accessed 10 September 2008).

Weeks, J. (2003) *Sexuality*, 2nd edn. Abingdon: Routledge.

Winnicott, D. W. (1965) Ego distortions in terms of true and false self. In D. W. Winnicott *The Maturational Processes and the Facilitating Environment*. New York: International Universities Press.

Chapter 5

Relational ethics in supervision

Val Wosket

I would like to start by outlining some of my own process as it unfolded around writing this chapter. My first reaction on being invited to make a contribution to this volume was to feel unsure that I knew enough about the concept of relational ethics to write anything useful. So while feeling energised by the prospect of tackling a new topic, I also experienced some apprehension about whether I might expose myself as having a lack of knowledge and expertise on the subject.

Then as I began to consider the topic I had been asked to write about – specifically relational ethics *in supervision* – I noticed a parallel with something going on in my own supervision experience at the time. I was in the process of moving to a new supervisor pending the retirement of my previous supervisor with whom I had been working for six years. In the initial meeting with my new supervisor I felt a mixture of feelings: sadness at the loss of my previous supervisory relationship coupled with excitement and anticipation at the prospect of working with another person with whom I might look at my clinical work from different and new perspectives. Sitting alongside these emotions were tangible feelings of anxiety and exposure. My scared feelings were around a number of 'what ifs?', including the following:

- What if he doesn't understand and accept the way I work?
- What if he doesn't think I'm competent to work with the issues/clients I am working with?
- What if he thinks I shouldn't be working with particular clients because of the complexity of their issues?
- What if he decides that he can't supervise me on some of my work?
- What if I am too unorthodox for him?

I was able to voice these concerns with my new supervisor in our first session together, although this felt uncomfortable and increased my feelings of exposure. It struck me later as I thought about this session that professional and ethical concerns were already beginning to surface right at the start of our relationship through my anxious self-questioning. As I reflected on this new beginning it dawned on me that the full and effective exploration of ethical issues in supervision is always rooted in the quality of the relationship between supervisor and supervisee.

So thinking back to my qualms about embarking on this chapter I can now see that the challenge for me was not so much about whether I 'knew enough' about relational ethics. Rather, I think the challenge was to find a way of putting together something of what I know and have experienced about ethics and about relationships in supervision into a form that communicates a little of that lived experience.

I have endeavoured to do this through including issues and examples that have arisen in my own practice of supervision – including one which seemed to turn out well and another where I felt I blundered in the process. I have included the latter as well as the former to emphasise the important learning potential to be mined from mistakes and omissions. In addition I hope that the examples of supervision practice included later in the chapter serve to illustrate the point captured by Frawley-O'Dea and Sarnat (2001: 69) that 'in effective supervision supervisor and supervisee may access new strands of their own life narratives'. It is my belief that good supervision can be a transformative experience for both supervisor and supervisee.

The supervisory relationship and quality assurance in supervision

As a supervisor I consider that the quality of relationship I manage to build and sustain with my supervisees is of paramount importance when it comes round to fulfilling my responsibility to monitor the quality assurance aspects of supervision. As a humanistic, integrative practitioner I hold that the relationship with my supervisees is important in two key ways. First, our relationship is about the quality of our emotional connection – including how real, human and vulnerable we are able to be with one another. Second, it encompasses our working alliance – our commitment to one another and our motivation to engage together in the tasks and process of supervision. Crucially in all of this, the quality of our relationship governs how freely and without fear of censure my supervisees can bring (both consciously and unconsciously) their mistakes, difficulties, fears and desires to supervision.

There is evidence to support the notion that the probability of whether supervisees will disclose ethical concerns in supervision is closely related to the quality of the supervisory relationship (Webb and Wheeler, 1998; Kaberry, 2000). This probability normally rests on the assumption that the ethical concern is in the conscious awareness of the supervisee whereas it is often the case, as Bramley (1996: 82) has observed, that 'most philosophical and ethical issues that come to supervision do so accidentally'. So what if the supervisee (and/or supervisor) is initially unaware of an ethical issue? In this case the supervisory relationship itself may become a conduit through which ethical concerns that are out of conscious awareness can surface and become available for exploration. An example of the emergence of an ethical dilemma in this way is given in the case illustration included towards the end of this chapter.

Because of the vital part played by the supervisory relationship in picking up clues to ethical issues that require attention, it follows that supervisor and supervisee need to place a high priority on maintaining the quality of that relationship and taking steps to review, nurture and repair it where necessary.

If the relationship between supervisor and supervisee is important for the informational value it may contain, it becomes pertinent to consider how this information might be made manifest. Frawley-O'Dea and Sarnat (2001) have suggested that information is frequently revealed in the way that the vicissitudes of the supervisory relationship mirror and parallel relational dynamics occurring between the supervisee and his or her client. An example of this would be where a supervisee brings to supervision an experience of feeling compelled to respond in an unusual or bizarre way to a client – that sense of finding myself acting as 'me and not me' which is familiar to many therapists. When this occurs it is important for the supervisor to pay attention to what the client seems to be evoking or provoking in the therapist and to consider with the supervisee how this projection may mirror or echo the client's fantasies, fears or yearnings in their (past or present) relational matrix. This may be picked up through a parallel process originating in the supervisor whereby he or she finds themselves, in turn, compelled to act out some unusual relational behaviour towards their supervisee. Hopefully the following example will make this clearer:

> My supervisee brought to supervision his unusual feelings of powerlessness and passivity in response to feeling berated by his client. He felt stunned by her critical onslaught and incapable of responding. It was an unfamiliar and extra-ordinary experience for him to feel paralysed and overwhelmed by the client's material in this way.
>
> In exploring this issue with him I made the error of pursuing what I thought would be a useful response he might make to the client. Unusually (I hope) for me, I did this in a didactic and directive manner that jarred with my supervisee's experience and resulted in a loss of meaningful contact between us. The more I 'banged on' about what I felt I wanted my supervisee to address with his client, the more I pursued my own agenda and lost contact with how my supervisee was feeling. At this point my empathy deserted me and it was only as he became visibly distressed that I had the grace to notice, pause in what I was saying and check out what he was experiencing. He was then able to let me know that he was feeling uncomfortable and put on the spot – at which point I had the sense to back off and start listening to him again.

At that moment I came up against my own capacity for arrogance, insensitivity, lack of awareness and abuse of power. Here I was trying to force a course of action onto my supervisee that he rightly resisted because it felt imposed and unhelpful. I felt ashamed and regretful when I realised what had happened. What had gone wrong was that I had failed to pay attention to how the relationship was between us as I wielded my ethical agenda as a very blunt instrument.

Later, as we processed what had occurred between us, we were able to understand the dynamic in our supervisory relationship as, in part, a reflection of the client's relational world wherein she had frequently experienced bullying and abuse of power. My supervisee had received two illuminating doses of what this might have felt like for his client – one from her in the counselling session and one from me in the supervision – and had also experienced what it might be like to feel unprotected and powerless under such an onslaught.

What eventually emerged from our understanding of this parallel process was useful awareness that helped my supervisee develop his empathy, resilience and resourcefulness when faced with further attacking responses from the client. As the supervisor I learned more about my own shadow side – about both its destructive and informational potential. Fortunately my relationship with my supervisee was robust enough to survive this rupture and to sustain the necessary processing we needed to do to understand the meaning and therapeutic potential of what had occurred between us. I recall that we had a warm and spontaneous hug at the end of the session which felt reparative for our relationship and not, I think, merely reassuring for us both.

Working with the supervisee's process

The example given above illustrates that something which is going on between therapist and client and not being addressed or acknowledged may be thought of and worked with in supervision in terms of transference, countertransference and parallel process (see Page and Wosket, 2001). However, it is important to remember that experiences such as this have real as well as transferential elements. Because therapy is a reciprocal process it is likely that the client becomes attuned to and astute at activating, albeit unconsciously, places where the therapist is wounded or vulnerable. This may be linked to what Frawley-O'Dea and Sarnat (2001: 53) have described as the client's determination (even if unconscious) to 'repetitively co-construct with another familiar maladaptive relational pattern'.

Because of the power and inevitability of this co-construction, supervisors need to give space, time, attention and care to the therapist's wounded self as well as to theoretical considerations of parallel processes. This is important in order to help the therapist understand and integrate wounded parts of the self into their authentic professional self and to free them from unconsciously acting out from a wounded part that might otherwise demand attention and fulfilment (Wosket, 1999). If this material is surfaced, named and given emotional expression, the supervisee is then freer to stand back and consider how their own issues and experiences are interacting with the client's.

For this reason I encourage my supervisees to bring their own process to supervision. Exploring the numerous ways that client material may overlap with or trigger the therapist's own issues can provide vital information on a number of levels, for instance:

- What might be going on for the client that the therapist is missing or overlooking?
- What might be contaminating (or enhancing) the therapist's response to the client?
- What support and self-care might the supervisee need in order to work effectively with the client?
- Where might the parallel processes be located?
- What informational value may those parallel processes hold?
- What learning, personal transformation or healing potential may there be for the therapist in working with the client's material?

A few examples from my recent supervisory practice may make this clearer:

When exploring a feeling of stuckness with one particular client, supervisee V connected to a sense of needing to be liked and admired by this client which seemed to have been triggered by the client's determination to put her counsellor on a pedestal. At the same time supervisee V experienced a fear of being found out as not knowing or of being clumsy or slow. Through exploring this in supervision she became aware of powerful echoes from her training which she had at times experienced as punitive, controlling, shaming and belittling, particularly in interactions with one particular tutor. Following this awareness she was then able to consider how best to show herself as real and vulnerable with her client, while retaining a sense of her strengths and resources as an effective practitioner.

Supervisee W brought an issue about boundaries with a child client. During supervision she realised that she felt drawn to offering more to this vulnerable young person because he reminded her of her own young self 'abandoned' as a child through a period of hospitalisation. Attending to the experience of her own 'child' in supervision allowed the impulse to 'rescue' her young client to diminish.

Supervisee X brought his emotional response to a client where he had felt deeply moved, open to and gratified by a recent interaction with her. He was worried by the overwhelming nature of his reaction which left him feeling raw, unprotected and exposed in relationship with the client. At the same time he also had the sense of feeling hugely validated by the deep connection he experienced with her in the session. The work of supervision was to help him think about what this experience meant for him as a counsellor and how to integrate it into his evolving professional self (Skovholt and Rønnestad, 1992).

Supervisee Y brought to supervision her ongoing process of loss and adjustment during a period in which she experienced family rejection and isolation. Supervision helped her to look at ways to protect herself when working with clients with similar issues and also at how her own experience could translate into greater empathic resonance with these clients.

Supervisee Z brought an organisational issue to supervision, part of which involved an experience of feeling bullied at work. During supervision he connected with his childhood experience of being raised in a care home and realised that his inclination not to complain or speak out at work was linked to memories of being punished for protesting as a child. Making this connection freed up a more 'adult' part of himself and could then think about addressing the situation at work more assertively.

The insights developed by these supervisees in their supervision sessions grew out of exploration that initially focused on a particular dilemma with a client or an organisational issue. Had the supervisory process not allowed and encouraged the expression of the supervisees' own process, awareness of these crucial connections and overlaps might have been missed.

Accommodating issues of power, authority and difference in relational ethics

Relational ethics, as I begin to understand it further, seems to encompass the concepts of balance and flow. The supervisor who fulfils the ethical functions of supervision through close attention to the supervisory relationship is able to move back and forth along a continuum that avoids the two extreme stances of either the 'passive optimist' or the 'ethical inquisitor' (Page and Wosket, 2001). Relational supervision gives priority to exploring and amplifying the relational dynamics between the supervisor and supervisee and between the supervisee and their client in the hope and expectation that, in so doing, issues that require ethical consideration will surface in a fluid and organic way.

The analogy that comes to mind is one from dentistry. So here it is not so much an act of teeth-pulling as a series of gentle and regular check-ups that may begin to show signs of possible damage, weakness or vulnerability well before an emergency extraction comprises the only possible course of action. Supportive, consistent and constructively challenging supervision that foregrounds attention to relational dynamics helps to develop ethical mindfulness in supervisees which in turn lessens the chances of sudden ethical emergencies arising in the process. This is an approach that views client safety and welfare as building on the counsellor's capacity to develop as a unique, autonomous and reflective practitioner – a capacity that is nurtured through supervision that is relational and process-oriented (Page and Wosket, 2001).

Research is beginning to support the notion that dynamic, process-oriented supervision enhances safe and ethical practice. For example, therapists who participated in Vallance's (2004) study exploring counsellor perceptions of the impact of supervision on client work reported that they experienced directive supervision as unhelpful and disempowering. In contrast, supervision that prioritised exploring counsellor–client dynamics increased a feeling of freedom and safety in client work. Frawley-O'Dea and Sarnat (2001) have criticised didactic supervision as predicated on an asymmetrical relationship where knowledge is conveyed downward and received by the supervisee. They advocate a relational model of supervision in which knowledge and meaning are co-constructed between supervisor and supervisee. Through the notion of relational ethics in supervision I believe we are beginning to explore this link between the quality of the supervisory relationship and its capacity to enhance autonomous and ethical practice by supervisees.

The monitoring of safe and effective practice in supervision is largely determined by how the supervisor wields their power and authority. Most forms of supervision are hierarchical (with the exception of peer supervision) and therefore imbued with an imbalance of power in favour of the supervisor. It is a bad mistake for the supervisor, and a denial of legitimate authority, to pretend that the relationship is entirely equal, when in many respects it is not. At the very least the supervisor has by virtue of their role the power and responsibility to express an opinion as to the quality of the supervisee's work. In many cases the supervisor finds themselves obligated to do more than this – they may be required to undertake formal assessments of a trainee's practice or provide written reports for the accreditation of experienced practitioners. Supervisors are bound by ethical principles and frameworks to invite supervisees to attend to issues of self-care, such as taking time out or having (more) therapy. The supervisor has powerful muscles to flex when required, even if those muscles are, for the most part, held at rest.

Hierarchy and power are inseparable components of supervision in that the supervisor uses their power to influence the supervisee by dint of their dominant position within the hierarchy. Nonetheless, the negative effects of hierarchy can be largely mitigated by the quality of the relationship between supervisor and supervisee. The supervisor has a responsibility to establish an effective climate and conditions for exploration and learning in supervision. Contracting which encompasses sensitivity to aspects of difference and diversity is central to establishing such a climate and to the emergence and sustainability of a robust supervisory relationship.

Relational ethics in supervision seems to me to be largely about using the relationship with my supervisees to mediate and work with issues of uniqueness and difference. Let me try to illustrate this by reference to my own experience. If I were to stand in a room with all my current and recent supervisees, to the casual observer we would look like a homogeneous group – all white, adult and seemingly able-bodied. Yet there are many differences between me and each of them – some visible on closer scrutiny and some not apparent in any outward form. A number of these differences are personal, cultural and ethnic. Many of them are professional. All of these differences affect the ways in which we engage together in the tasks and process of supervision – some profoundly. Table 5.1 provides a snapshot of the main ways in which I experience my supervisees as different to me. I have teased these out into personal and professional differences to give two separate lists – they are not 'matching pairs'.

Bradley and Ladany (2001: 115) speak about 'relationships of choice' in supervision and assert that 'relationship stances or styles should be differentially customized for the particular needs of the supervisee'. A question such as 'What would you like me to know about you that may help us to work

Table 5.1 Difference and diversity in supervision: a personal analysis

Personal differences *Eastern European*	*Professional differences* *Counselling service manager*
Male	Uses translators with non-English-speaking clients
Amputee	Counselling psychologist
Experiences ongoing debilitating illness	Works only with drug and alcohol issues
Visually impaired	Departmental manager with multiple roles
Hearing impaired	Works within health service
Significantly older	Student welfare officer
Significantly younger	Works for crisis service
Single parent on low income	Works for an Employee Assistance Programme (EAP)
Gay	Works exclusively to short-term contracts
Jewish	Predominately person-centred in approach
Catholic	Voluntary counsellor
South African in origin	Newly qualified
Widowed	Trainee
Unemployed	Predominately relational/existential in approach
Approaching retirement	Predominately Gestalt in approach
Brought up in care	Works with asylum seekers
Grandparent	Works with children and young people

together effectively?' posed by the supervisor at the start of a new supervisory relationship can begin to identify the style and stance of relationship that will best suit the needs of individual supervisees.

Working sensitively with a range of differences such as those tabled above begins with clear contracting. Attending to relational ethics at the contracting stage of supervision involves planning ahead and not fighting shy of ethical requirements. This is an occasion where the supervisor needs to work from their sense of power and authority while adopting a collaborative stance with supervisees to work out how ethical issues will be managed between the two of them. A question I always ask new supervisees at the start of our relationship is 'If I have concerns about your practice how would you like me to raise these with you?' A question such as this can effectively take the sting out of the need to address ethical concerns as, if, and when they arise in supervision.

After discussion, we write down our agreed procedure at the contracting stage. My supervisee now knows what will happen in the worst case scenario and also hopefully is reassured that I will bring any concerns into the open as soon as they start to form. As Scaife (2001: 61) asserts, contracting about how to manage ethical issues 'sets a context which gives a message that these matters are subject to some negotiation within the boundaries of ethical practice. That they might arise is seen as normal rather than pathological'.

Other areas of clear contracting that help to establish a climate in which ethical concerns are addressed in a consistent way involve clarity about how emergency supervision or extra supervision will be arranged if and when this is needed. Again I discuss and write this down as agreed with supervisees at the start of our supervision relationship.

Relational ethics and the embodied supervisor

Finally, in order to pull together these thoughts on relational ethics in supervision, with supervisee consent, I now present a further example from my supervision practice. I have chosen this example because I believe there is a tendency to think that paying attention to ethics in supervision is about looking outward and catching what may be going on around the edges of the work – for instance, where there are frame or boundary ruptures. Conversely, attending to ethics in a relational context will often involve the supervisor directing their attention inward and tracking their own embodied responses to the supervisee. The supervisor's interventions will then be closely informed by their internal responses to the supervisee's presentation.

The example illustrates how this process may unfold around the ethical principle of beneficence (what is likely to be of most benefit to the client). In the spirit of reciprocity which I hope to have conveyed in this chapter I have invited my supervisee to comment on his experience of the incident outlined below. His comments and observations follow on from my description of how I experienced this supervisory session. At the time the following incident occurred my relationship with my supervisee, called here Joshua, was fairly new and I had very little background information on the client brought to supervision:

> My supervisee is leaving his organisation in three months time and is moving into an ending phase with a number of his clients, some of whom he has been seeing long term. He brings to supervision one of these clients, called here Michael, whom he has been seeing for over two years. Joshua asks for my help in responding to Michael's request to move into more practical work before they finish – specifically Michael has asked Joshua to give him some techniques to better manage his anxiety.
>
> I feel an immediate resistance to giving Joshua what he is asking from me and I have a strong sense that to agree to his request might be to avoid Michael's and possibly Joshua's own anxiety about ending. I tell him that I feel a resistance to moving into practical issues and I ask him to tell me a little more about Michael's anxiety.
>
> He tells me that Michael's mother died when he was a young adult and that throughout his childhood she had failed to respond adequately to his attachment needs. Michael's anxiety started as a child trying to win the approval of his father who was a violent, alcoholic, neglectful parent from a travelling background. However hard Michael tried to be a good son, his father never seemed to care or to stay around for him.
>
> As Joshua calmly and unemotionally tells me this story I feel immensely sad – so sad that I know my eyes are filling with tears. To begin with I am merely overtaken by this feeling and I take a drink of water to steady myself. As I follow this feeling it leads to a thought and I say to Joshua, 'I feel so sad that I could cry and I have a strong feeling that Michael may be overwhelmed with grief at the thought of his attachment to you ending.'
>
> Joshua says, 'It doesn't feel like that for me. It feels more like if only I could have been a better therapist perhaps he might have been able to feel more attached to me.'
>
> I ask, 'Does what you have just said there resonate with your client's experience in any way?' and he replies, 'That must have been what *he* felt like with his father – if only he could have been a better son his father might have loved him and stayed around.'
>
> We are near the end of the supervision session at this point and don't have time to do much more with this – except for Joshua to say that what has just happened between us feels very powerful.
>
> In our next session a fortnight later we reviewed what had happened in the previous session and Joshua said, 'The supervision helped me to see that I had spent all my time in my relationship with Michael not feeling good enough.' He

was again able to see the parallel with his client's experience here. He then said something very revealing about his countertransference reaction to the client. 'I hadn't been able to see the wood for the trees. My feeling of not being good enough for him to feel attached to me has been so pervasive throughout our work that I have mistaken it for reality.'

About the supervision Joshua said that he had appreciated me sticking with my intuition because it gave him what he *needed* rather than what he thought he *wanted*. The phrase he used was, 'You smelled a rat and went after it.'

The key to picking up on this parallel process was, I think, my trusting my emotional experience and speaking from it, even though it felt risky. In our review Joshua mentioned that he had noticed me becoming tearful and would have felt confused and unsettled by this if I had just ignored or tried to suppress my reaction.

The final echo of a parallel came in Joshua's last words about the incident. He said, 'I never thought I could be important enough for someone to feel so attached to *me*.' This is the point at which – as inevitably happens in these incidents – the therapist uncovers aspects of his or her own process that overlap with the client's.

After this supervision Joshua reported a major shift in the depth of his empathy for the client and the two of them managed to talk about endings instead of cognitive behavioural strategies for anxiety management, although this was not easy for either of them.

Here are Joshua's comments on the session and about what I have written above:

Val offers a fascinating insight into how the supervisor's skilled use of self can serve to highlight countertherapeutic dynamics in a supervisee's clinical work.

Michael might quite reasonably be described as a difficult client. I started seeing him halfway through my Diploma training; such was his anxiety that, for the first four sessions, he was unable to make eye contact. Michael's anxiety led him to present in therapy as a wall of words, and it was easy for me as a rookie to feel deskilled and inadequate to the task of helping him, all the more so as inadequacy was a familiar feeling for me.

Although I had grown in confidence and effectiveness in the two-and-a-half years during which I had worked with Michael, the work remained hard and my view of our relationship was still heavily coloured, as I now appreciate, by those painfully difficult early sessions. The supervision discussed above enabled me to see that in agreeing to shift the focus of our work on to coping strategies, I was allowing my own need to feel – at last – really helpful to override Michael's therapeutic need for deeper relational contact. In this, I was probably assisted by Michael's transferential casting of me in the role of the mother who, as well as being unable to protect him from his father's malice, was never able to attune sufficiently to his emotional needs. The upshot was my unwitting collusion with Michael's view of himself as not good enough for me, or anybody.

Processing this episode with Val enabled me to see how I had come to hold what I described to her as a long-term countertransference belief – in discord with my humanistic stance – that Michael was damaged beyond repair, by me at any rate. This is a classic example of what Paul and Pelham describe as a therapist being drawn into a client's relational dance. In theory, the therapist is alerted to this by the kind of 'me, yet not-me' feeling described by Val elsewhere in this chapter, and is then able to take a step back and facilitate a novel outcome to the familiar drama.

On this occasion, my personal blind spot resulted in the countertransference remaining unquestioned and mistaken for reality. As a result of Val's input, I learnt, in her words to me, 'the distinction between acknowledging and respecting the client's reality and buying into it'. As well as allowing for a more therapeutic ending to my work with Michael, our identification of this long-term countertransference, as opposed to specific, moment-by-moment countertransference, has subsequently helped me to identify countertherapeutic dynamics in my work with other clients. As Val suggests, this episode also alerted me to the need for more personal development work around attachment issues.

Finally, on the theme of parallel processes, I'm struck by Val's description of my 'calm, unemotional' tone in the session in question. Although not the most expressive of people, this doesn't sound quite like me. It does, however, remind me of Michael.

In the work described above it may have become apparent that paying attention to ethical practice – in this instance working with the principle of maximising the benefit of the work to the client – is subsumed within a dynamic process that takes account of several relational matrices: the client and his relational world; the supervisee and his client; the supervisee and the supervisor; the supervisee and his relational world and (if only in fantasy) the supervisor and the client. Exploring and doing our best to understand the various facets of these relationships as we experienced them together on an emotional and cognitive level seemed to give us greater insight into the experience of the client and what he might need than a more directive or didactic approach might have done.

The incident also provides a useful example of an asymmetrical parallel process. The feelings of sadness that unexpectedly welled up for me as the supervisor did not immediately resonate with my supervisee's experience and yet further processing revealed that they may well have had currency in the client–counsellor dyad as giving clues to a dissociated process. In this sense the supervisor's experience here may be thought of as enacting a missing piece of the dynamic jigsaw, or as Frawley-O'Dea and Sarnat (2001: 190) neatly term it 'a postcard from the edge' of the relational scene between client and counsellor that is being re-enacted here by supervisee and supervisor.

In closing this discussion of relational ethics in supervision I will offer a few concluding thoughts about ethical frameworks for good practice, such as that produced by the British Association for Counselling and Psychotherapy (BACP, 2002). I believe that we need ethical frameworks governing supervision that are specific enough to provide clear guidelines and parameters for effective practice and at the same time flexible and inclusive enough to enable practitioners to develop their own autonomy, personally and culturally unique ways of working and internal loci of evaluation.

If ethical frameworks are too rigid and cumbersome they carry a danger of ossifying practice and reducing it to a level of average neutrality by privileging the approach of doing least harm. Ethical frameworks have the potential to become malleable, creative and resourceful mechanisms for containing and shaping counselling and supervisory practice when they are played out in a lived relationship. It now seems to me that relational ethics at its best can and must allow for creative, spontaneous and even unorthodox practice that privileges the needs of individual clients and supervisees over the limits and constraints of externally imposed professional protocols.

References

Bradley, L. J. and Ladany, N. (2001) *Counselor Supervision: Principles, Processes and Practice*, 3rd edn. Philadelphia, PA: Brunner-Routledge.

Bramley, W. (1996) *The Supervisory Couple in Broad-Spectrum Psychotherapy*. London: Free Association Books.

British Association for Counselling and Psychotherapy (BACP, 2002) *Ethical Framework for Good Practice in Counselling and Psychotherapy*. Rugby: BACP.

Frawley-O'Dea, M. and Sarnat, J. (2001) *The Supervisory Relationship: A Contemporary Psychodynamic Approach*. New York: Guilford Press.

Kaberry, S. (2000) Abuse in supervision. In B. Lawton and C. Feltham (eds) *Taking Supervision Forward: Enquiries and Trends in Counselling and Psychotherapy*. London: Sage.

Page, S. and Wosket, V. (2001) *Supervising the Counsellor*, 2nd edn. London: Brunner-Routledge.

Scaife, J. (2001) *Supervision in the Mental Health Professions*. London: Brunner-Routledge.

Skovholt, T. M. and Rønnestad, M. H. (1992) *The Evolving Professional Self: Stages and Themes in Therapist and Counselor Development*. Chichester: Wiley.

Vallance, K. (2004) Exploring counsellor perceptions of the impact of counselling supervision on clients. *British Journal of Guidance and Counselling* 32, 4, 559–574.

Webb, A. and Wheeler, S. (1998) How honest do counsellors dare to be in the supervisory relationship?: an exploratory study. *British Journal of Guidance and Counselling* 26, 4, 509–524.

Wosket, V. (1999) *The Therapeutic Use of Self: Counselling Practice, Research and Supervision*. London: Routledge.

Chapter 6

Ethical research in reflexive relationships

A dialogical process

Kim Etherington

Introduction

As a practitioner-researcher in the field of counselling and psychotherapy I am increasingly engaged in using narrative and life story research methodologies, and reflexive practices that are based upon forming research relationships with people who can help me discover new knowledge by telling me their stories (Etherington, 2000, 2003, 2004). Although this chapter[1] focuses on research, many of the issues can also be related to therapeutic practices.

These narrative and life story methods are based upon gathering, analysing and re-presenting people's stories as told by them. The philosophy that underpins my preferred approaches is based upon my view of reality as socially constructed, and of knowledge as situated and created within contexts, and embedded within historical, cultural stories, beliefs and practices (Gergen, 1985, 1994; Crossley, 2000). These ways of researching challenge the accepted nature of 'grand narratives' and modernist certainties, and question how we come to what we know (Polkinghorne, 1988; McLeod, 1997).

I have also been strongly influenced by feminist principles relating to equality and power that challenge researchers to make transparent the values and beliefs that lie behind their interpretations and to let slip the cloak of authority, lower the barrier between researcher and researched, and allow both sides to be seen and understood for who they are (Etherington, 2004). Those challenges have helped legitimise the reflexive use of 'self' in research: reflexivity being at the heart of feminist methodologies and increasingly other methodologies too. 'It [reflexivity] permeates every aspect of the research process, challenging us to be more fully conscious of the ideology, culture, and politics of those we study and those we select as our audience' (Hertz, 1997: viii).

In this chapter I will present two stories and a poetic representation from my own research that illustrates the challenges and learning gained by my own attempts to conduct ethical research within reflexive relationships. In doing so I hope to add to the recent body of work that increases our understanding of the complexities of relational ethical research, notably Guillemin and Gillam (2004), Hegeland (2005), Adams (2006) and Ellis (2006), all of which encourage us to challenge our research practices to ensure that we sustain a state of what Bond (2000) refers to as 'ethical mindfulness' that contributes to 'an ethic of trust' (Bond, 2006) in our relationships with research participants and ourselves.

Stories as relational

My interest in these issues is embedded in my fascination with stories as a form of knowledge creation and inquiry. Stories are produced and created within social relationships and between storytellers and their audiences; they are also told in professional counselling relationships. Frank (1995: 3) reminds us that stories are told or written to someone, 'whether that other person is immediately present or not. Even messages in a bottle imply a potential reader'. The researcher or therapist, as 'audience', may become actively involved in co-constructing previously untold stories by asking curious questions that help thicken and deepen existing stories and invite the teller into territory beyond what is already known to them. Even when we read stories we might silently fill in the gaps with our own assumptions and beliefs. The stories that are told, and received, are therefore influenced and informed by what tellers and listeners bring to the relationship from their own lives and contexts. All of these notions contribute to a greater recognition of the importance of the relationship between the storyteller and the listener, and between the knower and what is known.

Reflexivity in research

Reflexivity is a skill that we develop as therapists: an ability to notice our responses to the world around us, to stories, to other people and events, and to use that knowledge to inform and direct our actions, communications and understandings (Rennie, 1998; Wosket, 1999). When we extend that skill into the practice of reflexive research we need to be aware of the personal, social and cultural contexts in which we (and others) live and work, and to understand how those contexts impact on our conduct, interpretations and representations of research stories (Denzin, 1997; Edwards and Christians, 2000; Mauthner, 2002).

Reflexivity is therefore a tool whereby we can include our 'selves' at any stage, making transparent the values and beliefs we hold that almost certainly influence the research process, the counselling process and its outcomes. Reflexive research encourages us to display in our writing/conversations the interactions between ourselves and our participants from our first point of contact until we end those relationships, so that our work can be understood, not only in terms of what we have discovered, but how we have discovered it. For myself and other like-minded individuals these are ethical, moral and methodological issues (Frank, 1995; Josselson, 1996; McLeod, 2001).

Ethical considerations

Traditionally, as ethical researchers we have been expected to think about informed consent, the right to information regarding the purposes, processes and outcomes of research (related to fairness); the participants' right to withdraw at any stage (related to autonomy); and confidentiality (to protect the right to privacy and do no harm). These ideas are usually held within guidelines or codes of ethical practice. However, many researchers are now asking if 'dutiful ethics' are sufficient to the cause of research that upholds the values of human worth and dignity, when 'it may not be possible to satisfy both the demands of the ethical guidelines and those maintaining standards for conducting research' (Hegeland, 2005: 553), if we do not also take into account the demands of the context (Villa-Vicencio, 1994; Denzin, 1997).

For instance, participants cannot be expected to give informed consent prior to knowing what they are agreeing to: the researcher can usually provide information about the purposes and practices of research in advance, but may not be able to provide information about processes that have yet to unfold, particularly when using heuristic or narrative inquiry (Etherington, 2004). Ethical conduct in these instances relies on our awareness of the need to recognise and talk about the potential dilemmas raised by the research and our openness to engage in 'the ebb and flow of dialogue' (Hegeland, 2005: 554).

Ethical considerations for reflexive researchers will also include the need to remain aware of, and sensitive to, cultural difference and gender (Denzin, 1997; Cloke *et al.*, 2000). This would mean being sensitive to the rights, beliefs and cultural contexts of the participants, as well as their position within patriarchal or hierarchical power relations in society and in our research relationship. This notion has often been addressed within the body of feminist literature on ethical research, in terms of power relationships when researching with counselling clients or ex-clients, but it may also be true of other research relationships where power imbalance is a feature.

Story 1: Clumsy but concerned

I am currently involved in one such relationship where my participant and I discussed ethical issues concerning power, culture, gender and difference. The section of our conversation below shows my clumsy attempts to address power issues between myself and a participant who was also a student on a research unit I taught. In my concern about taking too much 'power over' him I was in danger of disallowing 'power with' him (Starhawk, 1990).

After speaking with a group of students about my current research topic (life story research with ex-drug users) I was approached by Joe (a pseudonym) who offered his story for my research. Joe was intending to use his own story to underpin an autoethnographic dissertation for his Masters degree – a form of self-narrative that places the self within a social context

(Reed-Danahay, 1997) – and he wanted to tell me his story in preparation for writing.

This seemed to be an instance where reciprocity was possible: by helping me with my research he would also be helping himself. But the potential power and boundary issues inherent in this situation needed to be addressed: I was the course co-ordinator, his dissertation supervisor, an older white woman, and a senior member of university staff. He was a black male, more than 20 years younger than myself, who was my student and whose work I had assessed (although I would not do so in the future). Our conversation began with me outlining the importance of consent as a 'process' rather than an 'event':

Kim: . . . and then . . . for us to . . . to make sure – all the way through – that you . . . are aware . . . that you can withdraw. That is really important . . . for you and me – *really* important . . ., because . . . um . . . because of my other roles with you . . .

Joe: [Quietly] Right, I'm with you.

Kim: . . . you know . . . at any point . . . you must never think that . . . that [withdrawal] would upset me or . . .

Joe: . . . or that I've *got* to do this . . .

Kim: No. Because you're a student . . . you know, . . . the fact that I'm your supervisor . . . this is going to affect . . .

Joe: I feel comfortable with that but uh . . .

As I speak, I am aware of my own discomfort: wondering what colleagues might say if they knew I was engaging with a student in this way, while also weighing up the potential benefits for both of us, and remembering that his involvement in the study was something he had asked from me. I notice how I re-emphasize his right to withdraw, and how in my anxiety I might come across as not listening or respecting his ability to say 'no':

Kim: It's really important for you to know that it'll be fine to say 'no' at any stage, and that I mean that.

Joe: Yeah. I hear you, and I'm aware of that . . .

Kim: . . . and to me, you know, it's much more important to be respectful and honouring of the person's rights in this . . . to . . . I'm not *relying* on your story. I've got other stories.

Joe: And . . I hear that but uh . . . I . . . I don't perceive any trouble . . . but if there was . . . at any point I would let you know.

In my effort to relieve him of any undue responsibility towards me – telling him that I'm not relying on his story – I fear I may have implied that his story was not unique and valuable in itself. I press the point again, needing to convince myself that he is aware that it might not be so easy to say no to me, because of his perception of the power held within my role:

> *Kim:*   Yeah. But I am also aware that you kind of view me as a bit of an authority figure . . .
>
> *Joe:*   Right. I know.
>
> *Kim:*   But . . . you know – that's the way it is.
>
> *Joe:*   And . . . a . . . [sighs] . . . when I say I view you as an authority figure . . . that's just your position – being a lecturer at the university. Actually I don't see you . . . I mean obviously you're in charge of the course, so yeah, you're in a position of authority, but I see you as someone I can approach, and disagree with or whatever. And so I'm not, I don't have that kind of . . . 'you're the boss, I better comply' feeling with you.
>
> *Kim:*   So . . . if you wanted to withdraw, if you didn't like the way I had construed your story . . .
>
> *Joe:*   I . . . I would inform you.

Listening to the tape of this conversation, and reading back over it, he seems more confident than I do. My thinking was that his relative naivety about the dynamics that can build up in research relationships, and my own awareness of how this can happen, might be a problem, even though he repeatedly reassures me.

Joe told me later that our conversation had made him think about the dual relationships he held within his own research context and how important it had felt to name those potential ethical problems. From examining that transcript, and writing about it, I have learned that even in my efforts to hold to the feminist ethic of care anxiety to get it right can cause me to lose sight of a participant as an 'independent actor' who possesses the power to say what he feels (Hegeland, 2005). However, I am encouraged by Josselson (1996: 70) when she writes:

> . . . I would worry most if I stopped worrying, stopped suffering for the disjunction that occurs when we try to tell the Other's story. To be uncomfortable with this work, I think, protects us from going too far. It is with our anxiety, dread, guilt, and shame that we honor our participants. To do this work we must contain these feelings rather than deny, suppress, or rationalize them. We must at least try to be fully aware of what we are doing.

Reflexivity as an ethical practice

Although reflexivity is sometimes recognised as a useful tool for ensuring rigour, for improving the quality and validity of research, and for recognising the limitations of the knowledge that is produced, it is not usually considered as a tool for ensuring ethical research processes and practices (Guillemin and Gillam, 2004). The link between reflexivity and ethical research seems to rest upon 'transparency'. When the reader is shown the interactions between researchers and participants (as above) we can observe the behaviours involved in respecting the autonomy, dignity and privacy of participants (or not!); the risks of failing to do so; the 'ethically important moments' that might have occurred; and the means by which they are ethically negotiated (Guillemin and Gillam, 2004).

Story 2: Consequences, confidentiality, ownership and collaboration

My second story relates to a previous study (Etherington, 2000) where I worked collaboratively with two ex-clients who are brothers. Mike is a GP and Stephen a nurse. Both men had been abused by their grandfather and had found their way to me for therapy via a book I had published out of my doctoral research in 1995. When our therapeutic relationship ended they told me they would like to use their experience to help others, so after a break of several years we came together to discuss that possibility.

We enter the conversation where we are discussing how to protect the men's anonymity, with me pointing out that there may be confidentiality issues between the two of them, as well as between them and the outside world. I had worked separately with them as a therapist and although during that period they talked with each other in some depth about their abuse experiences and their therapy, I was aware that there might be some details they wanted kept private from each other.

Kim: . . . we need to ensure that your privacy is respected – from each other, if necessary, as well as the wider world. Just to have that awareness . . . as a starting point and to know that just because you have agreed to do this together, it doesn't necessarily mean that you lose your own material – you still have ownership of that.

Mike: I have been really surprised at how unfrightening it has been. I have been much less worried than I ever thought I would be about the world reading the story . . . and that's really surprising.

Stephen: I find it incredible. As you know, when I first came to see you I was terrified that anybody would find out [about the abuse]. Whereas now, I think I'm in danger of going too far the other way – not like shouting from the rooftops – but I think I'll have to be careful. I feel safe with you . . . so

Mike: [to Stephen] But from the times you've discussed with me about disclosing to other people Stephen, you've been fairly certain of your judgement.

Stephen: I think I have – yes. But I think it's because it was so difficult in the beginning – incredibly difficult – it seemed impossible. It's almost immeasurable. I just can't believe it really.

As they spoke I held in mind that we might need to revisit this part of the conversation to check exactly what they expected or needed in terms of anonymity. We moved on to talk about how it might affect them to revisit their stories of abuse, and the differences between our former therapeutic relationship and new research relationship, which might also turn out to be therapeutic even though that was not now the intended purpose (Gale, 1992; Hart and Crawford-Wright, 1999; Wosket, 1999; Etherington, 2001).

Because of the boundaried nature of therapeutic relationships, research with current or ex-clients can raise complex ethical issues (Gabriel, 2005). However, I believe we can learn most about our practice from those with whom we practise and, providing we establish clarity about the purposes, expectations and norms of different roles and relationships, we can negotiate the sometimes tricky pathway in dialogue together. I had an opportunity to raise these issues when Stephen began to speak about rereading the diary he had kept throughout his therapy, which he had offered to use in the book. Mike asked him how he felt after reading it at this point in his life:

Stephen: I've read it three or four times when I'm feeling low sometimes – to see how far I'd come – to reassure myself, but erm – I find it is a bit uncomfortable. I was saying to Kim, I realised how much pain I was in when I was writing it by the style of writing – it was a different me. It was very interesting . . . [laughs] It reminded me how scared I was; what a terrible place I was in; how desperate I was feeling.

Kim: Mmm. That's reminded me of the other thing that I wanted to bring into focus. The process of doing this may very well open up things again, and I wonder what that would be like for you and what you would do then?

Stephen: I feel like I'm ready for that. I think I could cope with that now – at this distance. I could deal with that now.

Kim: How about you Mike?

Mike: [Pause] Mmm. Yes I think so. I think I've demonstrated by recent events [his separation from his wife] that I can mobilise support if I need to.

Kim: But here we are now, moving into a different relationship, when I'm not your counsellor. What would that mean if anything did come up? What might be your expectations of me if you got very distressed about something that was happening as part of the research process? I suppose my concern is – that if you needed counselling – I don't think it would now be appropriate for me to offer that.

Stephen: That would be OK.

Kim: [to Stephen] But I am also aware that you have financial limitations that would make it hard for you to get counselling elsewhere. I just wondered if you had thought about that.

Stephen: [indistinct] . . . talk to Mike [laugh] – it's exciting – just go for it.

Kim: So you have some contingency plans that might be possible? There are other options too that I can put you in touch with. There are other agencies where you can go for low fee or reduced fee coun-selling, but I think for me to get involved again with you as a counsel-lor – at this point in time – would be too messy if we are contracting a different kind of relationship now. That's not to say that I don't expect this to be therapeutic, or that I'm not going to be able to be supportive as a researcher, and I certainly wouldn't leave you in the lurch and abandon you – either of you. But I think it's important for you to know that this is a different kind of relationship.

Stephen: Of course.

Mike: I suppose that was what I thought it would be.

Stephen: I hadn't really thought about it until you mentioned it. I know what you mean.

Mike: [to Kim] Shall I push you a bit then?

Kim: Yes.

Mike: Can I ask you how much you see this being three people working together, and how much you see us two helping you to write a book?

Kim: Yes. That's what the publisher asked me and I said that I would have to talk to you about this. I was thinking that it would be me writing a book, and you giving whatever you wanted to give as part of that process. If you wanted your name in there, then we would have to talk about that – my understanding was that you probably wouldn't. [Pause] I think what we are trying to capture is *your* work, *your* process, *my* work, *my* process but I want to put that into the context of the wider work that I do with men – and I will be drawing on other material as well. I think I will be doing most of the work.

Mike: I have a picture in my mind then – of we three together being a source . . .

Kim: Yes . . . and there is another source that I bring to this, which is my other research, my client work, my own therapy. When I spoke to the publisher I said, 'I'm not quite sure whether this is going to be just these two men or whether it would be more "proper" to include others.' I was wondering what if there isn't enough material? But . . . actually there's a huge amount of material; but maybe it would be easier to anonymise you if there were more of you . . .

Mike: It's just going to be harder to hide our identity . . .

Kim: That's right.

Mike: I suppose if in the end it is your book to which we are contributing as a source – then the power relationship is going to be unequal . . . and that has to be faced up to in that sense.

Kim: Yes, insofar as that is true. But what I want is for everything that happens – as far as it is possible and practicable – to be up front and talked about. So what I was hoping is, that I would interview each of you separately; I would then transcribe those tapes . . . then I would send it back to you and you would go through it, and ensure that it was saying what you had intended it to say. And if there was anything in there that you did not want said, then you would have a chance to remove it – or to anonymise it. In that sense, the material would be given back to you to take ownership of and for you decide how and whether you wanted it used. If . . . you said 'no I don't want that used', then you have the power to say 'no'. So in that sense the power would be . . . Yes, we have to face up to the fact that it would be *my* book and it would be my name on it – although I would be prepared to talk about it if you wanted your name on it as well.

Mike: So it's not just sitting down and writing a book.

Later, after discussing the possibility of them writing their own books at some time in the future, we came back to thinking about what it would mean if they used their real names, and the chances of being identified – even if they used pseudonyms. It was clear that if one brother used his real name then the other would be identifiable. At this point the conversation entered the realm of 'ethics of consequences'. Having already established the potential positive consequences of their involvement, in order for them to make an informed choice, I now needed to help Mike and Stephen become aware of the negative consequences that could arise from being recognisable:

Stephen: I want to look after my own [anonymity] which would also mean Mike's – but I trust you to use your judgement. I don't think I would be very easily identified but that might not be so for Mike, being a professional man.

[Laughter from all] It's an old habit for the two brothers to always present the needs of the other and ignore their own.

Kim:	So you think if a book was written about a [height and appearance] man who was a [his job] in a [place of work] who had [x] number of children . . . you wouldn't be recognisable?
Stephen:	Yes, well that would be going a bit too far. I wouldn't want that for the sake of my children.
Kim:	No – right.
Stephen:	That's one extreme – the other extreme is leaving out what happened – but we need somewhere in the middle.
Kim:	Did you have any thoughts about that Mike?
Mike:	Yes I did and isn't it funny [mockingly] that I was more worried about Stephen than I was about me [laughter] because I was thinking, 'Well, who's likely to read this that I know' or 'Who would work out who I was?' I suppose I was thinking, 'Well if they've gone to the trouble to read this book (if the book is how I imagine it will be), then I probably don't mind them working out that it's me.' But that might seem very 'gung-ho'.
Kim:	I think what we mustn't lose sight of – is that *you* are very important in this – and the people who you care about are important.
Stephen:	Yes.
Mike:	Right – and then there's *their* confidentiality.
Kim:	Yes.
Stephen:	Needs a lot of thinking about.

[Long pause] I think it's the first time they have really thought about other members of their family being in the public domain.

Kim:	It's important for you to really know what it means. One of the things that happened after the last book was published . . .

I tell a story about how people's life stories can be recognisable to others who know them (even when written about anonymously), because of the uniqueness of the narrative; and how that can cause distress to people who may be included in that story but who have had no part in the decision-making process – not having given *their* informed consent.

Kim:	. . . so those two incidents have made me very cautious and . . . we don't always know until it happens – even when we take as much care as we can at the time. And when you open that book and see your words and your story out of your control, in the public eye

	– it's potentially a very disturbing experience – and I think you really need to think about that.
Stephen:	Yes. You've really made me think about it in a wider way now – thanks.
Mike:	So I think that needle is moving further to the left now.
Kim:	What's at the left?

[Laughter]

Mike:	Towards changing things – identities I mean. I guess it's not just me in the end that I have to think about . . .
Kim:	When you actually see that in print – it's a powerful medium for something that has been for so long very private for you, even secret and shameful – suddenly 'aaahhh!' And you've been through abuse and overexposure and I didn't want to be a party to that happening to you again.

[Long silence]

Kim:	So in a way I hope I'm answering some of your questions about the power . . .
Mike:	Yes, what you've done for me now, is to show me how complicated the anonymity side of it is going to be.
Stephen:	Yes – I was looking at it in a too narrow way.
Mike:	Yes, it's about other people as well as us.

[Long pause] I am wondering if I should offer them an explicit opportunity to withdraw at this stage.

Kim:	You might change your mind altogether?
Stephen:	No. I've been thinking about the reasons for doing it and maybe the reasons for not doing it. What I said already is: I think that to relook at it again from this perspective will help me; the other thing is [that] I want to help other people in the same situation, people who are victims. People like yourself are doing so much to help. I really want to give some of that back – I want to help. This is my chance. It was chance that you lived near enough for me to have counselling. I felt very fortunate and I don't think I've put anything back and I want to . . .
Kim:	You don't have to put anything back.
Stephen:	No, but I want to.

As the work on the book progressed the relationship between Mike and Stephen deepened and they became closer than ever before – their abuse experiences having isolated them from each other early since childhood. All three of us were in regular communication throughout the process and when we finally met for a meal to celebrate the publication of the book, Mike referred back to the conversation quoted above and thanked me again for helping them see the potential consequences for their families of using their own names. He added that if I hadn't done that he might have ended up feeling abused.

This story also has a sequel: At the end of 2004 I was approached by a television editor who wanted to turn that book into a television film. I felt very uncertain about how to handle this because it was now four years since publication and I was not in contact with Mike and Stephen, apart from a very occasional letter from them and Christmas cards. I was reminded of Ruthella Josselson's words:

> Do you really feel like interfering in his or her life? Will you be able to live with the consequences of this encounter or intervention? Is it justified from the interviewee's own perspective?
>
> (Josselson, 1996: 9)

I was aware that Mike and Stephen might have put those abusive life episodes behind them and by inviting them to think again about their stories being made into a television film I might risk opening up feelings and thoughts they had left behind. However, I also felt they had a right to know of this request and a right to make a choice. So I copied the letter to them and sent it to their separate addresses, with no additional comment except to say that I would go along with whatever they decided. Nearly two weeks passed before I heard from them, and in this silence I worried that they might be angry with me for interfering in their lives; that they might have moved house (but surely not both of them?) and not received the letter; that I might not receive a reply – and what then? But after two weeks Mike wrote:

> It has been really affirming to know . . . someone else has been fired up by our stories . . . Stephen and I have discussed this at some length and he has asked me to reply for both of us; sadly we are going to have to refuse our consent. This is largely a reluctant decision, as we both see the good it could bring about, both around the issue in general and for particular survivors.
>
> We two have rehearsed again the discussion the three of us had preliminary to the book. One difficulty is the far greater risk of hurt to other family members – in that the potential audience will obviously be much broader, as well as numerically larger in a TV film than in a 'specialist' book . . . Another is that Stephen is rather vulnerable at the moment [he goes on to say why]. Thirdly, while in principle and individually I am not averse to disclosing, I do not think I would cope well with uncontrolled public discovery about someone in my profession – we are very much public property . . .

> We both feel a little sad and ungrateful to say no; but we do need to protect ourselves, and those around us. (There is also a little spark of interest in what the process and product would have been like.) Please convey our best wishes to [the editor] and that it was a decision reached with reluctance.

This letter warmed my heart in recognising how both men had used their learning from our first meeting about the book and reminded me how important it is to trust our participants to make the choices that are right for them when they have the information they need.

The vulnerable researcher

Reflexivity in representing texts can expose and rebalance power relations between researcher and researched. Being transparent about our presence within a research relationship requires a shift from using the objective voice of 'the researcher' to the subjective 'I'. It also means that researchers have to emerge from behind the secure barrier of anonymity and own up to their involvement (Crotty, 1998). This requires varying degrees of self-disclosure for the researcher.

Although some respected researchers value the adoption of a reflexive approach as a way of dealing with moral dilemmas and sharing them with readers, there are still relatively few who embrace this concept fully within the counselling and psychotherapy research literature, although this is increasingly being seen within research from disciplines such as psychology, social work, sociology, communication studies, humanities and medicine (Frank, 1995; Martin, 1998; Cloke *et al.*, 2000; Ellis and Bochner, 2000; Riessman, 2002; Maracek, 2003), among others.

Traditionally, counselling and psychotherapy have been heavily influenced by psychodynamic practices that encourage 'the transference', valued as an important tool for therapeutic change. Those practices discourage any form of self-disclosure. Even though person-centred, existential, humanistic and co-constructionist therapists use judicious self-disclosure as part of their practice, psychodynamic thinking still holds powerful influence. When psychodynamic ideas are put alongside traditional research beliefs about subjectivity being a 'contaminant' of scientific objective research, it is hardly surprising to find within the counselling and psychotherapy world a reluctance to be transparent in research. Clandinin and Connelly (1994: 423) comment on the risks that come with using a personal voice and self-disclosure in research writing or presentations:

> The researcher is always speaking partially naked and is genuinely open to legitimate criticism from participants and from audience. Some researchers are silenced by the invitation to criticism contained in the expression of voice.

This 'self-silencing' became evident in a research conversation between myself and William, a participant in a study I conducted with social scientists who were becoming 'reflexive researchers' (Etherington, 2004). I asked William about something he had written in one of his published papers in which he had expressed his doubts about the wisdom of my use – and clients' or ex-clients' use – of self-disclosure in research writing (West, 2002). His tentative response to my question, arranged below in stanza format, explains his basis for those doubts:

> What's kind of coming up for me
> is a sort of ambivalence
> about my *own* exposure
> and my *own* hiding,
> that, yes I want to be in print
>
> and, no I don't,
> you know?
> It's like I want to be seen
> and I don't want to be seen
> and, yes,
> I want to be on the stage
> and I want to be hidden under the chair
> at the same time.
>
> My coming into print,
> and coming out as a reflexive researcher
> and coming out heuristically,
> has been a gradual process of:
> is this going to be OK?
> And then pushing it a bit further
> and selecting the media,
> the journal
> or the conference,
> where I can go that next step.
>
> Yes, it's all a risk
> and it's all a kind of a question
> of knowing what I can . . .,
> knowing what I can get away with.

Another example of researcher vulnerability is described in a remarkable study with young people about adolescent transition. Fay Martin (1998: 2) describes how she gathers her stories using 'direct scribing', in which she sits side by side with the young people who are telling their stories while watching her type their words verbatim into her computer. They edit, change and direct as the stories unfold and help to analyse the data. She describes in detail how she 'democratizes the ownership of written material' and 'flattens the power imbalance', and writes of her heightened sense of vulnerability whilst working in this way:

> In thirty years of interviewing, often under observation and within strin- gent accountability frameworks, I have seldom felt as exposed – or as fluent – as I have in this project. I think it has something to do with the torque between leading and following. Both players play both roles in the course of the interview and are equally represented in the same medium. It creates the sense of a level playing field with no place to hide, which is perhaps evidence of a real shift on power relations, at least within that micro-world.
>
> (Martin, 1998: 10)

As researchers we cannot deny our position of power, neither should we deny that participants also have their power. However, no matter how much we include participants' views and voices and negotiate our relationships, in the end the research is our work. Fay Martin describes how she acknowledged this to her participants:

> I then explained that the research protocol was drawing to a close and that the time was nearing when the story would become independent of its author and exist on its own in the world.
>
> (Martin, 1998: 7)

Power issues permeate every aspect of research relationships: from con- siderations of who owns the data and outcomes of the research; how we interpret and represent others; if and how we make transparent the decision- making processes between researcher and participant; to the potential fluidity of power between the parties involved.

Conclusion

In this chapter I have highlighted our ethical and relational responsibilities to work with interpersonal integrity, negotiate decisions, provide information, and clarify our roles, taking into account principles of mutual respect, justice and beneficence (Kohlberg, 1984). I have drawn attention to the need for awareness of the context in which the work is undertaken and particularities in participants' circumstances that might increase the inherent imbalance of power that already exists between researchers and participants.

Reflexive relational ethics pays attention to the balance required between our own needs as researchers and our obligations towards, care for and connection with those who participate in our research (Gilligan, 1982). It requires that researchers not only acknowledge and reflect upon these obligations, but that we also put them into action through practice with those who help us with our research, a point made by Fisher (2004): 'Relational ethics conceives personhood and autonomy as social constructions which can best be respected through mutual understanding and dialogue'.

The storied dialogue used in this chapter reminds us that all parties are potentially vulnerable when undertaking ethical reflexive research that requires us to come from behind the protective barriers of objectivity and invite others to join with us in our exploration of being a researcher and remaining human.

Note

1 A version of this chapter was published in 2007 in *Qualitative Inquiry* 13, 5, 599–616.

References

Adams, T. E. (2006) Seeking father: relationally reframing a troubled love story. *Qualitative Inquiry*, 12, 4, 704–723.

Bond, T. (2000) *Standards and Ethics in Counselling in Action*, 2nd edn. London: Sage.

Bond, T. (2006) Intimacy, risk, and reciprocity in psychotherapy: intricate ethical challenges. *Transactional Analysis Journal* 36, 2, 77–89.

Christians, C. G. (2000) Ethics and politics in qualitative research. In N. K. Denzin and Y. S. Lincoln (eds) *Handbook of Qualitative Research*. Thousand Oaks, CA: Sage.

Clandinin D. J. and Connelly, F. M. (1994) Personal experience methods. In N. K. Denzin and Y. S. Lincoln (eds) *Handbook of Qualitative Research*. Thousand Oaks, CA: Sage.

Cloke, P., Cooke, P., Cursons, J., Milbourne, P. and Widdowfield, R. (2000) Ethics, reflexivity and research: encounters with homeless people. *Ethics Place and Environment* 3, 2, 133–154.

Crossley, M. L. (2000) *Introducing Narrative Psychology: Self, Trauma and the Construction of Meaning*. Maidenhead: Open University Press.

Crotty, M. (1998) *The Foundations of Social Research: Meaning and Perspective in the Research Process*. London: Sage.

Denzin, N. K. (1997) *Interpretive Ethnography: Ethnographic Practices in the 21st Century*. London: Sage.

Edwards, R. and Mauthner, M. (2002) Ethics and feminist research: theory and practice. In M. Mauthner, M. Birch, J. Jessop and T. Miller (eds) *Ethics in Qualitative Research*. London: Sage.

Ellis, C. (2006) Telling secrets, revealing lives: relational ethics in research with intimate others. *Qualitative Inquiry*, 13, 1, 3–29.

Ellis, C. and Bochner, A. (2000) Autoethnography, personal narrative, reflexivity: researcher as subject. In N. K. Denzin and Y. S. Lincoln (eds) *Handbook of Qualitative Research*, 2nd edn. Thousand Oaks, CA: Sage.

Etherington, K. (1995) *Adult Male Survivors of Childhood Sexual Abuse.* London: Pavilion Publishers.

Etherington, K. (2000) *Narrative Approaches to Working with Male Survivors of Sexual Abuse: The Clients', the Counsellor's and the Researcher's Story.* London: Jessica Kingsley Publishers.

Etherington, K. (2001) Research with ex-clients: an extension and celebration of the therapeutic process. *British Journal of Guidance and Counselling* 29, 1, 5–19.

Etherington, K. (2003) *Trauma, The Body and Transformation.* London: Jessica Kingsley Publishers.

Etherington, K. (2004) *Becoming a Reflexive Researcher: Using Our Selves in Research.* London: Jessica Kingsley Publishers.

Fisher, C. (2004) *Research Involving Persons with Mental Disorders that Might Affect Decision-Making Capacity Paper 3: Relational Ethics and Research with Vulnerable Populations.* Online Ethics Center for Engineering and Science. http://onlineethics.org/reseth/nbac/mpaper3.html. Accessed 10 September 2008.

Frank, A. W. (1995) *The Wounded Storyteller: Body, Illness and Ethics.* Chicago: University of Chicago Press.

Gabriel, L. (2005) *Speaking the Unspeakable: The Ethics of Dual Relationships in Counselling and Psychotherapy.* Abingdon: Routledge.

Gale, J. (1992) When research interviews are more therapeutic than therapy interviews. *The Qualitative Report* 1, 4, 31–38.

Gergen, K. (1985) The social constructionist movement in modern psychology. *American Psychologist* 40, 266–275.

Gergen, K. (1994) *Toward Transformation in Social Knowledge,* 2nd edn. London: Sage.

Gilligan, C. (1982) *In a Different Voice.* Cambridge, MA: Harvard University Press.

Guillemin, M. and Gillam, L. (2004) Ethics, reflexivity and 'ethically important moments' in research. *Qualitative Inquiry* 10, 2, 261–280.

Hart, N. and Crawford-Wright, A. (1999) Research as therapy, therapy as research: ethical dilemmas in new paradigm research. *British Journal of Counselling and Guidance* 27, 2, 205–215.

Hegeland, I. M. (2005) 'Catch 22' of research ethics: ethical dilemmas in follow-up studies of marginal groups. *Qualitative Inquiry* 11, 549–569.

Hertz, R. (ed.) (1997) *Reflexivity and Voice.* London: Sage.

Josselson, R. (ed.) (1996) *Ethics and Process in the Narrative Study of Lives,* Vol. 4. London: Sage.

Kohlberg, L. (1984) *Lessons on Moral Development.* San Fransisco: Harper and Row.

McLeod, J. (1997) *Narrative and Psychotherapy.* London: Sage.

McLeod, J. (2001) *Qualitative Research in Counseling and Psychotherapy.* London: Sage.

Maracek, J. (2003) Dancing through minefields: towards a qualitative stance in psychology. In P. C. Camic, J. E. Rhodes and L. Yardley (eds) *Qualitative Research in Psychology: Expanding Perspectives in Methodology and Design.* Washington, DC: American Psychological Association.

Martin, F. E. (1998) Tales of transition: self-narrative and direct scribing in exploring care-leaving. *Child and Family Social Work* 3, 1–12.

Polkinghorne, D. E. (1988) *Narrative Knowing and the Human Sciences.* Albany, NY: State University of New York.

Reed-Danahay, D. E. (1997) *Auto/Ethnography: Rewriting the Self and the Social.* Oxford: Berg.

Rennie, D. (1998) *Person-Centred Counseling: An Experiential Approach.* London: Sage.

Riessman, C. (2002) Doing justice: positioning the interpreter in narrative work. In W. Patterson (ed.) *Strategic Narrative: New Perspectives on the Power of Personal and Cultural Stories.* Oxford: Lexington Books.

Starhawk (1990) *Dreaming the Dark: Magic, Sex and Politics.* London: Mandala.

Villa-Vicencio, C. (1994) Ethics of responsibility. In C. Villa-Vicencio and J. de Grucy (eds) *Doing Ethics in Context.* New York: Orbis Books.

West, W. (2002) Some ethical dilemmas in counselling and counselling research. *British Journal of Guidance and Counselling* 30, 3, 261–268.

Wosket, V. (1999) *The Therapeutic Use of Self: Counselling, Practice, Research and Supervision.* London: Routledge.

Chapter 7

Relational ethics

A perspective after the essays and marking

Nic Neath

I was invited to contribute this chapter as a recent graduate from a diploma course; to recount my experiences of relational ethics as a student and in the early stages of my career. This chapter will cast an experiential and philosophical view of my context, training, orientation and practice. I will offer an example of walking through the framework, my thoughts on ethics, relation, time and the learning contract. I do not offer a conclusion but a myriad of questions.

As parallel process (a comparable and experiential replication of a client's process in the process of the counsellor) becomes the bread and butter of my practice it feels appropriate that I parallel the training experience with the counselling process. So like a novice client, it was a novice trainee that stepped into the training room, not even knowing I would need to consider relational ethics, let alone how to. The learning in the first place is, therefore, to know to ask, to know what to ask and who to ask. This manner and method needs to be taught, but what is the ethical standpoint of the tutor and how might they model asking the questions? How might you take this learning and apply it to work with clients? What might you learn in supervision and what do you do with controversies?

My context

My personal ethical context comes from my western culture and it will clash, at times, with others whose ethical context emanates from an entirely different ideological background. My exploration of ethics began in philosophical study undertaken prior to and outside of my counselling training. This study led me to consider the heuristics of knowledge, belief, systems, perception and expression. This occasionally deconstructive and phenomenological method leads me to believe that whatever my current relational ethics are, they are grounded in what I know now about the world, what the others know now and how that knowledge is shared, communicated and understood. My learning is to pay attention and listen out for differences. As I initially cast around to see who was writing about relational ethics, I discovered it arises as a topic for debate in the world of medicine and nursing. Medical practitioners consider how to manage conflicting ethical responses in relation to patients and institutions, where consideration of appropriate choices in care are pondered against rights to choice, imposition of treatment and advocacy. Such discursive articles ponder beliefs and values and the changing roles of care givers and point to:

> . . . sometimes conflicting concepts. These concepts are defined as follows:
> - beneficence – the principle of doing good;
> - nonmaleficence – the principle of doing no harm;
> - unitary-transformative paradigm – a perspective that views human beings as unitary, self-organizing energy fields interacting with a larger environmental energy field; and
> - utilitarianism – an ethical doctrine in which actions are focused on accomplishing the greatest good for the greatest number of people.
> (Falk and Adeline, 1995: 25–32)

Consider also current debate on euthanasia: who in that relation holds the ethical cards, the patient, the doctor, the family, the legal system? This all feels reassuring and overdue at the same time. When I think about relational ethics I consider what is important about relation. Adams (2007: 29) writes about the primacy of interrelating and the work of Martin Buber who . . . 'emphasizes that humans are essentially interrelational beings. He goes on to demonstrate that from birth to death we are always involved in relationships, whether these be with oneself, others, the world, nature, or God'.

This is my starting point then. We are in relation all the time and ethics come from a range of places and there can be power differentials in ethical weight according to what and who we believe. I invite you to form a relation with me and to help you do so, I choose to tell you where I am coming from.

My orientation and practice

My theoretical orientation is integrative with a strong person-centred bias. I had an instinctive and intuitive inclination in training towards the work of Carl Rogers (1902–1987). His movement towards the client through his career (Rogers, 1951, 1961) and the establishment of client as the framework if you like (as opposed to a framework for behavioural change placed upon an issue or a client as might be described in some cognitive behavioural techniques) felt and still feels right for how I choose to operate as a counsellor. That said, some of my therapeutic practice is based in a student counselling centre where sessions are limited unless the case is considered severe enough to warrant the funding of extended contracts. This work forces my hand and through this I develop a practice there that is more framed in the allocation of sessions and more issue- as opposed to client-focused than is my preference. Occasionally I hear myself ask a Stage II Egan Skilled Helper Model question on possibilities for the future (Egan, 2002), inwardly gasp, but recognise that it can have its place, if that place has arisen from the need of my client.

This practice brings me into contact with a diverse student population, both in terms of culture and ethnicity. The service offers counselling to students and provides a varied and well-considered groupwork programme. Contracts of four sessions are currently offered. The service is higher education funded; therefore clients do not pay for their sessions directly but through whatever financial mechanism moves fees and funding around the higher education sector. It is a fantastic resource and support for them. I have worked in this setting for three years to date. It was my placement while I trained and has also offered me great support and opportunity as I develop.

My second practice is working with a small business devoted to forming relationship with clients and organisations. It seeks to understand and engage in the world of others and offer tailored help and support through training, counselling and coaching. It offers short, mid- and long-term contracts, and supports the clients' right to choose and empower self in deciding how many sessions are enough wherever possible. Therefore contracts range from two to 20-plus. The organisation is not funded but keeps its charges to a minimum and provides access to free counselling to organisational employees through the organisational funding while maintaining client autonomy and confidentiality. It also works with private clients. Clients range in age, ethnicity, background and gender. It is a rare place to work, where I develop longer-term relationships with my clients often against the climate of shorter-and-shorter-term 'quick fix' approaches that seems to be growing in the counselling environment. This practice facilitates growth through holistic practice, multi-issue work and integration of theory into practice. I have worked there for over a year.

I use my integrative approach in both settings, working also with creative techniques. I am fortunate therefore to have a very broad client base, both male and female, from manual workers to senior management, working class to privilege class. I have worked with issues including bereavement, bullying, addiction, self-harm, sexuality, relationships, anxiety, depression, suicide, identity, communication, managing others, existential exploration, . . . to name but a few. Prior to this I worked as a Samaritan for two years.

So, to return to what relational ethics meant for me as a student, ultimately I feel they were the principles of engagement that extended from me to others, covertly or overtly, principles that informed, framed or structured contact. As a student, the landscape seemed littered with potentiality for perilous adventure or shortfall in relational engagement. Why, because of that unconscious incompetence. I did not know what I did not know.

Upon willingly choosing to embark on my graduate diploma in counselling to gain therapeutic skill, I contracted with myself to some degree to engage with the work and business of learning; with the educational establishment, with a willingness to engage with and manage institutional responses, tolerance of bureaucratic systems; with course directors, to trust their choices in designing the course; with the course curriculum, as that which needed to be learnt and evidenced; with individual tutors, that they are fit, willing and able to promote the learning; with peers, whose shared learning, feedback, support and challenge informed aspects of me and my process of learning further; with clients in training settings, who are the training ground of the newly acquired and occasionally clumsily executed skills; with placements offering training contracts, who put their trust in my selection and the educational setting to endorse my work as a trainee; with family and friends, who may be expected to endure some shift in whatever lifestyle or pattern existed before. I list these in one sentence to demonstrate that it can feel overwhelming. You may well need to catch your breath when you get to the end.

Most of these contracts, these engagements, are unknown feasts. Some proved more important than others; many were unspoken, informal, learnt on the hoof. Do we know what we sign up to when we engage in these contracts? And would knowing beforehand change how we engage? The parallel is here again then – would the client proceed if they had an inkling as to what might happen in the process?

Using the BACP framework

One of the first tasks of the trainee is to begin the process of understanding and absorbing the code of ethics set by whichever body oversees their training, BACP in my case. Understanding these means to some degree debriefing the self of the ethics consumed as an indigenous citizen, in order to recognise and reconcile any differences in perception and concept. Then what feels like a transition happens as one begins to understand where there may be conflict, to begin to discover a process for deciphering one ethic over another, and like any other good rule, it is tested case by case – it follows the same parallel to the legal system: trust it works until you find a case where it doesn't. But unlike the legal process, in the room the judges are both the counsellor and the client; outside of the room although embodied in the process are the supervisor, internal and passive, outside external and active, and behind them BACP.

Ethical decisions may need to be made in a split second in the counselling room. They may need to be reviewed in supervision, but how does one choose which aspect of the work to debrief; how does one self-select and offer enough to the supervisor overtly or covertly to look at and work through? In every case, every scenario, trust and exploration are essential. But in order to trust we need to know what it is we are to expect, how to decipher when trust is being stretched, when to trust, even if it feels difficult, which is the right way to proceed. In my early practice I was drawn to cover all scenarios in my personal supervision. I had the urge to check every client in with my supervisor, to offer her what I believed at the time as a wide a view of my practice so that she might spot where I was in the shadows, caught in parallel process, as I so often am. However, as our relational ethics develop I learn to understand that in fact it is the transparency of myself which offers her greatest scope on my practice. If we can learn and grow to know those areas of me where I wobble, where my personal material may interfere, then we can work to support my clients better. I can learn to know myself and in turn both offer the experience of my learning to the encounters I have with my clients. This relational ethic then begins to inform my approach to ethical issues with my clients; using my supervision and developing self-supervisory skills I begin to notice ethical conflicts. I imagine what my supervisor might ask me, as instructed I may take the Ethical Framework and work through point by point, but sometimes those points clash.

Consider a ruffle in the status quo on my course. Some of my training cohort (myself included) began to experience a loss of contact with our tutors as the requirement to cover different theoretical approaches meant that other specialists were brought in to teach us. In our questioning this loss we were faced with a relational ethic problem.

Considering trainees as clients, trainers as counsellors, should we prize: *Fidelity: honouring the trust placed in the practitioner*? In this case the practitioner can be paralleled to the institution, the tutors. Should we trust their judgement in their choices on the facilitation of the learning?

Or should we prize: *Autonomy: respect for the client's right to be self-governing*, and pay attention to our own right to decide what is best for us, to participate in our own learning process as we were so often encouraged to do? How does that impact when it isn't the whole cohort who feels that way? Where does our informed consent begin to get informed? What do we do with the conflict? Who are the interested parties here? The curriculum has to be covered, but the curriculum includes learning about relationship. We are in relationship with our tutors, but there are limits upon the resources available and different needs from both the individual group members and the tutors.

How do we all prize: *Beneficence: a commitment to promoting the client's well-being*, if as trainees we are paralleled as clients to the course direction, and there is our well-being but also the consideration of our future clients' beneficence which depends upon our professional competence, which is about our ability to form relationship? Who decides what is the 'the best available means' (BACP, 2007b)? How does the cohort engage with those means and who judges 'best' when as trainees perhaps our 'autonomy is diminished because of immaturity, lack of understanding . . .' (BACP, 2007b)?

How do we perceive: *Non-maleficence: a commitment to avoiding harm to the client*, when the course is based upon financial exchange, where the limits of resources may mean there are inadequate chairs, rooms, funding for external tutors, where video players don't work, where the tools for developing self-reflective practice are not available? What then of the non-maleficence? What might we in turn pass on to our clients who wait in the wings of our training? As trainees how do we learn to exercise our 'responsibility to challenge, where appropriate, the incompetence or malpractice of others'? How can we know as trainees what is the best for us? How indeed does the client know that they should be getting more for their money?

Who decides on the lines of: *Justice: the fair and impartial treatment of all clients and the provision of adequate services*, when different members of the cohort have different ideas on 'fair', parallel to an individual's subpersonalities, where one aspect of self may actively war and contradict the needs of another? Which subpersonality gets precedence, which individual view of the cohort? What happens when trainees are not all able to get adequate placements (BACP, 2007a: 44). Is it the responsibility of the accredited training organisation? In which case who funds them to inspect the placements? Who provides the cover while the tutors are away? Is it the trainee's responsibility? How do they make the judgement? Is it potential work environments? How does BACP reconcile different ethical standpoints of different organisations? How can anyone actually judge for certain before a counsellor/client contact happens, what is a *'suitable match'* (p. 44)? Does BACP abdicate its responsibility by informing policy without enabling it in practice? Do they fund these enquiries in return for the fees we pay them? If we can only pursue placements open to this scrutiny do we discriminate against others? Do we in turn exclude colleges that cannot fund this scrutiny? Which relation in all of those above is the one to draw the ethic from? Who decides justice for us?

In consideration of relational ethics and relation to self then perhaps 'self respect' is the most cognisant. In the scenario above, the trainee's facilitation, engagement and direction in learning is surely driven by care for self. The requirement some had for more contact with tutors correlates to the need for some to further themselves in relation with their tutors. In this instance a compromise was reached where the group and tutors found ways of increasing contact. It was negotiated – could this parallel a negotiation that happens between therapist and client about the frequency of sessions, length of contract – is it self-respect that fosters a model of self-respect to the client? What also of relationships that develop after the training process. Could it be this learning that helps the trainee therapist negotiate their own way to have collegial or other relationship with tutors? Does this parallel change in relationship with ex-clients with significant mindfulness to a client's welfare but also mindfulness to a client's autonomy? Is it okay if the tutor, if the therapist, proceeds and negotiates with care and transparency? Or does this stretch the parallel too far so that it is still difficult to consider relationship with clients after therapy because of our fears, because of what the rule setters say, because there is no safe space to say it?

It is interesting that I use the framework to review this training experience.

We didn't use it at the time, nor were we encouraged to, what we did was try to find practical compromise.

So what is an ethical relationship? And who judges it to be so? And how do these ethical principles get formed. My understanding is that our society is based on a hierarchical system of rule setting. We nod to democracy, but live in a country which has an average political voting rate of 61 per cent (Electoral Commission, 2005), leaving thereabouts 23.2 million people who don't vote, eligibility to vote being a whole other issue. We vote with our consumer power but only 1 per cent of the populous hold 21 per cent of the wealth (National Statistics Online, 2007). We believe in education and are at the hands of the choices made by our educators on what to teach us. We have copious rules for good behaviour, rules that seem to increase every year, regulation of counselling included. Indeed, there are rules for me in the writing of this chapter. The context of rules for this study on relational ethics is enormous if only I choose to view it in that broad a perspective. Every statement I make is therefore contentious. The question behind the question seems to be: where does the power to set the ethic come from? When I practise in an institutional setting, it is set by that institution. Both my clients and I exist in that system and are there times when the institutional ethic conflicts with mine and with the relational ethic developed between my client and myself? What do I do when the consensus rule overrides the uniqueness of each client? How can I practise in a client-centred way when the engagement paradigm is already predetermined? Where does the relational ethic fit?

Relation

Relational ethics must be about relation. What do we know about relation? Adams (2007) combines the work of Martin Buber, Emmanuel Levinas and Maurice Merleau-Ponty. He asserts that 'humans are primarily relational beings, not separate egoic subjects'. Coining the compound noun 'interrelating', he continues to 'emphasize the active, ongoing, dynamic quality of our participatory engagement with the rest of the world' (Adams, 2007: 27).

These three authors offer a deep relational perspective on the world. Buber (1923) asserts how relation is everything: 'I become through my relation to *Thou*; as I become *I*, I say *Thou*. All real living is meeting' (Buber, 1958: 17). Of Levinas, Adams shows how 'his entire work centers on establishing the "primacy of the ethical, that is, of the relationship of man to man – signification, teaching, and justice – a primacy of an irreducible structure upon which all other structures rest" (Levinas, 1961/1969: 79 in Adams, 2007: 33).

Merleau-Ponty is referenced as he expounds the phenomenological perspective and the 'primacy of perception' (Adams, 2007: 48), moving from a scientific experience of the world towards a holistic, subjective felt experience of the world. That is a kind-of how is it for me, how is it for you and how do we communicate that to each other? What are the signs and signifiers that we use to gesture to each other (Merleau-Ponty, 1973)? These three views feel key when we consider what is my relation to the world.

An ethical approach that is relational seems essential in any business that claims to have human beings as its subject, in any business where one has potential for power over the other. Are ethics the principles that keep everyone safe; that ward off abuse; that inform appropriate behaviour; that give meaning to the process that two people engage in? Indeed, can that ever be true, and should we even try to keep everyone safe – doesn't learning and evolution actually come through risk taking, making mistakes, being out of comfort zones? These ethics will have a sociological and cultural reference and they may not necessarily translate from one culture to another, and therefore used inappropriately may be used to abuse others. If we impose one set of ethics and beliefs from one onto another culture, do we become the abusers? Do we predetermine the outcome in the language (signifiers) that we use, in the culture that we impose as Ranjana Khanna asks of colonialism (Neath, 2007)?

As a trainee I came with some expectations and assumptions and much unknowing, parallel again to a novice client. All the power lies with the trainer, the trainer's establishment – as with in those first few moments (and for some always) with the therapist. Somehow it is the job of the trainer to impart the training, to empower the trainee, to pass on the rules but maybe not pass on the power. There are limits to resources in both scenarios, limits to personal engagement, and limits on time. You need to complete the course in two years – you need to end your counselling (if you are lucky these days) in ten sessions – if you wish to carry on learning or developing you will need to privately finance that, or join another queue, or join another course. My first experience of relational ethics is with my college, course, tutors and peers. How will I be with them? How will they be with me? Who knows the rules? Who has the power? Who leads the way? The huge difference between relational ethics in training to that in therapy, is in training more can be written down and established at the outset. You are given course outlines, essay titles, deadlines, explanations of modules, requirements for writing personal journals. These pointers to what will come offer you some insight into the process. However, like almost any definition of therapy, can you actually know what that is until you get into it? It is 'unscripted' (Yalom, 2002). When perhaps you start to realise what all the fuss about having appropriate support behind you really means. Informed as I felt I was, there was an 'Ah ha' moment which was also the equivalent of jumping out of a plane without a parachute. After all, can you describe coffee if you haven't tasted it?

How long should we take?

My second ethical disquiet from training concerns practice. I did not get my placement until late October in my first year and some trainees have gone much further into the course without a placement. What other vocational training would accept this? My personal struggle was not being able to attach my learning to experience with clients, to find myself theorising and drawing as much as I could from training triads but not being able to ground my practice. The experience of sitting in a room with one other still a million miles away from sitting in a room with many. I was fortunate to get up and running relatively soon. How can a trainee work through relational ethics without practising in relation? What pressure does a training organisation put on a trainee who struggles to get a placement? Where do the relational ethics lie, between college and trainee, trainee and learning, trainee and future clients, college and clients?

What are the beliefs around the time it takes for an individual to learn – to embed learning, to benefit from counselling? What are the ethics of courses that churn out trainees that haven't actually gathered the learning, that don't fail trainees? Parallel again the counsellor who finishes because the sessions have run out. Is some better than none? Consider the student writing in 1992 who regarded 'six months' short term counselling' (Jarrett, 1992: 194). Six months seems luxurious now. I still don't know that I am reconciled to this relational ethical problem. I need to work to survive, if I row with those who provide my work because I want to do it differently do I then risk not working at all? What are the ethics of the college that actually needs to get you through the course in order to promote its own financial survival?

But limits are a fact of life, you may say. Indeed they are, but sometimes I feel we accept the limits imposed through lack of resources and tolerate it with a shrug and get on with it. But then where is the push to ask for more and challenge that very ethical basis, why should we assume that two years is enough or that ten sessions are enough. How do I manage that? I still push, I do what I can to work for longer where my client and I agree a need, and not a dependency, I try to work with others and organisations that are willing to see the greater benefit in extending support and engaging in deeper relationship over time. I talk about it. I engage with processes that talk about regulation and setting rules. With Yalom, I also must wonder:

> Does the patient engage his or her [the therapist's] service as a guide to existential awareness? Or do not most patients say in effect, 'I feel bad, help me feel better'; and if this is the case, why not use the speediest, most efficient means at one's disposal – for example, pharmacological tranquilization or behavioural modification? Such questions, which pertain to all forms of treatment based on self-awareness, cannot be ignored, and they will emerge here again and again. (Yalom, 1998: 238)

Who has the choice here, and what might I do with my anger at feeling under pressure to accommodate a client in what might be perceived as a 'very tight time schedule' (Jarrett, 1992: 200)? I find comfort in knowing that there are others out there who recognise the 'uniqueness' of the client and 'psycho-therapies [that] seek to give symptoms a voice: to hear what is being expressed in them, rather than stifle them' (Leader, 2007).

An existential experience

I came face to face with another ethical conundrum after an experiential weekend. During the weekend we were introduced to a guided visualisation technique and through this I had an experience of my mom who had died two years previously. At the time I was moved, elated, overjoyed by having an encounter with her, she was a great absence in my life. However, as time passed I found myself in a conflicting dualism with the experience. I wondered if I had actually spoken with her, in which case while that had offered me solace it put me into an existential spin – what world had I experienced, was she a ghost, had I pulled her out of her Christian post-death setting into my non-religious one? If I had experienced a being, was that even her? And had I experienced another at all? Or had it been a conjuring of my own mind, to fulfil my own need and lack and spoke more of my ongoing grief and ongoing relationship with her? I became overwhelmed, frightened and starting to doubt the perceptive tools I could rely upon in order to function in the world. What was true? I came close to deciding to stop training – how could I now knowing how destabilising this business can be, continue on and possibly, intentionally or not, bring another person into that very destabilised place. I now had information to make a very significant relational ethical choice.

When I raised my concern with my college I found no satisfaction. The fact that I was a trainee was seen to absolve some responsibility for my welfare. Apparently I had the tools to look after myself – at the time I did not feel I did. While I heeded the warnings given on my interview for the course that this training could be upsetting, disturbing, life changing, how could I possibly give informed consent to have a chat with my mother? I did not know what landscape would form around the corners. Informed consent is therefore a dubious notion per se. Informed by what experience, by what perceptual beliefs, by trust in whose understanding of the world? I envied those of my peers whose religious beliefs at that time offered them absolute certainty, for some who's beliefs and ethical reasoning gave them reason not to engage in the exercise at all. I was fortunate to have support and understanding elsewhere, two people who held me in that philosophical fright and guided my learning through it. It still sits with me as an unknown but the questions posed by them were absolutely right for me. It was essential that I embodied this key relational ethical conundrum: that as counsellor I did have the power to move another into a place that they may not wish to be in, that may call their beliefs about themselves and the world into question. It is an ethical concern I walk with in my practice all the time. Some reassurance was also given that it made me a better counsellor for having stopped in my tracks and battled with the ethical issue. I hear loud and clear Clarkson's (2001: 44) wondering that 'philosophical training is essential since some research has indicated that the intellectual ability to deal effectively with complexity is a prerequisite for dealing intelligently, compassionately and competently with ethic issues'. And I wonder where is this philosophical training on counselling courses?

There is no conclusion

So, after much meandering, what is relational ethics after the training environment? Is it commitment to trust? To trust the self; the educational establishment; course directors; individual tutors; peers; clients; family and friends. Where does the trainee start?

My experience suggests it begins with the desire to help others, to recognise what it is you can give and what it is that you need to offer and learn to do. We take our guidance, our learning from ourselves and very much from our tutors and each other. We begin by learning to listen, to set ourselves to one side in order to truly hear the words, the colours, the tones, the echoes of another. We have to learn to trust ourselves not to get lost in their story, to see the parallels, to hold them and their story and stumble in that process – and as I learn, we stumble often, and these are the places where we learn to check ourselves. But we have to learn to know what to check. When are you making a relational ethical choice? When does your personal choice clash with the ethics of where you study, where you practice? What are the ethical differences of establishing relationship in someone's home, with a student, with a tutor, with an organisation, with an elder, a juvenile, a convict, an abuser, an abused? How do you walk through this minefield of difference with consistency – while all the time you are changing, evolving, learning, bending against or towards an ever-changing world of phenomenological encounter?

It seems to me that relational ethics are almost insupportable perceptual conflict. We carry on because we agree the principles but the principles clash – is that the human experience? But as I draw to the end of my allotted space here I realise I have just scratched the surface but there just isn't enough time to explore it deeper! I know I have raised a lot of questions in this chapter, and perhaps have whetted your appetite. These are just some of the questions I had after training, some of the philosophical, theoretical, relational issues that aren't given enough time in training. If you are frustrated, you have a good idea of my experience.

Acknowledgements

I would like to thank Jill Burns and Gayle-Anne Drury for their invaluable comments on this chapter and for being supportive and inspirational.

References

Adams, W. W. (2007) The primacy of interrelating: practicing ecological psychology with Buber, Levinas, and Merleau-Ponty. *Journal of Phenomenological Psychology* 38, 24–61.

British Association for Counselling and Psychotherapy (BACP, 2007a) *Therapy Today*, 18, 7, 44.

British Association for Counselling and Psychotherapy (BACP, 2007b) *Ethical Framework*. http://www.bacp.co.uk/ethical_framework/ (retrieved 30 September 2007).

Buber, M. (1958) *I and Thou*, 2nd edn. Trans. R.G. Smith. London: Continuum.

Clarkson, P. (2001) Reporting others' transgressions. In F. Palmer and L. Murdin (eds) *Values and Ethics*. Maidenhead: Open University Press.

Egan, G. (2002) *The Skilled Helper Model*, 7th edn. Pacific Grove, CA: Wadsworth.

Electoral Commission (2005) *Election 2005: Engaging the Public in Great Britain. An Analysis of Campaigns and Media Coverage*. http://www.electoralcommission. org.uk/files/dms/Engaging_19456–14157__E__S__W__.pdf (retrieved 30 September 2007).

Falk, R. and Adeline, R. (1995) Advocacy and empowerment: dichotomous or synchronous concepts? *Advances in Nursing Science* 18, 2, 25–32.

Jarrett, M. (1992) The man no one wanted to see. In E. Noonan and L. Spurling (eds) *The Making of a Counsellor*. London: Tavistock/Routledge.

Leader, D. (2007) A dark age for mental health. *The Guardian*, Saturday 13 October.

Merleau-Ponty, M. (1973) *The Prose of the World*. Evanston: Northwestern University Press.

National Statistics Online (2007) http://www.statistics.gov.uk/CCI/SearchRes.asp? term=wealth&x=43andy=7 (retrieved 30 September 2007).

Neath, N. (2007) Book review of *Dark Continents: Psychoanalysis and Colonialism*. By Ranjana Khanna. *Psychotherapy and Politics International* 5, 2, 155–158.

Rogers, C. R. (1951) *Client Centred Therapy*. London: Constable.

Rogers, C. R. (1961) *On Becoming a Person*. New York: Houghton Mifflin.

Yalom, I. D. (1998) *The Yalom Reader*. New York: Perseus Books.

Yalom, I. D. (2002) *The Gift of Therapy*. London: Piatkus Books.

Chapter 8

Relational ethics in psychiatric settings

Subodh Dave

> We live in a world that places a high premium on standardisation and objectivity; subtlety and complexity are imperilled in that world.
>
> (Andreasen, 1995)

Personal reflections

Soon after I had moved to the UK 12 years ago as a young psychiatrist, a helpful senior professor took me aside and asked me with some concern whether I was experiencing 'culture shock'. I was indeed in culture shock. I had moved from the bustling city of Mumbai (then Bombay), to Wolverhampton. Email was an unknown quantity in the NHS in those days and I had to travel to Birmingham to send an email back home. I had no family or friends in the UK but what assisted me in my transition as a migrant psychiatrist was my relationship with my patients which seemed remarkably similar 5000 miles away in a land with a vastly different socio-cultural milieu.

The physical environment could not have been more starkly different. I had moved from a public hospital in inner city Bombay where I was managing 60 inpatients in a ward with 20 beds – 40 had to lie on mattresses on the floor! In the outpatients clinic patients had to often wait as long as three hours to see a psychiatrist. The UK, in contrast, was a richer country and this was evident in the service design and delivery. Inevitably, I was asked the question whether the care was any better in the UK compared to that in India. The answer was not as readily available as I thought it would be. Certainly, the material aspects of care were better – better wards and clinics, more staff, better documentation, but was the overall care better? I was used to scheduling a detailed interview with family members soon after a new assessment (in fact it would be fair to say that I had little choice in the matter as family members would clamour to see the psychiatrist themselves). In contrast, in England, it was often the social worker in the team who did a 'social assessment'. It could be days or even weeks before I saw a family member. Rehabilitation was assisted by the occupational therapist that offered woodwork and art. In India there were no occupational therapists but the community often supported reintegration, for example by offering employment as shop assistants or 'helpers' in local businesses. Some of my very ill psychotic patients had even landed the role of a priest in a temple on account of the presumed spiritual association of their mental illness.

Interestingly, however, despite all these differences, the stigma against mental illness and the mentally ill (as also against psychiatrists) was no different. What was also notably the same was my interaction with my patients and their carers (the UK term). While I struggled with my personal acculturation, which happened at an expectedly slow pace, my professional acclimatisation was almost instantaneous. I experienced in myself the same level of care, concern and feeling for my patients here as I did in India. The feeling aroused in me by their distress was no different. The shared experience with my patients and their significant others was no different. I did not label it as such then but this *shared experience*, the connectedness which bound me to my patients and helped *me* find my feet in a new country, is what relational ethics is all about (Bergum and Dossetor, 2005).

Clinical ethics in medicine

When I was a medical student in India in the 1980s, quite like the medical schools in the UK (Hope, 2001) there was no formal training in medical ethics. When I passed out of medical school, I and my colleagues all took the Hippocratic Oath, but without much reflection or philosophical analysis. Good ethical practice to us was taught to mean a sense of duty to our patients and the supremacy of their best interests. The textbooks then still talked about paternalism without too much of an apology. This was what Gadow (1999) has called a period of uncritical certainty of a profession united in its values and beliefs (Pellegrino, 1999). A lot of progress has been made since then. As the lessons learnt from the unethical experiments in the Nazi era and the Nuremberg trials filtered through, the principle of autonomy gained ground especially in the western world (Burt, 1996).

A significant and very influential development in western bioethics was the four principle approach of Beauchamp and Childress (1979). The four pillars of *autonomy*, *beneficence*, *non-maleficence* and *justice* have dominated ethical thinking in medical practice and have been used extensively to resolve clinical ethical issues (Pellegrino, 1993). The period since then has seen a dramatic increase in research publications and funding of medical ethical issues but the authors also acknowledge that despite progress in clinical ethics there has been scant improvement in patient outcomes (Singer *et al.*, 2001).

These developments in ethics have occurred alongside the traditional business of clinical medicine which has a strong belief in expert knowledge. The last two decades of the twentieth century offered hopes of dramatic improvements in patient care with a wider commitment to and dissemination of knowledge through evidence based medicine (EBM; Sackett *et al.*, 1996). While there is some evidence for improvements in healthcare efficacy relating to the practice of EBM at an organisational level – implementation of guidelines etc. – (Yealy *et al.*, 2005), similar evidence of improvements in clinical outcomes at an individual practitioner's level is lacking (Coomarasamy and Khan, 2004).

This failure has proved disappointing, especially as clinicians had hoped that the dual certainty afforded by advances in medical knowledge and moral knowledge would lead to improved clinical care. The failure of clinical ethics in general and the tetrad of Beauchamp and Childress's (1979) principles in particular to deliver on their promise has invited criticism on several grounds: (a) focusing on individual autonomy to the exclusion of wider family and community (Hardwig, 1990); (b) lack of focus on care and relationship (Gilligan, 1988); (c) allowing for the growth of a clinical ethics 'industry' without concomitant benefits to patient care (Daar, 2002).

Psychiatric clinical ethics

Psychiatric ethics as a subdiscipline of the wider medical ethics has not been untouched by the problems described above (Roberts, 2002). With issues such as involuntary treatment, capacity and diminished responsibility, tension between public safety and autonomy, etc., psychiatry has additional issues unique to it. There are some encouraging signs with increased publications (Anzia and la Puma, 1991; Roberts and Roberts, 1999) and funding of psychiatric ethics (Shore *et al.*, 2001) and also increased representation of psychiatrists on ethics committees (Engel, 1992; Leeman, 2000). However, as Singer *et al.* (1990) have warned, ethics committees can lead to 'abrogation of moral decision making by the referring physician, usurpation of moral decision making by the ethics consultant and diffusion of responsibility within the ethics committee'. Moreover, within medical education psychiatric ethical issues have been ignored, despite their clear relevance to all, not just psychiatric clinical practice (Harrison, *et al.*, 1995).

In my role as a Clinical Teaching Fellow at the University of Nottingham, I find that while formal teaching of biomedical ethics has indeed become a part of medical school curricula following the publication of the General Medical Council's *Tomorrow's Doctors* (GMC, 1993, updated 2003) and *Good Medical Practice* (GMC, 2001), psychiatric ethics teaching remains the Cinderella element, despite the awareness that mental illnesses create a disproportionate amount of suffering and loss of productivity (Murray and Lopez, 1997) and the richness of clinical information and diversity usually available in psychiatry. Unfortunately, this has persisted at the postgraduate level in the UK, though there have been some efforts by the Royal College of Psychiatrists (2007) at addressing this in the new curriculum.

The end result is that clinical ethics teaching is often reduced to a mechanical learning and application of principles (usually the four principles mentioned above) without an understanding of the ethical framework underpinning those principles. There seems to be an acceptance of these principles as 'inventions' rather than as derivatives of common shared values. This creates the risk of reducing a professional from 'an ethical agent to an automaton' (Gadow, 1999), which in turn has practical consequences. Discusssion about ethical practice is not mere armchair theorising. Clinical moral issues arise in day-to-day practice for most psychiatrists, whether it is about diagnosis, or the use of the Mental Health Act, or breaking confidentiality, or medico-legal reporting.

So what is the alternative? The place for relational ethics

Nancy Andreasen, noted American neuropsychiatrist and neuroscientist, and architect of the DSM classification system, has captured the issue in the epigraph to this chapter (Andreasen, 1995). In our quest for certainty, both moral and medical, anything that is deemed subjective is considered unreliable and unscientific. And yet, even the definition of evidence based practice explicitly talks about the importance of patient values – 'The best care results from the conscientious, explicit, and judicious use of current best evidence and knowledge of patient *values* by well trained experienced clinicians' (Sackett *et al.*, 1996).

Clinical care has been considered as much an ethics using activity as a science using activity (Wright, 1991). Siegler (1979) makes the point that *good clinical practice* (emphasis mine) means both good technical and ethical care. Singer *et al.* (1990) also state that 'clinical ethics is not founded in philosophy, law or theology but, instead, is a subdiscipline of medicine, centering upon the *doctor–patient relationship*' (emphasis mine). Fulford, the British philosopher and psychiatrist, has highlighted the fact that clinical practice involves conflict in values (for example, of patients, carers, psychiatrist) and that one can only achieve efficient clinical decision making by becoming aware of these value conflicts (Fulford, 2004). Laura Weiss Roberts (2002) also argues that such value conflicts are inherent in the clinical world, whether between clinician and patient, between social policies and systems of care delivery, or between scientific discoveries and society.

What these various authors are advocating is essentially a relational approach allowing for input of differing views and perspectives in clinical decision making. In the clinical context, this involves taking into account 'the shared experience', whether it is shared with patients, carers or even managers or health policy makers. This is the very premise of relational ethics – that 'human experience is shared experience' (Bergum, 2004). It was this shared experience with my patients that helped me adapt in a foreign land. It was not merely encountering similar psychopathology, indeed the presentations were understandably a bit different, but more so the feelings and emotions generated within me which were the same. Oliver Sacks, neurologist and film maker, has described this relational space as the place 'which is neither subjective nor objective, but . . . a place where the physician must proceed . . . sharing his experiences and feelings and thoughts . . . and make it possible for his patient to do likewise' (Sacks, 1990).

Over the years, as I have graduated from being a trainee to a clinical research fellow in psychiatric genetics to my current job as consultant psychiatrist and clinical educator, I have become increasingly aware of this relational space. This is curious in some ways as I had moved from a largely interdependent culture to an autonomous independent culture, but as Walter Jeffko (1999) argues, relationships do not occur in a vacuum, and personal autonomy is contextually linked with human interdependency and reciprocity (Sherwin, 2002). The awareness of this relational space has clinical consequences as there is increasing evidence that the quality of clinician-patient encounter and other similar relational variables can significantly improve the quality of care at both individual and organisational levels (Greenfield et al., 1985; Boumbulian et al., 1991; Fowler, 1995; Sobel, 1995; Laine and Davidoff, 1996; Lorig et al., 1999). I will illustrate this with a clinical case example.

Clinical scenario

Sharon Smith, a 40-year-old single Caucasian lady, presented with a six to seven years old history of tiredness, body ache, lethargy, low mood and loss of interest. She used to work as a medical secretary but had stopped working five years ago and now found it too tiring to work. Her sleep and appetite were both quite disturbed. She also described ideas of worthlessness and poor self-esteem. There was no evidence of any psychotic symptoms or any ideas of self-harm. She had consulted two medical physicians, an orthopaedic surgeon and a rheumatologist, for her body ache and tiredness which she perceived as her main problems. None of them had identified any medical problem and her general practitioner (GP) had now referred her to a psychiatrist on the recommendation of the consultant physician who had suggested that she was suffering from depression. Sharon disagreed with the diagnosis vehemently and had only reluctantly accepted fluoxetine (an antidepressant) prescribed by her GP about twelve weeks ago. She admitted that of late she had not been taking her medication regularly. She said that she had derived no benefit from it. She was perplexed as to why she had been referred to a psychiatrist and felt that little could be achieved in this consultation.

Discussion

When I have discussed this case in clinical fora, questions have been raised about the 'ethical issues' in the case. It has been seen as a 'straightforward clinical problem' and in fact that is the reason I have chosen this case rather than some other where there is a 'more obvious ethical issue' at play. In clinical discussions, Sharon is deemed to meet the criteria for a major depressive disorder but lacks insight.

Evidence based medicine

Evidence based medicine guidelines such as National Institute of Clinical Excellence guidelines (NICE, 2007) would suggest initiating treatment with a selective serotonin reuptake inhibitor (SSRI) which the GP seems to have adhered to, although detection of depression has been delayed by years. NICE guidelines for depression do acknowledge that patient care is hampered by their unwillingness to seek help for a variety of reasons (Meltzer *et al.*, 2000) including stigma (Priest *et al.*, 1996) and also due to poor recognition by clinicians, especially when the presentation is somatic (as in Sharon's case), rather than psychological (Kisely *et al.*, 1995).

Detection of depression does not improve with use of guidelines (Thompson *et al.*, 2000) but by clinicians with better communication skills, who are not only better at recognising depression (Goldberg and Huxley, 1992; Üstün and Sartorins, 1995), but also at managing it merely by acknowledging distress and providing hope and social support (Ormel *et al.*, 1990), even if they do not identify the problem as depression (Van Os *et al.*, 2000)! The importance of a therapeutic relationship in improving treatment outcome has been emphasised by Safran and Muran (2000), Norcross (2002) and Schaap *et al.* (2003). The guidelines do recommend, in line with Sackett *et al.* (1996), taking into account 'the patient's values and preferences', but provide no guidance on dealing with patients' failure to engage or indeed on the ethical or moral imperatives of the clinician in such a common clinical scenario (NICE, 2007: 23).

Good medical and psychiatric practice

The professional codes of ethics are more explicit about the ethical duties of the doctor/psychiatrist. The general code of practice for doctors – *Good Medical Practice* (GMC, 2001) – outlines the core attributes/duties of a doctor relevant in the above case:

As a doctor you must:

— make the care of the patient your first concern
— treat every patient politely and considerately
— respect patients' dignity and privacy

— listen to patients and respect their views
— give patients information in a way they can understand
— respect the rights of patients to be fully involved in decisions about their care
— keep your professional knowledge and skills up to date

The psychiatrist's professional code of ethics – *Good Psychiatric Practice* (Royal College of Psychiatrists, 2004) – echoes this: 'Psychiatrists must consider and explain to patients the risks and benefits of acting in accordance with or against their expressed wishes and act decisively but sensitively, and always in the best interests of the patient'.

Faced with the principles/edicts mentioned in the codes, the clinician is caught in the traditional bind between the patient's best interests and respect for the patient's views and rights. Resolution is typically attempted in such cases by recourse to Beauchamp and Childress's (1979) tetrad of ethical principles leading to a trade-off between autonomy and beneficence. Sharon does not have psychotic symptoms, does not pose a risk to herself or others, and therefore in the traditional view her autonomy trumps beneficence.

Relational ethics perspective

Relational ethics is an action-oriented approach based on nurturing positive and healing relationships. In direct contrast to a competing rights perspective, the focus here is on co-operation and mutual accommodation (Zohar, 2003). There is no loss of respect for autonomy but rather than blind application of principles, attention is paid to the particular context of the situation and the relational space created in the specific situation.

Relational ethics in Sharon's case

Sharon's mental state examination suggested that she lacked 'insight' or that she had only 'partial insight' and was unwilling to co-operate with treatment. She was rather unhappy at having been referred to a psychiatrist and refused to have anything to do with medical treatment. In a relational ethics perspective, rather than view her refusal to co-operate as intransigence or lack of insight, her perspective was viewed as an essential and valid component in the development of a therapeutic relationship with me. From her perspective, her main complaints were physical in nature and she felt rebuffed by her physicians who had passed the buck on to a psychiatrist. Sharon, an independent lady, had not worked for years and now felt significantly disabled by her symptoms. Relational ethics involves a two-way process of giving and taking between doctor and patient. I felt moved to tell Sharon that I felt distressed about the suffering she had endured for years which to me seemed needless. Sharon, on her part, suspecting an agenda of me pushing drugs her way, reacted non-committally. Genuine mutual respect, a cornerstone of relational ethics, involves respect for the other and for oneself in the relationship. My respect for Sharon meant that for me she was an equal partner in the therapeutic endeavour. This was not a token gesture but an enterprise where both of us were stakeholders on a par. My self-respect was based on my role as an expert in the field of psychiatry fuelled by my training and experience in the science and practice of psychiatry. Equally and truly, I acknowledged Sharon's expertise in her own symptoms and her story and invited her to join me so that we could jointly use our expertise in solving the clinical problem.

An important caveat is that this is emphatically neither political correctness nor posturing to 'empower' patients, nor a device to achieve any other goal, but is an end in itself. I could have analysed this situation in a cognitive-rational way using the four principle approach but that would have focused only on Sharon's autonomy (her right to make decisions about her treatment) and beneficence (my ability to help her). The finer nuances of the case – Sharon's mistrust of medical professionals, her fundamental disagreement with the non-medical conceptualisation of her problems, her anxiety and distress – would have been lost in this dry impersonal analysis.

Seeing Sharon as a whole person truly respects her autonomy in the context of her personal story and affords her true respect. Mutual accommodation and respect, however, do not mean the absence of disagreement. True respect is a byproduct of therapeutic engagement which occurs when there is genuine empathy and sensitivity for the other. When Sharon asked me what I thought was the matter with her, I replied truthfully that from my perspective she was suffering from depression, but equally that the diagnostic label was not particularly important if we both agreed on the symptoms she was presenting with. As an expert I had the privilege of making a diagnosis. Similarly, as an expert she had the privilege of rejecting the diagnosis as inapplicable to her. The resulting disagreement, rather than mutual confrontation, leads to a co-learning situation where the two experts work together on finding a solution to the agreed problem of troubling symptoms. It is a strength of relational ethics that experts can disagree without compromising on professional or personal integrity.

Another strength of this model is that it fosters a true therapeutic alliance, which, as we have discussed (Safran and Muran, 2000; Norcross, 2002), seems to be a key ingredient in treatment outcomes. Again, the therapeutic alliance here is viewed as an end in its own right rather than a means to an end. Moreover, in a sprit of true shared experience, the experts share the credit for a successful outcome or the blame in case of an unsuccessful outcome.

Sharon agreed to work jointly with me in an exploration of her symptoms. She decided to discontinue her medication, but after a few sessions when we jointly looked at the evidence, she and I decided to restart antidepressant medication. Crucially, working relationally does not involve rejecting evidence. Instead, it integrates factual knowledge with personal knowledge

(Bergum and Dossetor, 2005). This is what Fulford has called integrating evidence based medicine with values based medicine (VBM; Fulford, 2004; Dave *et al.*, 2005; Fulford *et al.*, 2007).

Awareness of values allows for a process of reasoning through conflicting values, sifting through evidence and arriving at the best practice decision. Respect for difference allows for successful co-working despite differences in values. Indeed, I challenged Sharon when she dictated the antidepressant that she would use (rather than blindly accepting her right to refuse) and equally she challenged me when she felt that I made presumptions about her symptoms. Sharon and I have now been working together for nearly two years. She feels 90 per cent better. Both of us are dissatisfied with the missing 10 per cent and looking for ways to improve on this. She is taking an antidepressant with an adjunct medication though she adjusts the dose seasonally. Both of us also agreed that finding work was a way forward for her and she sought the help of the local occupational therapy service in finding work as a volunteer with a local charity.

Service delivery scenario

Background

Modern-day clinical practice goes beyond the doctor–patient relationship. A number of diverse professionals such as psychologists, community psychiatric nurses, social workers, occupational therapists, support workers, etc. comprise the modern multidisciplinary team. The last ten years under a Labour government have seen a raft of changes in the working of the National Health Service (NHS) (Secretary of State for Health, 1997, 2000). Several agencies may be involved in the care pathway of a patient from family members, employers, voluntary agencies, primary care to the other professionals mentioned above. With the purchaser–provider split and money following the patient for payment by results under the umbrella of clinical governance, the role of managers has increased significantly in the new NHS (Scally and Donaldson, 1998). Understandably, many of these agencies have differing values and beliefs, different (but occasionally competing) funding streams, are informed by different knowledge systems and skill sets and with poor integration and lack of mutual accommodation operate with great mistrust of one another (Mechanic, 1996).

Scenario A

Continuing with Sharon's case, let me take you back to the time she was referred by her general GP to the community mental health team (CMHT). Under the stepped care criteria of NICE guidelines for depression, Sharon did not meet the criteria for referral to the CMHT. According to the gatekeeping criteria for referrals, the multidisciplinary central allocation team suggested that Sharon ought to be managed in primary care with psychosocial support if needed, from primary care mental health workers.

Discussion

Under the new NHS system, the CMHT has clear criteria for accepting new referrals. Anything that is not serious mental illness is batted back to primary care with alacrity by the multidisciplinary central allocation team that deals with all new referrals to the CMHT. Clearly, there is an issue of distributive justice of allocation of scarce resources. But also at play is the issue of non-maleficence, which is likely, considering it is obvious from the referral that the patient has already suffered for years. Resolving the issue using the four principles is difficult, especially when distributive justice in the NHS situation is perceived as being remote and 'too big'. Under the circumstances, clinicians tend to take shelter in central guidelines such as NICE. In my opinion, this does, however, lead to what Singer *et al.* (1990) called abrogation of moral decision making by the allocating team. The concept of serious mental illness as a criterion for involvement of secondary care has been criticised by Barker *et al.* (1998) as 'seriousness' is contextual, and identifying serious mental illness with psychotic illnesses risks ignoring a person's human needs at a particular point of time (Barham and Hayward, 1995). Bowers (1997) has argued that the so-called worried well receive vital support from the CMHT at a critical time in their lives.

I would argue that the same is true in Sharon's case. From a relational ethics perspective, moving from ideology to action, viewed within the context of a longstanding misdiagnosed illness in someone who feels stigmatised and is unlikely to engage in a seven-minute interview with her GP, batting back the referral seems immoral and unethical. This still leaves the issue of distributive justice. We have seen that at an individual level evidence based medicine alone does not lead to improved patient outcomes, but needs the addition of the relational value based medicine. Similarly, at an organisational level, dealing with interfaces by creating rigid guidelines (even if evidence based) to gatekeep entry or exit will not be sufficient in improving clinical outcomes unless this occurs in the context of relational values of respecting organisational diversity, working in partnership with mutual accommodation towards the common goal of providing person-centred care, highlighting the need for awareness of clinical ethical issues in medical managers (Sharpe, 2002).

The challenge for service organisers is to use this 'shared experience' to create integrated models of service delivery and funding. Leutz (1998) and Kodner and Spreeuwenberg (2002) have put forth a case for how such an integrated model may work in practice.

Other clinical issues

There are several psychiatric ethical issues not covered in this chapter due to space constraints: for example, involuntary treatment; confidentiality issues; balancing risk; public protection vs autonomy; autonomy of carers vs that of patients; covert vs forcible administration of medication, etc. Each of these issues raises conflicts in values which are self-evident. However, routine psychiatric practice throws up issues where the values are covert (Sadler, 2005) and conflicts not easily evident. Issues of diagnosis, impairment, transcultural psychiatry, 'good' psychiatrist, 'good' treatment, etc. are all value-laden concepts. However, personhood does not end with someone being detained under a section of the Mental Health Act. In each of the examples mentioned above it should be possible to view the situation not impersonally but sensitively and empathically within a relational context. The case example I have chosen focuses on the individual patient but, as is obvious, engaging the family and the wider community is an integral aspect of relational practice.

Drawbacks of relational ethics in psychiatric practice

1   '*I already practise it.*' Valuing patients and their community is such a truism that relational ethics can justifiably attract the charge that it is old wine in new bottles. I have often been told by clinicians that they would not dream of practising in any other way. Yet evidence suggests otherwise (Gerteis *et al.*, 1993; Botelho *et al.*, 1996). The analogy is to evidence based medicine which when introduced in the early 1990s led to clinicians protesting that they were already practising in an evidence based manner (Rosenberg and Donald, 1995) but using EBM explicitly has integrated it into routine medical practice.

2   '*It is resource intensive – I don't have the time.*' The practice of medicine is not a technology based cocktail where one can add the 'humane' bits whenever required (Siegler, 1979). As I have shown above, ethical care is an integral part of medical practice. Failure to work in an ethical patient-centred way is not only morally indefensible but also clinically unacceptable. The experience with EBM has shown that with adequate support and investment at the organisational level, it should be relatively easy for individual clinicians to engage in values based medicine.

3   '*It is too vague, diffuse, naive.*' Working in a relational way can seem to be too idealistic. However, as I have discussed in my case study, relational ethics is situational and contextual, valuing the 'particular over the general' (Gadow, 1999). It does not reject evidence based medicine, guidelines, ethical theory or principles, but rather places them in their individual context. It may seem unachievable in practice, but like any other clinical craft it is about learning and over-learning the skills and

attitudes from the particular, extending it to the general to be reapplied in a particular case. The key is to root relational working in clinical practice.

4   '*It promotes ethical relativism – it is too individual – anything goes.*' Ethical relationalism with its emphasis on individual context may seem like ethical relativism and raise fears of situational ethics (Macklin, 1998). However, relational ethics is about recognising that an individual is not an island and that we are what we are based on how we relate to others. Legal-ethical principles such as justice or humane-ethical perspectives such as the care perspective are then interpreted using this insight of valuing interdependency over independence.

Conclusion

Scientific and technological progress, with its relentless strides towards objectivity, does not eliminate values but in fact raises more, newer ethical issues (Singer *et al.*, 2001; Fulford, 2004). In the UK context, the NHS has embraced the clinical governance structure with the aim of striving towards excellence in clinical care. So far, this has been driven by the implementation of EBM through the widespread dissemination and use of guidelines, reducing and managing risk in the workplace using risk management groups and clinical audits. This seems to have had some positive effect in terms of care delivered at the organisational level. Clinical ethics, though not mentioned explicitly, is a core element of themes such as patient and carer involvement, team working, risk management, etc. In the wake of these changes, clinical ethics teaching has become routine practice in undergraduate teaching of medicine and postgraduate psychiatric education. However, this has not resulted in improvements in clinical care. I have argued that clinical ethics teaching has largely been theoretical, principles based teaching leading to an impersonal, legalistic application in clinical situations. This leads to the practice of resolving conflicts in values by referring to rules (or vicariously by referral to ethics committees or on-call ethicists) in an attempt to find the 'right' answer.

Relational ethics with its focus on persons and their context shifts the emphasis from finding the right answer to asking the 'right questions'. Eliciting facts is important, but so too is not brushing complexity under the carpet. Eliciting multiple relational perspectives is a practical way of achieving this clinically. This clearly shifts the focus from the individual as a bearer of rights to a situation where the rights are embedded in social reciprocity. This also lifts the restriction of the location of ethical matters from the individual patient to the larger community, policy makers, administrators and institutions.

Whether virtue can be taught remains a moot question (Kopelman, 1999). There is evidence to show that focused courses can lead to improvements in knowledge (Sulmasy and Marx, 1999) and healthcare outcomes (Davis *et al.*,

1999). At my medical school, we have used various techniques such as role play, case vignettes and simulated patients to teach psychiatric ethics in its clinical context, which is what students want (Charon and Fox, 1995).

The real hope for the future is that this training will create a new wave of *ethical governance* – a framework of learning and working that will enable individuals and organisations to achieve and maintain highly ethical practice; a framework which will facilitate and encourage diverse individuals and organisations to work in partnership with mutual respect for each other as moral beings.

References

Andreasen, N. C. (1995) Post-traumatic stress disorder: psychology, biology and the Manichaean warfare between false dichotomies. *American Journal of Psychiatry* 152, 7, 963–965.

Anzia, D. and la Puma J. (1991) An annotated bibliography of psychiatric medical ethics. *Academic Psychiatry* 15, 1–17.

Barham, P. and Hayward, R. (1995) *Relocating Madness: From the Mental Patient to the Person*. London: Free Association Books.

Barker, P. J., Keady, J., Croom, S., Stevenson, C., Adams, T. and Reynolds, W. (1998) The concept of serious mental illness: modern myths and grim realities. *Journal of Psychiatric and Mental Health Nursing* 5, 247–254.

Beauchamp, T. and Childress, J. (1979) *Principles of Biomedical Ethics*, 1st edn. New York: Oxford University Press.

Bergum, V. (2004) Relational ethics in nursing. In J. L. Storch, P. Rodney and R. Starzomski (eds) *Toward a Moral Horizon: Nursing Ethics for Leadership and Practice*. Toronto: Peason.

Bergum, V. and Dossetor, J. (2005) *Relational Ethics: The Full Meaning of Respect*. Hagerstown, MA: University Publishing Group.

Botelho, R., Lue, B. and Fiscella, K. (1996) Family involvement in routine health care: a survey of patients' behaviours and preferences. *Journal of Family Practice* 42, 572–576.

Boumbulian, P., MacGregor, D., Delbanco, T., Edgman-Levitan, S., Smith, D. and Anderson, R. (1991) Patient centred care, patient valued care. *Journal of Health Care for the Poor and Underserved* 2, 338–346.

Bowers, L. (1997) SPN caseloads and the 'worried well': misspent time or vital work? *Journal of Advanced Nursing* 26, 930–936.

Burt, R. (1996) The suppressed legacy of Nuremberg. *Hastings Center Report* 26, 5, 30–33.

Charon, R. and Fox, R. C. (1995) Critiques and remedies: medical students call for change in ethics teaching. *Journal of the American Medical Association* 274, 767–771.

Coomarasamy, A. and Khan, K. S. (2004) What is the evidence that postgraduate teaching in evidence based medicine changes anything? A systematic review. *British Medical Journal* 329, 7473, 1017.

Daar, A. S. (2002) Failure of clinical ethics to deliver on its promise. *BMC Biomedical Ethics* 2,2 (http://www.biomedcentral.com/1472–6939/2/2).

Dave, S., Fulford, K. W. M. and Williams, R. (2005) *Values based practice: case studies, clinical skills and service development.* One day workshop presented at the Annual Meeting, Royal College of Psychiatrists, Edinburgh, UK.

Davis, D., O'Brien, M. A. T., Freemantle, N., Wolf, F. M., Mazmanian, P. and Taylor-Vaisey, A. (1999) Impact of formal continuing medical education: do conferences, workshops, rounds, and other traditional continuing education activities change physician behavior or health care outcomes? *Journal of the American Medical Association* 282, 867–874.

Engel, C. C. Jr (1992) Psychiatrists and the General Hospital Ethics Committee. *General Hospital Psychiatry* 14, 29–35.

Fowler, F. (1995) Using patients' reports to evaluate medical outcomes. In *Tools for Evaluating Health Technologies: Five Background Papers, BP-H_142 US Congress Office of Technology Assessment.* Washington, DC: US Government Printing Office.

Fulford, K. W. M. (2004) Values in psychiatric diagnosis: developments in policy, training and research. *Psychopathology* 38, 4, 171–176.

Fulford, K. W. M., Adshead, G., and Dave, S. (2007) *Patient centred care and values based practice: a training course.* Paper presented at the Annual Meeting, Royal College of Psychiatrists, Edinburgh, UK.

Gadow, S. (1999) Relational narratives: the postmodern turn in nursing ethics. *Scholarly Inquiry for Nursing Practice: An International Journal* 13, 1, 57–70.

Gerteis, M., Edgman-Levitan, S., Daley, J. and Delbanco, T. (1993) *Through the Patient's Eyes: Understanding and Promoting Patient-Centred Care.* San Francisco: Jossey-Bass.

Gilligan, C. (1988) Remapping the moral domain: new images of self in relationship. In C. Gilligan J. Ward, J. M. Taylor and B. Bardige (eds) *Mapping the Moral Domain: A Contribution of Women's Thinking to Psychological Theory and Education.* Cambridge, MA: Harvard University Press.

General Medical Council (GMC, 1993) *Tomorrow's Doctors.* London: GMC.

General Medical Council (GMC, 2001) *Good Medical Practice.* London GMC.

General Medical Council (GMC, 2003) *Tomorrow's Doctors.* London: GMC. http://www.gmc-uk.org/education/undergraduate/undergraduate_policy/tomorrows_doctors.asp (accessed 25 October 2007).

Goldberg, D. P. and Huxley, P. J. (1992) *Common Mental Disorders: A Bio-Social Model.* London: Tavistock/Routledge.

Greenfield, S., Kaplan, S. and Ware, J. (1985) Expanding patient involvement in care. *Annals of Internal Medicine* 102, 520–528.

Hardwig, J. (1990) What about the family? *Hastings Center Report* 20, 2, 5–10.

Harrison, J., Barrow, S. and Creed, F. (1995) Social deprivation and psychiatric admission rates among different diagnostic groups. *British Journal of Psychiatry* 167, 456–462.

Hope, T. (2001) Clinical ethics in the UK. *BMC Medical Ethics* 2, 2. http://www.biomedcentral.com/1472-6939/2/2 (accessed 25 October 2007).

Jeffko, W. (1999) *Contemporory Ethical Issues: A Personalistic Perspective.* Amherst, NY: Humanity Books.

Kisely, S., Gater, R. and Goldberg, D. P. (1995) Results from the Manchester Centre. In T. B. Üstün and N. Sartorius (eds) *Mental Illness in General Health Care: An International Study.* Chichester: Wiley.

Kodner, D. L. and Spreeuwenberg, C. (2002) Integrated care: meaning, logic, applications, and implications – a discussion paper. *International Journal of Integrated Care* 2.

Kopelman, L. R. (1999) Values and virtues: should they be taught? *Academic Medicine*, 74, 1307–1310.

Laine, C., and Davidoff, F. (1996) Patient-centred medicine: a professional evolution. *Journal of the American Medical Association* 275, 152–156.

Leeman, C. P. (2000) Psychiatric consultations and ethics consultations: similarities and differences. *General Hospital Psychiatry* 22, 270–275.

Leutz, W. (1998) Five laws for integrating medical and social services: lessons from the United States and the United Kingdom. *Millbank Quarterly* 77, 1, 77–110.

Lorig, K., Sobel, D., Stewart, A., Brown, B., Bandura, A., Ritter, P., Gonzalez, V., Laurent, D. and Holman, H. (1999) Evidence suggesting that a chronic disease self-management program can improve health status while reducing hospitalization: a randomized trial. *Medical Care* 37, 5–14.

Macklin, R. (1998) Ethical relativism in a multicultural society. *Kennedy Institute of Ethics Journal* 8, 1, 1–22.

Mechanic, D. (1996) Changing medical organisation and the erosion of trust. *Millbank Quarterly* 74, 171–189.

Meltzer, H., Bebbington, P., Brugha, T. *et al.* (2000). The reluctance to seek treatment for neurotic disorders. *Journal of Mental Health* 9, 3, 319–327.

Murray, C. and Lopez, A. (1997) Alternative projections of mortality and disability by cause, 1999–2000. Global burden of disease study. *Lancet* 349, 1498–1504.

National Institute of Clinical Excellence (NICE, 2007) Depression: management of depression in primary and secondary care – National Collaborating Centre for Mental Health. http://guidance.nice.org.uk/CG23/fullguideline/pdf/English (accessed 25th October 2007).

Norcross, J. C. (ed.) (2002) *Psychotherapy Relationships that Work: Therapist Contributions and Responsiveness to Patients.* New York: Oxford University Press.

Ormel, J., Van den Brink, W., Koeter, M. W., Giel, R., Van Der Meer, K., Van De Willige, G. and Wilmink, F. W. (1990). Recognition, management and outcome of psychological disorders in primary care: a naturalistic follow-up study. *Psychological Medicine* 20, 4, 909–923.

Pellegrino, E. (1993) The metamorphosis of medical ethics: a 30 year old retrospective. *Journal of the American Medical Association* 269, 9, 1158–1162.

Pellegrino, E. (1999) The commodification of medical and health care: the moral consequences of a paradigm shift from a professional to a market ethics. *Journal of Medicine and Philosophy*, 24, 3, 243–266.

Priest, R. G., Vize, C., Roberts, A. *et al.* (1996) Lay people's attitudes to treatment of depression: results of opinion poll for Defeat Depression Campaign just before its launch. *British Medical Journal* 313, 7061, 858–859.

Roberts, L. W. (2002) Clinical ethics as a parent discipline. *BMC Biomedical Ethics*, 2, 2. http://www.biomedcentral.com/1472-6939/2/2 (accessed 25 October 2007).

Roberts, L. W. and Roberts, B. (1999) Psychiatric research ethics: an overview of evolving guidelines and current ethical dilemmas in the study of mental illness. *Biological Psychiatry* 46, 1025–1038.

Rosenberg, W. and Donald, A. (1995) Evidence based medicine: an approach to clinical problem-solving. *British Medical Journal* 310, 1122–1126.

Royal College of Psychiatrists (2004) *RCPsych Good Psychiatric Practice*, 2nd edn. http://www.rcpsych.ac.uk/files/pdfversion/cr125.pdf (accessed 25 October 2007).

Royal College of Psychiatrists (2007) *A Competency Based Curriculum for Psychiatry: Core and General Module*. http://www.rcpsych.ac.uk/docs/Curriculum%20-%20core %20and%20general%20modulecd.doc (accessed 25 October 2007).

Sackett, D. L., Rosenberg, W. M., Gray, J. A., Haynes, R. B. and Richardson, W. S. (1996) Evidence based medicine: what it is and what it isn't. *British Medical Journal* 312, 7023 71–72.

Sacks, O. (1990) *Awakenings*. New York: Harper.

Sadler, J. (2005) *Values and Psychiatric Diagnosis*. Oxford: Oxford University Press.

Safran, J. D and Muran, J. C. (2000). *Negotiating the Therapeutic Alliance: A Relational Treatment Guide*. New York: Guilford Press.

Scally, G. and Donaldson, L. J. (1998) Looking forward: clinical governance and the drive for quality improvement in the new NHS in England. *British Medical Journal* 317, 61–65.

Schaap, C., Bennun, I., Schindler, L. and Hoogduin, K. (1993) *The Therapeutic Relationship in Behavioural Psychotherapy*. Chichester: Wiley.

Secretary of State for Health (1997) *The New NHS: Modern, Dependable*. London: The Stationery Office.

Secretary of State for Health (2000) *The NHS Plan: A Plan for Investment, A Plan for Reform*. London: The Stationery Office.

Sharpe, V. (2002) Broadening the foundation. *BMC Biomedical Ethics* 2, 2. http://www.biomedcentral.com/1472-6939/2/2 (accessed 25 October 2007).

Sherwin, S. (2002) A relational approach to autonomy in health care. In S. Sherwin *The Politics of Women's Health: Exploring Agency and Autonomy*. Philadelphia: Temple University Press.

Shore, D., Goldschmidts, W., Wynne, D. and Hyman, S. (2001) NIMH perspective: meeting national needs of psychiatrist researchers. *Academic Psychiatry* 25, 9–11.

Siegler, M. (1979) Clinical ethics and clinical medicine. *Archives of Internal Medicine* 139, 914–915.

Singer, P. A., Pellegrino, E. D. and Siegler, M. (1990) Ethics committees and consultants. *Journal of Clinical Ethics* 1, 263–267.

Singer, P., Siegler, M. and Pellegrino, E. (2001) Clinical ethics revisited. *BMC Medical Ethics* 2, 1.

Sobel, D. (1995) Rethinking medicine: improving health outcomes with cost-effective psychosocial interventions. *Psychosomatic Medicine* 57, 234–244.

Sulmasy, D. P. and Marx, E. S. (1997) Ethics education for medical house officers: long term improvements in knowledge and confidence. *Journal of Medical Ethics* 23, 88–92.

Thompson, C., Kinmonth, A. L., Stevens, L. *et al.* (2000) Effects of good practice guidelines and practice-based education on the detection and treatment of depression in primary care. Hampshire Depression Project randomised controlled trial. *Lancet 355*, 9199, 185–191.

Üstün, T. B. and Sartorius, N. (eds) (1995) *Mental Illness in General Health Care: An International Study*. Chichester: Wiley.

Van Os, T., Van den Brink, R., Tiemens, B., Jenner, J., Van der Meer K. and Ormel, J.

(2002) Are effects of depression management training for general practitioners on patient outcomes mediated by improvements in the process of care? *Journal of Affective Disorders* 80, 2–3, 173–179.

Wright, R. A. (1991) Clinical judgment and bioethics: the decision-making link. *Journal of Medical Philosophy* 16, 71–91.

Yealy, D. M., Auble, T. E., Stone, R. A., *et al.* (2005) Effect of increasing the intensity of implementing pneumonia guidelines: a randomized, controlled trial. *Annals of Internal Medicine* 143, 12, 881–894.

Zohar, N. J. (2003) Co-operation despite disagreement: from politics to healthcare. *Bioethics* 17, 121–141.

Chapter 9

Therapy as evidence

Legal perspectives on the relationship between therapist and client

Peter Jenkins

Therapists are increasingly aware that their work with clients is not only a helping relationship and a therapeutic activity, but also one which is framed by powerful ethical considerations, and even ultimately one which is constrained by the law. This is not to suggest that legal considerations should be the dominant perspective in work and relationships with clients, with the unwelcome consequence that a fear of legal repercussions results in the development of heavily defensive forms of practice. There will always be a tension between therapeutic, ethical and legal elements of practice. This would be the case, for example, in deciding whether or not to report child abuse, in the case of a client resisting this course of action, where there is no apparent immediate risk to the client, or to a third party. As Bond has argued, 'What is ethical may not be legal. What is legal may not be ethical' (Bond, 2002: 124).

This chapter will explore some of the key legal aspects of the therapeutic relationship between practitioner and client. Given that the therapy relationship is central to developing an effective relational ethic in any given client–practitioner relationship, this is a significant feature in relation to legal aspects of counselling and psychotherapy. The chapter will include legal definitions of the boundaries of safe practice, and the legal responses to perceived breaches of such boundaries. The irony is that, for the therapist, their actual practice may later be presented in court by the client as material supporting a claim for negligence – hence this chapter's theme of *therapy as evidence*. This discussion will then be followed by a more personal reflection on my approach to ethical practice, in my work as a counsellor trainer.

Law and ethics

It is perhaps important to start with some definitions. The term 'law' used here relates to all forms of civil and criminal law, including statute, common and case law. The discussion will focus mainly on the law applying to England and Wales. There are some differences to be found regarding the legal systems of Scotland and Northern Ireland, but the general principles outlined here will broadly apply to these jurisdictions as well. Most of the law relating to therapeutic work is civil, rather than criminal, in nature. The main purpose of civil law is to regulate relationships between parties, or to resolve conflict, rather than to punish crime. Within civil law, the term 'common law' describes a form of law which has grown up over centuries. It is based on incremental decisions made by the courts, rather than coming from a single authoritative set of codes, as in the European tradition. Within a common law system, such as applies in the UK, former Commonwealth countries and the US, there are key cases, which decide contentious issues. These then set a precedent for future contests, as in the *Gillick* case, with regard to the rights of young people to confidentiality and consent to treatment. Specific case law relating to therapy in the UK is still limited, perhaps fortunately. Nevertheless, the basic principles for deciding cases brought against therapists, or their organisations, are well established with reference to other fields such as medicine (Jenkins, 2007).

Returning to definitions, ethics is 'a generic term for various ways of understanding and examining the moral life' (Beauchamp and Childress, 2001: 1). Developing sensitivity to these ethical aspects of therapeutic work is now recognised as an essential part of every therapist's role. Every decision about working with a client, starting from the initial decision as to whether even to accept a client for therapy, is necessarily bound up with ethical considerations. The therapist might ask himself or herself a number of questions, such as: Am I the right therapist for this particular client? Is there any pre-existing contact or knowledge about the client which might prejudice the work? Am I competent to work with the presenting issues, as far as initial information might suggest? Even before starting therapeutic work (and for some schools, the relationship will begin before actually meeting the client) ethical considerations rapidly come to the fore.

Ethical frameworks

There has been a major, and welcome, shift in the ways in which therapists are now obliged to take note of ethical considerations in their practice. Whereas previously therapists were bound by prescriptive codes of ethics, setting out what must be done, or what must not be done, therapists now are increasingly bound by more flexible, if still intransigent, frameworks of ethical principles. This is premised on the realisation that, for some dilemmas, such as working with a suicidal client, there may be no single correct course of action to follow. A number of different approaches may each be supported by equally sound, if conflicting, ethical arguments. Thus, the therapist might seek to break client confidentiality in order to obtain psychiatric help for a severely distressed client, following the principle of non-maleficence, or avoidance of harm. Equally, another therapist might respect the client's right to take their own life (Currey, 2005). This could be argued on the basis of respecting the client's right to autonomy, as, for example, is found in the practice of befriending organisations such as the Samaritans.

The main reference point in this shift to an empowering approach to therapeutic ethics is the BACP Ethical Framework (2002). This describes a complex, but accessible, framework for practitioners, which includes ethical *principles*, such as autonomy and avoidance of harm, ethical *values*, such as integrity and *personal qualities*, such as humility. Practitioners are required to use the framework as a toolkit, in order to clarify and devise the appropriate responses to the very real challenges encountered every day in their own work. This ethical framework thus provides the conceptual underpinning, or philo- sophical scaffolding, for developing their own finely tuned and well-thought- out, or indeed heartfelt, responses to ethical dilemmas, in the context of their relationships with clients and colleagues.

The key ethical principles in this framework include fidelity (trust), auton- omy, beneficence (welfare), non-maleficence (avoiding harm), justice and wel- fare. These principles, in turn, derive from a well-established philosophical tradition, namely the deontological, or rule-following, approach, proposed by Kant and further developed by authors such as Beauchamp and Childress (2001) in the field of biomedical ethics, and by Thompson (1983) with regard to therapy.

Ethical principles and legal concepts

When it comes to exploring relational ethics, it is useful to translate these key ethical principles into a legal context (see Table 9.1). While ethics may supply the underpinning framework for a therapist's decision, for example, whether or not to report a client's threat against a partner, in a domestic violence situation, the law will bring a separate and quite distinct set of principles to apply in court. Therapeutic practice may be shaped, and hopefully informed, by sound ethical principles, but, in the final instance, is subject to the sanctions of the law. Thus, a therapist might breach confidentiality on the basis of avoiding harm, but could be subject to the full weight of the law, in any subsequent legal action for breach of confidence.

Table 9.1 is not intended to formalise any exact correspondence between ethical principles and legal concepts, but simply to suggest how these two discourses may be linked. Thus, the central ethical principle of respecting client autonomy finds expression, in legal terms, in the client's right in law to choose whether to engage in, or decline, a contract with a therapist, assuming the existence of a fee-paying relationship. The legal concept of informed consent is steadily gaining prominence, particularly in National Health Service (NHS) work. However, it holds much weaker status in UK law than in the US, where there is extensive supporting case law. The doctrine of informed consent points to the right of the client, or patient in medical treat- ment, to have possession of all relevant information, in order to decide on the

Table 9.1 Relationship of ethical principles to legal concept

Ethical principles (BACP)	Legal concepts
Fidelity (trust)	Duty of confidence Fiduciary duty
Autonomy	Informed consent Contract
Beneficence (welfare)	Duty of care
Non-maleficence (avoiding harm)	Standard of care Duty to warn
Justice	Non-discrimination
Self-respect	Preconditions necessary to fulfil duty to apply 'reasonable care and skill'

risks of accepting, or declining, treatment. Other ethical principles equally find some kind of translation in corresponding legal concepts, with the ethical principle of fidelity, or trust, linking across to the legal concept of the therapist's duty of confidence towards the client, or furthermore, of the much broader 'fiduciary duty of trust' towards the client.

Legal boundaries of ethical practice

So, given the ethical and legal frameworks surrounding therapeutic work, how does this take form as a set of relational ethics towards the client? The law, just like therapy, is concerned with maintaining appropriate boundaries, both for practice and for the professional relationship between practitioner and client. These boundaries include the use of touch, provision of formal consent to treatment, the requirements for a contract, the protection of sensitive client confidential information and the maintenance of appropriate professional standards of care. Breach of any of these boundaries carries the risk of legal sanction, primarily via action brought by an aggrieved client, but also potentially by the state in the case of a serious criminal matter, such as assault.

Therapeutic use of touch

Many therapists would not routinely use touch as part of their therapeutic work, but for others, touch, including massage or bodywork, would constitute a central part of their repertoire. Therapists using touch as an intentional part of their therapy need to obtain prior client consent, and to remain within established boundaries of safe and competent practice (Hunter and Struve, 1998). Breach of boundaries for touch could lead to a client bringing a civil action against a therapist for assault or battery. Assault includes a threat, or reasonable fear and apprehension of immediate force or violence. Battery includes the actual application of some degree of force to another person, but does not include the normal, unavoidable touching which is part of everyday life. The following example illustrates some of the hazards involved in therapeutic use of touch:

> Mary was an enthusiastic member of a therapy group, which routinely used group hugs to hold and physically support members requesting this activity. Mary, now seven months pregnant, asked for the group to help her embody the sense of 'maternal role pressure' which she was experiencing, in the form of an intense group holding exercise. This was entered into with spontaneous enthusiasm by the group, but without careful direction by the group leader. Mary quickly felt physically and emotionally overwhelmed by this experience, and shortly later had a miscarriage, and unfortunately lost the baby.

Obtaining the client's informed consent

Linked to the above case, the developing concept of informed consent requires, certainly in medical practice, for the patient or client to be given sufficient information about alternative treatments, or non-treatment, in order to make an informed decision. This process is now routine, even for minor medical procedures in the NHS, but has yet to become firmly established as a legal principle in wider therapeutic treatments, however desirable it may be in ethical terms. However, in several cases involving a request for a termination of pregnancy, it has been argued that the patient or client did not receive sufficient counselling to enable her to provide fully informed consent to a difficult and irrevocable decision (*The Guardian*, 30 July 2007). In this type of case, counselling is essentially an ancillary step towards a wider medical procedure, or a means towards an end.

There is a stage even before this, however, for the client to consider their informed consent to the therapeutic process itself. This would require the therapist to outline and explore the possible positive and negative outcomes of engaging in therapy, or in not undertaking therapy for depression, as compared, perhaps, with undergoing (or not undergoing) antidepressant medication. Positive effects, related to research findings, might touch on the effectiveness of the particular kind of therapy being offered, for example, person-centred counselling, as compared with cognitive behavioural therapy. Negative effects might include the possible short-term worsening of mood, a destabilising effect on key supporting relationships, perhaps if the client becomes more angry or assertive about their emotional needs, or any number of possible outcomes. For some schools of therapy, this kind of discussion is a key part of a mutual assessment process, which is essential before therapy proper can begin. For other approaches, this kind of discussion may be less formal and becomes inevitably intertwined with the development of the actual therapeutic alliance itself. Legal principles might seem to be intrusive and cumbersome within this delicate unfolding process, which is much more about the construction of a trusting relationship, than a description of a specific therapeutic technique.

Use of contracts with clients

Informed consent is linked to the relational concept of respect for client autonomy. Similarly, the legal concept of a contract, namely an agreement enforceable in law, is based on the acknowledgement of the client's right of choice. Therapists tend to use the term 'contract' quite widely, with 'contracting' seen as a necessary stage of the therapeutic process. However, in strictly legal terms, a contract between a therapist and client will not necessarily constitute a formal legal document, unless, broadly speaking, there is an exchange of money for therapy. Therapy provided without direct payment, as under the NHS, or by a voluntary organisation offering relationship counselling, will not be based on a contract as such. Under the classic private practice model, a therapist (or supervisor) providing therapy (or supervision) for direct payment will be bound by contract, even if only a verbal one. The terms of such a contract can be implied, namely that the therapist possesses the necessary level of skill and expertise required for the job, and that confidentiality will ordinarily be maintained. Express, or explicit, terms will usually include reference to the cost of sessions, their frequency, arrangements for cancellation, holidays and notice of ending. The contract may also include information about the therapist's theoretical orientation, training, qualification, membership of professional bodies, supervision and avenues for complaint. Therapists clearly need to be cautious about overoptimism in setting out their contract of agreement with clients, as the following example illustrates:

> Mr and Mrs Aziz brought their teenage daughter, Parveen, to see a private therapist, Melissa Shaw, for help with an apparent eating disorder. Ms Shaw's contract made reference to a published research study on which she had, apparently, taken a key part as a researcher. The therapist's promotional leaflet indicated 'an almost 100 per cent recovery rate' using the therapeutic approach developed in the survey. Parveen did not respond to Ms Shaw's therapeutic approach, and the parents subsequently brought a successful case for breach of contract against the therapist in the small claims court.

Therapist's duty of confidence

The ethical principle of fidelity, or trust, can be seen at work in the legal concept of the therapist's duty of confidence. Therapists are required by law to keep confidential any personal information of a sensitive nature, which is disclosed to them by the client, in the course of their work. This duty of confidence arises from several sources, including both common law and statute. Under common law, the therapist has a duty to maintain confidentiality, due to the special trusting nature of the relationship with the client. Confidentiality can also be expected via a legally binding contract, either as a specific or express term, or as an implied term of the contract to provide therapy. Statute law provides further protection for client confidentiality in the form of the Data Protection Act 1998, and the client's right to respect for private and family life, under Article 8 of the Human Rights Act 1998.

However, therapists are well aware that this duty to strive to maintain client confidentiality is not absolute. The ethical concept of fidelity, namely of keeping trust with the client, can be counterbalanced, or even outweighed, by competing ethical alternative responsibilities, such as the avoidance of harm, or non-maleficence. In law also the duty of confidence, or the therapist's fiduciary duty of trust towards the client, may be outweighed by considerations of the potential for harm to others. Confidentiality can be broken in the public interest, i.e. for the greater good of society, in order to prevent terrorism, or serious crime. Therapists in the UK are not legally protected in the same way as some of their counterparts in the US are. Legal opinion has asserted forcibly that '"confidentiality" is not a separate head of privilege' (*Alfred Crompton Amusement Machines v Customs and Excise* [1974] at 433). Roughly translated, this means that therapists cannot claim professional confidentiality as a cast-iron, or ready-made, defence against enforced disclosure, for example, of their notes to a court. Therapists may, however, seek to take action to breach client confidentiality where it is clearly in the public interest, as occurred in the case of *Egdell*. Here, a psychiatrist breached medical confidentiality to make essential information available to the authorities concerning the continuing and substantial risk to the public presented by a psychiatric patient.

Therapists will generally try to communicate the potential limitations on confidentiality to clients at the outset. They will discuss any exceptions to confidentiality, which are set by law, or determined as policy by an employing agency. Mandatory limitations to confidentiality, such as the obligation to report terrorist activity, are comparatively rare in the UK. However, many therapists will signal other limits to confidentiality via a discussion during the first session, or refer the client to a leaflet setting out their agency's policy on this issue. While many describe this as agreeing the contract with the client, in cases where there is no exchange of services for money, this will be more accurately termed as an advance client consent to disclosure. Many therapists will clarify with the client that disclosures of serious crime, or a threat to a third party in the context of domestic violence, incidents of child abuse, or evidence of suicidal ideation, will be passed on to the appropriate authorities, on the basis of this advance agreement. However, some situations may arise which are not covered by the terms of such an agreement, as the following example illustrates:

> Carl worked as a counsellor for a voluntary agency specialising in outreach work with young people requiring information and advice on sexual health issues. While working with Marlon, he became concerned that the latter was apparently reckless about infecting his current long-term partner, Kevin, with the HIV virus, perhaps as a form of unconscious revenge for his own condition. After taking advice from a medically qualified supervisor, Carl took the radical and unprecedented step of contacting Kevin by text message, to invite him in for a confidential discussion. The text message prompted a bitter exchange between Kevin and Marlon. Marlon then sought legal advice as to whether any legal action was possible against Carl, and his employing agency, for 'gross and deliberate breach of confidence'.

The case above illustrates some of the tensions inherent in the therapist's role of containing, or disclosing, highly sensitive personal information. Disclosure of personal information, even when apparently in the public interest, will not necessarily be supported by the courts, particularly in the relatively untried area of HIV counselling. Therapists may have to live with very real tensions and dilemmas about holding information concerning risk to other parties, without possessing a clear legal or ethical mandate for its disclosure.

Breach of standard of care

In ethical terms, the therapist has a responsibility to act on the basis of the principle of beneficence or welfare, in order that the therapy is of benefit to the client. In legal terms, this would translate as the therapist owing a duty of care to the client. The therapist must work within accepted professional standards, and be judged against the standard of the 'reasonably competent practitioner', according to the *Bolam* test, derived from medical case law. The client could bring a case against the therapist on the grounds of negligence, under civil law. It would need to be proven that a breach of duty of care had materially caused the client a psychological injury, such as clinical depression. This is referred to as the test of causation, which proves to be an almost insurmountable obstacle for many clients bringing litigation against their therapist. One of the major problems for the client lies in actually bringing sufficient credible evidence of negligence on the part of the therapist, given the intentionally private, and even closeted, nature of much therapeutic work.

Case law illustrating this aspect of relational ethics is quite limited. The key reference point illustrating how the courts define the therapist's duty of care, in a legal sense, can be found in the case of *Werner v Landau* (1961), described below:

> Alice Landau successfully sued her therapist, Dr Theodor Werner, for 'willful misconduct and/or negligence', following her attempted suicide. She had taken part in 24 sessions of therapy. After the first tranche of therapy sessions, Dr Werner had developed a social relationship with her, which took the form of an exchange of letters, a visit to her flat, and talk of a weekend away together. Therapy had then resumed for some months, after which it was again terminated, leading to her attempted suicide. Dr Werner appealed against the original court's decision in favour of Ms Landau, but this failed, when expert witnesses found that his actual therapeutic practice was completely incompatible with his declared adherence to psychoanalytic principles.

This is the only reported case of its kind at Appeal Court level, with significant implications for how the law views relational ethics as applying to therapeutic practice. The standard applied is that of the ordinary, competent practitioner, rather than the higher one of the practitioner claiming to hold specific expertise. Unusually, the client in this case possessed credible evidence, in the form of letters from Dr Werner. Also, unusually, there was a close, and, in the eyes of the court, a causal relationship between the therapist's breach of professional duty of care and the psychological harm experienced by the client. This took the form of a suicide attempt, presumably in the absence of any previous psychiatric history on the client's part.

The *Werner* case stands as an isolated, if instructive, example of the legal perspective on the therapist's duty of care. Subsequent medical case law, such as *Maynard*, has recognised the existence of a variety of medical or therapeutic practices, rather than a single paradigm or model. *Bolitho* has further required that a rational basis of research evidence must underpin practitioner claims to competent practice.

Implications for innovative therapy

Action for breach of duty of care perhaps represents the ultimate backstop of enforcing ethical and professional standards for therapists, but its rarity suggests that this is not an easy system for clients to activate. For therapists also the notion of breach of duty of care may not always be so straightforward and unproblematic. Keeping to the rules of profession may largely protect the therapist from litigation, but innovation may, at times, lead to the breaking or at least the bending of such rules. Val Wosket has discussed the concept of rule-breaking in this context:

> By rule-breaking, I mean where the therapist breaches the guidelines or

dictates of accepted practice as established by their education and training, chosen therapeutic approach, or professional association, in favour
of responses determined by more internally located standards of self-
regulation.

(Wosket, 1999: 133)

Carefully distinguishing between boundary *crossing* and boundary *violation*,
Wosket argues that the former can have positive, creative benefits for the client,
as for instance in the more extensive but still therapeutic use of the practitioner's own personal material. From this perspective, innovative or experi-
mental therapy runs the serious risk of being seen by peers, and perhaps by
the courts, as breaching well-established norms of practice.

It may be, as a result, that the practitioners working with sexual and erotic
material are most at risk. David Mann, for example, explicitly acknowledges
that 'psychotherapy is an erotic relationship between the analyst and patient'
(Mann, 1997: 12). He develops this argument, claiming: 'Probably more than
any other subject, the erotic takes both the patient and the therapist into the
unmapped territory, the hinterland, where something new may be discovered
or occur' (p. 185). This may have happened in the case of Dr Margaret Bean-
Bayog, a psychiatrist sued for malpractice by the estate of her former patient,
Paul Lozana, after his suicide. Court-ordered disclosure of therapeutic records
revealed the extensive use of sexual fantasy countertransference material
by Dr Bean-Bayog, which led to a malpractice case against her. This was
later settled for $1 million by her insurance company (McNamara, 1995).
Therapists working at the margins of accepted practice with sexual or erotic
material are possibly, therefore, those most at risk of professional censure and
challenge in the courts.

Therapeutic work needs to be guided by the conscious application of clear
ethical principles, including respect for client autonomy and the avoidance of
harm. Ultimately, however, these relational ethics are subject to oversight
and enforcement by the law. Problematic areas for therapeutic practice can
include the use of touch, growing requirements for informed consent by clients, the expectations arising from a legally enforceable contract, the therapist's duty of confidence and the obligation to meet the standard of care of a
reasonably competent practitioner. The law represents a valuable means of
redress for clients, and provides a necessary framework for safe and effective
practice, but does so, perhaps, at the potential cost of acting as a brake on the
emergence of new, innovative forms of therapy.

Personal reflection: ethical values and interpersonal conflict

In applying relational ethics to my principal role as a counsellor trainer, I am
very aware that this activity seems to be inherently tied up with conflict. This

conflict can take various forms, involving conflict with students, university or college managers, colleagues and even with professional counselling associations. Holding to deeply felt ethical positions seems inevitably to bring me into conflict with other parties, who are, no doubt, holding their own ethical values, which are, presumably, also equally strongly felt. Perhaps part of developing an ethical sense as a practitioner requires also nurturing a high level of tolerance for such conflict with others, without being in the position of necessarily wanting, or seeking out, such conflict.

A consistent part of my experience as a counsellor trainer in colleges and universities has been that, as a gatekeeper to the profession, selection and assessment of students involves making difficult decisions about suitability for training and fitness to practise. This has brought me into repeated conflict with those students, whose perception of their own suitability for training or progression was decidedly at odds with mine and that of my colleagues. Failing a student's work, or professional practice, is not an easy or pleasant task. It really requires strong evidence that a particular student has failed to reach a necessary, well-defined standard, or, more accurately, has failed to produce evidence of their competence and suitability, over an extended period of time. This can be for a variety of reasons, and I can relate this to specific situations, where a particular student:

- is consistently unable to accept or act on critical, supportive feedback from trainers
- has enduring mental health problems, producing significant lapses in their ability to relate consistently to others in distress
- is pursuing a covert, personal agenda of seeking power and influence over others, which is not open to reflection, discussion or supervision.

These judgements on students' fitness to practise are clearly not made in an organisational vacuum. A good deal of counsellor training seems to operate in a rule-bound institutional setting, often to be found in further education, where there is a strong 'culture of entitlement'. The rights of students to enter training, to progress and to qualify, are thus pitched up against the seemingly vicarious professional judgement of trainers, apparently claiming a self-awarded right to decide on fitness to practise. The exercise of professional judgement will thus often clash here with this dominant discourse of rights and entitlement. From a professional and ethical point of view, this situation has led to my developing a strong sense of how to operate tactically within large bureaucratic organisations, and how to gain essential support from colleagues, in order to sustain the kind of resilience required to see this kind of conflict through to a satisfactory conclusion.

In other training settings, there can be, instead, the pervasive influence of charismatic individuals. These are often those who have set up and defended the training courses in a hostile environment, against the odds, whether in a private training institution, or university setting. Disagreements about student fitness to practise, or challenges to the existing way of doing things, can be experienced here as a covert attack on the absolute right of the charismatic leader to rule the roost – and, in a sense, this characterisation is absolutely correct. However, this charismatic culture runs the very real risk of degenerating into a culture of narcissism, where challenge to the traditions or practices of the established way of doing things simply cannot be tolerated. In my experience, this kind of conflict is hard to resolve, and has led, in one case, in my deciding to give up my job and look for work elsewhere, after attempts to challenge the dominant leadership style had ultimately proved to be fruitless.

Influences on my personal sense of ethics

Where does my own ethical stance come from? My own continuing interest in the law probably owes a great deal to the example of my father, who was something of a self-taught 'barrack-room lawyer', rather than a lawyer of the more conventional kind. This Oedipal role model is that of the 'rule-following maverick', where knowing the rules inside out can become a useful tactic in arguing against authority. Again, in my own case, this led to me checking out the law on trade union and employment law when the college for which I was working wanted to alter and remove my existing conditions of service. Becoming convinced that this was unjust and indefensible brought me into direct conflict with both college management and the trade unions supposedly representing the interests of college staff. I refused to sign the new contract, against their advice, and held out for several years, before eventually leaving to work elsewhere. This position was not simply about rejecting a worsening of my own individual terms and conditions of service, but was based on a strong conviction that these very conditions should not be up for sale or renegotiation.

In terms of relational ethics, my own interest in the law has taken the form of a strong defence of the client's right to autonomy. The main expression of this has been in my work defending the rights of children and young people to confidentiality, under the *Gillick* principle, and in my work more generally in devising training activities around the theme of children's rights. This perspective has brought me into conflict or disagreement with colleagues, for example, in exploring the limitations to the counsellor's duty to report suspected child abuse in different contexts. Within my work in counselling training in a wider context, my other strong commitment has been to the principle of avoiding harm. This stance has infused my concern to act as an effective 'gatekeeper' to training and access to practise, where issues of risk to clients, or lack of fitness to practise, are concerned.

My other enduring interest, as a counsellor trainer, has been in relation to record keeping. In part, this has been, at an intellectual level, simply to defend the importance of confidentiality. At a more personal level, this is connected with my own experience of my need for, and indeed facility for, keeping secrets within my own family. My experience of growing up as a child was of the gradual piecing together of my parents' closely guarded secret – that an elder sister of mine, Ann, had died soon before I was born. As children, we painstakingly pieced together the truth of this tragic event from fragments of information, allusions and unguarded slips of the tongue made by parents or relatives. In time, our covert knowledge transmuted into yet another family secret. It also became a secret, namely that, now, as children, we knew the secret. Keeping confidentiality is thus second nature to me, and my interest in protecting counsellors' rights to keep professional secrets from disclosure no doubt has its ultimate roots in this formative family experience. My recent work within professional counselling associations to safeguard counselling records from disclosure to the courts, and my admiration for figures like Ann Hayman, a therapist who risked being sent to jail for refusal to breach therapeutic confidentiality, can thus be traced back to this experience of keeping powerful secrets within my own family.

References

Beauchamp, T. and Childress, J. (2001) *Principles Of Biomedical Ethics*, 5th edn. Oxford: Oxford University Press.

Bond, T. (2002) The law of confidentiality – a solution or part of the problem? In P. Jenkins (ed.) *Legal Issues in Counselling and Psychotherapy*. London: Sage.

British Association for Counselling and Psychotherapy (BACP, 2002) *Ethical Framework for Good Practice in Counselling and Psychotherapy*. Rugby: BACP.

Currey, H. (2005) Is suicide a function of the actualising tendency or its ultimate distortion? *Person-Centred Quarterly* May, 4–7.

Hunter, M. and Struve, J. (1998) *The Ethical Use of Touch in Psychotherapy*. London: Sage.

Jenkins, P. (2007) *Counselling, Psychotherapy and the Law*. London: Sage.

McNamara, E. (1995) *Breakdown: Sex, Suicide and the Harvard Psychiatrist*. New York: Pocket Books.

Mann, D. (1997) *Psychotherapy: An Erotic Relationship. Transference and Counter-Transference Passions*. London: Routledge.

Thompson, A. (1983) *Ethical Concerns in Psychotherapy and their Legal Ramifications*. Lanham: University Press of America.

Wosket, V. (1999) *The Therapeutic Use of Self: Counselling Practice, Research and Supervision*. London: Routledge.

Legal references

Alfred Crompton Amusement Machines v Customs and Excise [1974] AC 405.

Bolam v Friern HMC [1957] 2 All ER 118.

Bolitho v City and Hackney Health Authority [1997] 3 WLR, 1151, [1997] 4 All ER 771 HL.

Gillick v West Norfolk Area Health Authority [1986] AC 112, [1985] 3 All ER 402, [1985] 3 WLR 830, [1986] 1 FLR 224.

Maynard v West Midlands Regional Health Authority [1984] 1 WLR 634, [1985] 1 All ER 635.

W v Egdell [1990] Ch 359, [1990] 1 All ER 835.

Werner v Landau, TLR 8/3/1961, 23/11/1961, Sol Jo (1961) 105, 1008.

Chapter 10

The role of practitioner self-care in practitioner–client relationship ethics

Alan Dunnett

Marion was a first-year trainee on a counselling diploma course at a further education college in a rural market town. The course advertised itself as person-centred in orientation. Although Marion – a former district nurse – coped well with the training, she found the practice element stressful. Her agency had no assessment systems: her first two clients had both made previous suicide attempts and were still clearly 'at risk'. The course required her attendance for regular supervision with a specified college-linked supervisor, whom she experienced as punitive and prescriptive. After 30 hours of practice, feeling increasingly exhausted and demoralised, she dropped out of the training.

The *Code of Ethics and Practice for Counsellors* published by the then British Association for Counselling in 1992 and subsequently revised up to 2002 provided clear guidelines and – in part – prescriptions for ethical conduct for practitioners within the emergent profession. The values underpinning these clear paragraphs of guidance were clearly stated in three principles: integrity, impartiality and respect (BAC, 1992: 2). The principles informed statements of application to practise: counsellors were urged to consider issues of responsibility, anti-discriminatory practice and client self-determination. The management of the three 'Cs' – confidentiality, contracts and competence – attracted particular attention. Pervading the whole document is the sense of a profound concern for the well-being of the client.

The first publication of the British Association for Counselling and Psychotherapy *Ethical Framework for Good Practice in Counselling and Psychotherapy* (2002) presented a new set of principles, albeit couched in a context and a language which encouraged and promoted autonomous reflection rather than prescription. Five of the principles enshrined in the framework appear to reflect the earlier concern to focus on the client and the professional relationship. The particular innovation lay in the sixth principle – labelled 'self-respect' – an aspect of ethical practice which had been the object of only oblique reference in the previous document. This last guiding principle focuses on counsellors as people: they too are human and they too have needs.

The recognition that the person of the counsellor constitutes a critical component in the therapeutic system is scarcely novel. If the history of millenia of therapy tells us anything, it is that characteristics residing in or ascribable to the therapist are key. The person who seeks help may well project qualities onto the therapist even before their first meeting. Expectations relating to expertise, competence and experience are common.

The therapist can operate through and within the therapeutic processes so long as the disjunction between client expectations and the lived experience of the counsellor is not too great. The recently retired client who discovers that her counsellor is a 24-year-old recently qualified graduate may find it difficult to manage her unfulfilled expectations and to settle into the therapy. The style of therapy itself places expectations on the counsellor: for example, the positive thinking embedded in the theory of cognitive behavioural therapy (CBT) seems to require that the therapist communicates belief in demonstrable client change. Pessimists should not apply.

Counsellors frequently report that clients believe them to be 'sorted'. The belief that the counsellor is healthy allows the client to be unhealthy ('unsorted'): it is a simple equation which works to the benefit of the therapy. The client feels held and cared for by a person who does not need to be held and cared for in that relationship: the one-way flow of nurturance does its job for the client. This imbalance, which in other human relationships may well create unstable and ultimately unsustainable conditions, has as its corollary the need for the counsellor to suspend her or his need for care within the therapeutic relationship. This is not to say that some indirect care may not be present – evidenced, say, in positive feedback from the client or through the status enhancement of the counsellor provided by the social structure of the therapy situation.

Since the profession requires that counsellors suspend communication of one of their fundamental human needs – for care and nurturance – inside the therapy room, it is reasonable to argue that this need must be met elsewhere. (The degree to which a particular counsellor does manage to suspend this need is, of course, sometimes open to question.)

The impact of client behaviour

The BACP Ethical Framework document referred to above provides a list of components which are held to constitute 'self-respect'. Regular supervision, still a key element in professional support, is now listed as only one among many possible sources of moral, emotional and physical replenishment. Counsellors are urged to take good care of themselves, to adopt a holistic view of their well-being and to engage in practices and behaviours aimed to promote wellness. A proactive approach to the business of self-care is encouraged. Counsellors – skilled at respecting and caring for others – are formally reminded of the need to respect and care for themselves.

The person who presents for counselling is, self-evidently, not expected to sign up to a framework of ethical behaviour. Aside from the caveat relating to harm to self or others, the contract is likely to set out responsibilities regarding attendance and the payment of a fee, together with any local requirements such as abstention from the use of drugs or alcohol prior to the session. Client behaviours which demand attention in the course of the therapy have to be dealt with as they arise. The service user who consistently arrives late, cancels at the last minute or simply fails to signal absences will incur a response which may be regulated by the agency or left to the discretion of the counsellor. The psychodynamic therapies expect that such behaviours – far from prompting a neo-legalistic response – become part of the material of the sessions. That framework provides the counsellor with a strategy to process and transmute irritation, frustration or feelings of rejection: converted into the countertransference, these become grist for the therapeutic mill. The humanistic therapies do not have recourse to this device: the counsellor may experience a similar range of responses, from irritation to hostility, from self-doubt to feelings of downright inadequacy. He is trained to be sensitive to the nuances of his own feelings, and to respond in ways which correspond to precepts of 'realness', congruence and immediacy. A pattern of sporadic attendances and poor time-keeping on the part of the client often necessitates more than just a cathartic expression of annoyance in supervision. When these events are conceptualised both as in breach of the working contract and as disrespectful in terms of everyday human relationships, the counsellor may be better placed to take action to care for himself. That action – if it is not itself to ignore the principle of beneficence – should incorporate considerations for the well-being of the client:

Sharon had been seeing an addiction counsellor for the last six months to try to reduce her use of cocaine and alcohol. Although she had a friendly relationship with the counsellor, Mike, she missed a lot of sessions because she was drunk or woke up too late. Mike seemed fairly laid back about her attendance, but one day told her he wasn't prepared to see her any more: he lived in the next town and was fed up with coming across to see her, and her not turning up.

Mike's response was understandable. One could argue that, ultimately, he was congruent with his client and that he was looking after himself. However, it scarcely served Sharon's needs. A more experienced counsellor might have challenged these behaviours earlier and set out a clearer contract, taking account of what Sharon said would motivate her to adhere to it. The contract would have needed close monitoring and reviewing if Sharon reverted to her previous pattern: if those strategies were failing, what others could be put in place?

On occasions, client behaviours render therapeutic progress impossible. At the most basic level, the client who fails to commit to regular attendance not only subverts the course of the therapy but may well exercise a delibilitating or demoralising effect on the counsellor. More serious breaches of contract may develop into situations which the counsellor is unable to resolve without third party intervention:

> Andrew worked in the student counselling service on a large city campus. Miranda initially presented with a history of self-harming behaviours. These appeared to increase in severity after the early sessions. Miranda expressed herself as increasingly drawn to Andrew: she stated that she thought about him 'all the time'. Andrew made repeated attempts to draw clear lines in the relationship and to challenge her leaving messages for him in between sessions. Miranda claimed to have well-developed plans to take an overdose if he discharged her or referred her on. At the point where Andrew's preoccupation with Miranda appeared to be compromising his ability to work effectively with other clients, Andrew's manager intervened to terminate the therapy.

It can, at the very least, be disorientating for the counsellor when adherence to ethical principles appears to be one-sided. The counsellor in training conscientiously learns the precepts underpinning ethical mindfulness, and then may begin to feel misused when a client appears not to be sticking to the rules. The client who arrives every week with what appears to be the same story, talks across the counsellor, becomes indignant if the counsellor attempts to make an intervention, seems bent on extracting the last drop of empathy for her situation from the counsellor, can leave the practitioner feeling drained, helpless and deskilled.

The inability to effect meaningful change which the counsellor experiences in a client may in itself be the source of the practitioner's feelings of inadequacy. It is not unusual for a person with a history of poor mental health and of successive interventions by mental health services to exhibit signs of helplessness. The counsellor may find herself listening to a story of failed attempts to seek assistance, of incompetence on the part of mental health workers, of not being heard or understood. While evidence may exist to bear out the client's assertions, parallel evidence of client resourcefulness and commitment to change may be scant. The counsellor can feel trapped in a cycle of failure similar to that of the client. She may blame herself or the client for the lack of progress – with predictable emotional consequences: frustration, guilt, reduced motivation. Unless appropriately tackled, these responses will leak into the therapy and into the counsellor's relationship to self and role.

The impact of clients' stories

The counselling profession can now draw on a fund of writing on the physical and psychological effects of secondary traumatic stress – that is, of working with those suffering from the impact of abuse, disaster, injury and loss. The consequences for the counsellor – feelings of helplessness or confusion or incompetence – have been clearly documented (Higgins, 2005). It is in the very nature of therapeutic activity that counsellors place themselves in the position of 'bystanders and . . . witnesses to damaging and often cruel events' (Pearlman and Saakvitne, 1995b: 155). At times there is likely to be tension between the desire to intervene or to rescue and the boundaries of the professional role. It is not unusual for practitioners to question their own abilities and the adequacy of their own training – as well as experiencing the need to reprocess traumatic events in their own lives. Belief systems may be tested: positive views of humankind and of the future may be hard to sustain in the face of the power of trauma.

Therapists are almost inevitably left with some residue of painful client material from their work – sometimes in the form of images or fragments of dialogue, or else as triggers which can restimulate memories of traumas of their own. Chidgey's (2004) study of primary care counsellors looks specifically at the impact of client work on the physical health of the practitioner. While her findings point to the prevalence of a range of conditions – from poor sleep patterns to fatigue to various physical ailments – it is difficult to separate the impact of client material from the effects of the counsellor's employment environment. Her conclusions draw on Winnicottian theory when she suggests that the counsellor, akin to a mother with her baby, requires a secure and supportive environment in order to hold and metabolise a client's distress.

The role of the organisation

The interactions between the counsellor and her organisation are highly influential on the conduct and effectiveness of the therapy. Counsellors who experience valuing and support in their workplace are, quite simply, able to sustain the emotional and psychological demands of the work more successfully. Negative situations – which may be characterised by an autocratic management style, resource reductions or the counsellor's inability to influence key aspects of the provision – are likely to impair the effectiveness of the therapy in the long term:

> Jenny was in her tenth year as a primary care counsellor when she began to develop worrying physical symptoms, ranging from shooting pains in her chest to breathlessness and insomnia. Medical investigations revealed no obvious physical disorder: she was offered a course of antidepressants by her GP and

signed off for four weeks. Jenny subsequently returned to work, whereupon the symptoms returned. The primary care trust for which she had worked had been systematically cutting down on funding for counselling provision for the past two years in an attempt to manage its budgetary deficit. Jenny had also been moved from a familiar local surgery environment to three small outlying surgeries where she was the lone counsellor. The new working schedule involved her in car journeys totalling 250 miles each week.

Over time, the effects of working in some organisational settings may engender a sense of isolation, rejection or low self-worth:

> The need to understand, accept as normal, and to neutralise harmful effects from the work is vital. Self-care must be a personal commitment (. . .) but it needs to be recognised that it can be hard to sustain wellbeing when battling with the complex dynamics and stresses of a large organisational context, compounded by a different, medical (or financial) mindset.
> (Chidgey, 2004: 42).

Expressed in these terms, a battle is being fought simultaneously on two fronts: the counsellor managing the effects of secondary traumatic stress from her client work at the same time as holding the line against the organisation (Cherniss, 1995). She is negotiating her relationship with her client, with her client's material, with her employers, with her employers' agenda and with her own responses to all of these.

Organisational structures may pose problems of their own, adding to the stresses on the counsellor. It is not unusual for a large regional health trust to offer a number of routes into psychological assessment and therapy. Different in-house services may either operate in what appear to be incompatible ways, or else compete for status and significance. The counsellor may find it difficult if the client requests referral to a service of which the counsellor has poor experience. Resource issues frequently surface in a disparity between service users' needs for longer-term therapy and levels of organisational funding for such work. How to prioritise this client over that client, when only one of the two can have access to the long-term therapy they require? How to accommodate to the dilemma of knowing that the waiting list of clients is so long that some will never be seen?

The presence of conflict or tensions on an individual level poses a further challenge. Fundamental differences of perspective between a team of counsellors and their line manager may turn on much more than a question of personal preference. In the end, it is the welfare of service users which is at stake. Counsellors who find themselves in an environment unsympathetic to their needs may have to rely on each other for nurturance and support. Occasionally, though, peer support can itself be a problematic area:

Jane found herself compromised in her efforts to support her counsellor colleague, Karen. They had both worked for the last 15 years in the psychological services department of a large NHS trust hospital. Jane had offered the help when Karen was signed off for three months with work-related stress, having become embroiled in a situation in which a client had begun to 'stalk' her at work and at home. Karen began telephoning and texting Jane several times a day. It was normal for Karen to be on the phone for an hour and a half in the evening. Jane found that time for herself and her family was seriously eroded, but didn't know how to say this to her colleague, whom she experienced as very vulnerable.

On occasions, situations like the one in which Jane found herself can be resolved if there is a line manager in the organisation who is prepared to act to protect the counsellor from further harm or distress. Jane was lucky: her manager, acting in the interests of both her junior colleagues, called a meeting at which both Kim's and Jane's strategies for managing the crisis were discussed. Transparency, naming the issues and allowing space for both individuals to state not just their own needs but also their level of care for each other – helped these individuals to move to a reconfiguration of their relationship.

Tracey had been appointed six months earlier to a post in a prestigious residential boarding school. She felt daunted by the social and cultural climate among the teenage students. In defiance of the school's clearly published rules, many students had access to alcohol and drugs. Eating disorders were common among the girls. Because Tracey had a dual role as counsellor and resident tutor, she was sometimes called out at night to go to a student who had been self-harming. Her own health began to suffer: she slept badly, and had recurrent nightmares in which blood and self-injury frequently figured. (Tracey had gone through a period of adolescent self-harming herself after her parents' divorce.)

Tracey's predicament is not unlike that experienced by other counsellors where a group of individuals in the organisation seem almost to be acting in concert to place them under pressure. It is as if there were a commonly agreed intention to act out, defend against change, operate in the counsellor's area of greatest vulnerability. The counsellor is apt to feel isolated and targetted, her personal beliefs and values attacked. By whatever means, the counsellor's need to access respite and refuge is paramount: a range of strategies may need to be worked out, including sufficient time away from the events to recuperate and to marshall the emotional resources to return.

It is difficult to dissociate the organisational from the macro-political agenda. Current promotion of the cognitive behavioural therapies suits the philosophy and talents of some practitioners far better than others. Counsellors required to retrain in these approaches to therapy may question the ethics of working with clients from a theoretical position about which they have serious misgivings. How likely are such individuals to practise effectively if they experience psychological dissonance with the model favoured by the organisation?

Many counsellors may prefer not to grapple with the mechanics of organisations. They may be highly effective in their therapeutic work and want their energies to go fully into their interactions with clients. They do not see themselves as skilled at institutional politics or at dealing in the negotiated truths which are the stock in trade of most organisations. The qualities which individuals typically bring into discussions about resources or conditions of service are not, first and foremost, the undiluted qualities of congruence and empathy, even though these may have a place. In the shifting landscape of institutional values, some counsellors will feel increasingly distanced from the principles which come to dominate the work environment. Situations in which there is a major disparity between the values embodied in organisational policies and the values espoused by the counsellor are those in which the need to attend to strategies of individual self-care can become critical.

Recognising good health

So far, this chapter has explored some of the challenges which professional activity can impose on the counsellor's health. I have also referred to the service user's belief (arguably, an act of idealisation related to the desire for nurturance) that the counsellor represents a pole of 'wellness' in counterpoint to clients' experience of their own poor health. Any discussion of gradations of psychological wellness presupposes an understanding of what constitute the components of good mental health. How might the counsellor recognise the status of her own functioning?

Descriptors of wellness in the literature of the psychotherapies conceal a variety of preferences and bias. For one school of therapy rational functioning constitutes the primary sign of good mental health; for another it resides in emotional responsiveness. Thus, psychoanalysis recognises good health in the presence of psychological insight, intrapsychic balance and a clearly boundaried self. Humanistic approaches privilege authenticity, openness to experience and autonomy. Cognitive therapies promote intellectual mastery, problem-solving capacities and self-responsibility. As MacNamee and Gergen (1992) remark, the unwitting client happens in on a particular professional narrative, according to the style of therapy chosen. And the conclusion of that narrative lies in the denouement – the arrival at a place of resolution in a particular version of good mental health.

Rather than relying on the sectarian preferences of the schools of therapy, a number of recent authors have developed transtheoretical models to describe the condition of well-being. In each case, the components of wellness incorporate composites of traits. The so-called 'Wheel of Wellness' is an example of these attempts: positive functioning is listed under five headings: 'spirituality', 'self-direction', 'work and leisure', 'friendship' and 'love' (Myers *et al.*, 2000). My own study of UK counsellors' constructs of wellness also elicited five components: 'good sense of self', 'good relationships', 'strategic capacities', 'engagement with the world' and 'experience and expression of affect' (Dunnett, 2004). Put simply, psychological wellness appears to reside in a cluster of factors. Healthy persons are reasonably confident in themselves, enjoy good self-belief and positive self-esteem. They have close enduring relationships with others. They can meet challenges and find a way through difficult times. They can look beyond themselves in the present and envision the future. Healthy persons can engage with others in work or recreation. They are in touch with their affective world and can express their emotions.

The counsellors in the UK study were able to recognise in others the presence of attributes of good mental health. It appeared that they could also recognise healthy features in themselves – or, in some cases, the aspiration towards positive features they perceived in others. It seemed likely that, by their personal definition, they would be attentive to any reduction in levels of psychological wellness in themselves. The major problem, though, is that it is precisely the ability to make reasoned judgements about the self which is frequently absent at times of declining mental health.

The danger with any definition of good mental functioning is that it could be both used and misused as a prescription. What begins as a set of personal preferences may come to have a fixed and essentialist existence, disconnected from any individual person and their experience of themselves. Neither my own attempt to circumscribe and define good psychological health, nor those of others, should be taken as some kind of absolute or as a tool for discriminating between the traditionally favoured and the traditionally disdvantaged (Foucault, 1977). Nonetheless, if the principle of self-care is to mean anything, it will need to have reference points for every counsellor. The BACP Framework for Good Practice places the responsibility on the practitioner to monitor and attend to her or his own state of psychological wellness. The document offers a yardstick against which individuals can judge their state of well-being. The relational ethic here is clear – and it resides in practitioners' relationship to themselves. We may recognise the effects of stress through a loss of humour, through sleepnessness, through somatic pain. We may notice our inability or unwillingness to make or sustain relationships. We may recognise that we are 'shutting down' and adopting a much more emotionally defended position. We may become less skilled at dealing with difficult or even everyday problems. We may become more pessimistic about our own future, that of our organisation, that of the world.

Guidelines for self-care

The professional situation of the counsellor embodies a particular set of circumstances. Our normal activity (which may seem anything but 'normal' to many outside the profession) consists in voluntarily entering into often highly intimate relationships with individuals who are experiencing psychological pain. Our task is to spend our working life in close connection to psychological suffering and to resonate with the impact of that suffering – at least to a sufficient degree to be able to intervene therapeutically. Whatever practitioners' theoretical orientation, they are required to some degree to be touched by the other person's pain – to have a relationship with it. The ability to connect with the sufferer and the suffering – and subsequently to reconnect with the self apart from that world – is a crucial element in professional survival. Stamm (1999: xvi) cites the possibility of a personal transformation through living at close quarters with trauma. While it has the power to harm, 'engaging it can bring us to the edge of the human condition and offer us opportunities to move beyond the common distractions of life, which frees us to deal with the unspeakable which is happening in our very experience'.

While there are no recipes which guarantee the maintenance of healthy functioning, there are sufficient pointers to self-care activities for the individual practitioner to develop her palette of options. Social networks can provide comfort and relaxation. Yassen (1995) writes about the 'restorative' connections with others which assist the counsellor to develop her sense of self outside of therapeutic relationships, and to experience the care of others. Supervision and meetings with colleagues can assist in conceptualising the situation and in reducing feelings of isolation. Creative and other replenishing activity – music, art, contact with nature – can provide the necessary contact with the world beyond the self so as to repair what Pearlman and Saakvitne (1995a: 396) describe as the 'spiritual damage of vicarious traumatisation'. Given the employment patterns in counselling, it may be possible to create a working pattern which includes counterbalancing roles related to counselling – training, supervision or mentoring – or else activity in a completely different sphere. Whatever strategies are applied, the maintenance of equilibrium – psychological, physical and spiritual – is essential for the health of the counsellor (Higgins, 2005). The self-aware counsellor needs the same level of attunement to self which he exercises in regard to his clients. Self-regulating and self-nurturing activity needs to be in place if the professional is to live a life characterised by energy, satisfaction and openness to experience.

The earlier discussion of tensions between the individual and the work setting implies that self-care strategies need also to be applied to the relationship with the organisation. Assertiveness, awareness of the organisational agenda and the landscape of power and an ability to intervene strategically are valuable assets. Where counsellors are unable or unwilling to discover such potential in themselves, they and their clients may suffer in the relationship with an employer who discounts the needs of the counselling service. Crucially, the nature of the counsellor's relationship with the organisation represents as much an ethical concern as the management of direct interaction with the client.

In practical terms, first, the counsellor is wise to obtain as much information as can be had on policies and negotiations – local and national – which bear on her position. Second, she should be willing to make clear statements, in well-documented written form, in person or through an ally in the organisation, so as to have a voice in the development of new structures, procedures and frameworks of delivery. Third, she should use colleagues either locally or in similar professional contexts for dialogue about her situation; to gain experience and assistance with putting forward her own case; and for collegial support. The alternative – feeling isolated, attacked and diminished – is an unappetising position from which to enter a day's demanding client work.

A systemic approach to supervision may alert the counsellor to the dynamic within which she is working – both in therapy and in the organisation. Exploration of her responses may enable her to deconstruct these and understand how she might intervene more productively, caring for herself and her client group. Effective supervision may remind the practitioner of her own patterns, those of clients and of the organisation: of her own triggers to action (say, the 'fixer' urge or the 'be perfect' driver); the client's (such as the need to remain within the secure, unchallenging realm of failure); that of the organisation (which may exhibit the need to deny uncertainty through the drive to action or through the discourse of success). The involvement of another person as consultant represents a significant component in pursuing strategies of self-care. The supervisor isn't – and needs the skill not to become – part of a poorly functioning dynamic. As witness to this dynamic she or he can comment on what they observe and experience, ask the questions of a naive enquirer, and notice, at one remove from the centre of the drama, the impact of intimate involvement in the action on the counsellor.

References

British Association for Counselling (BAC, 1992) *Code of Ethics and Practice for Counsellors*. Rugby: BAC.

British Association for Counselling and Psychotherapy (BACP, 2002) *Ethical Framework for Good Practice in Counselling and Psychotherapy*. Rugby: BACP.

Cherniss, C. (1995) *Beyond Burnout: Helping Teachers, Nurses, Therapists, and Lawyers Recover from Stress and Disillusionment*. New York: Routledge.

Chidgey, E. (2004) *Taking our own medicine: an inquiry into the impact of counselling in the primary care context on the counsellor's general health and wellbeing*. Unpublished MA dissertation. York St John University, UK.

Dunnett, A. D. (2004) *A study of constructs of mental health and emotional well-being held by counsellors and psychotherapists.* PhD Thesis, University of Leeds, UK.

Foucault, M. (1977) *Discipline and Punish: The Birth of the Prison.* Harmondsworth: Allen Lane.

Higgins, C. R. (2005) *Balance is the key: Coping with secondary traumatic stress.* Unpublished MA dissertation. York St John University.

MacNamee, S. and Gergen, K. J. (eds) (1992) *Therapy as Social Construction.* London: Sage.

Myers, J. E., Sweeney, T. J. and Witmer, J. M. (2000) The Wheel of Wellness counselling for wellness: a holistic model for treatment planning. *Journal of Counselling and Development* 78, 251–266.

Pearlman, L. A. and Saakvitne, K. W. (1995a) *Trauma and the Therapist: Countertransference and Vicarious Traumatisation in Psychotherapy with Incest Survivors.* New York: Norton.

Pearlman, L. A. and Saakvitne, K. W. (1995b) Treating therapists with vicarious traumatisation and secondary traumatic stress disorders. In C. R. Figley (ed.) *Compassion Fatigue: Coping with Seconday Traumatic Stress Disorder in Those Who Treat the Traumatised.* New York: Brunner/Mazel.

Stamm, B. H. (ed.) (1999) *Secondary Traumatic Stress: Self-Care Issues for Clinicians, Researchers and Educators,* 2nd edn. Lutherville, MD: Sidran Press.

Yassen, J. (1995) Preventing secondary traumatic stress disorder. In C. R. Figley (Ed.) *Compassion Fatigue: Coping with Seconday Traumatic Stress Disorder in Those Who Treat the Traumatised.* New York: Brunner/Mazel.

Chapter 11

Training matters

On the way in

William West

In writing this chapter I am aware of how easy it is to read ourselves into someone else's story. When people interview me for research purposes and I see a copy of their report or conference paper, sometimes I look in vain to find myself there. On other occasions I can be convinced that they must have interviewed me when I know they have not. However, I am not presenting research as such in this chapter. What I am doing is drawing on some of my experiences, some of my story as a trainer, as well what other trainers have told me over the years. I have taken steps to disguise some of the facts so that people are not recognisable as far as possible. If you do read yourself into this writing then it may well be coincidence or synchronicity and should perhaps illustrate the relevance of the issues I am raising.

I have been involved in training counsellors and psychotherapists (I will use the word 'therapist' to cover both) since 1981. In these various training programmes I have been in a number of roles: courses director, course director, core tutor, member of the training team, visiting specialist tutor, personal development group leader, group supervisor, case discussion leader, group tutor, personal tutor, supervisor of trainers and external examiner. In some situations I have combined more than one role. In this chapter I am particularly interested in exploring aspects of the working relations between training team members as I have experienced them and heard others tell me about. The content of this chapter raises issues that are important in developing relational ethics within training teams and training contexts.

You might view this writing as narcissistic, you might more charitably regard this as more of a heuristic offering (West, 1998). Certainly my understanding of my own story is informed by many conversations with trainers over the years (see Acknowledgements). I also am currently involved in ongoing research into the experiences of trainers training counsellors in different cultures and this has impacted on my thinking here (West, 2007).

The area of concern

Working in a therapist training and research team presents its own challenges of an ethical nature. Most training teams in higher education (HE), further education (FE) and private institutions typically consist of perhaps one full-time tutor, possibly two, and a number of part-time tutors. In some cases the whole team will be part-time. Many of the part-timers will come in, do a task (for example, personal development group facilitator) and then leave, having a very limited relationship with the rest of the institution. The question of who actually belongs in the team as a whole and how even to get everyone together in the same place at the same time for a team meeting or team supervision can be an all but impossible task.

All of this in itself presents a huge managerial challenge. Indeed, the question of what constitutes the 'team' is open to debate. Is the team the group that delivers the overall programme of therapy courses which typically might include introduction, certificate, diploma, supervision course and possibly Masters programme? Or does each course have a 'team'? To which 'team' do trainers have allegiance to?

However, the (part-time) tutors are often chosen from the best ex-students from previous trainings. This typically means they were trained by the full-timer and by (some) other part-time members of the team. The part-time members of the team will often have been appointed informally and on casual contracts of employment rather than by a process of advertising and selection for their posts. Such practices are fairly common in other courses within FE and HE and private therapy institutions but they have a profound downside. First, there are equal opportunity issues not addressed – your face fits so you are invited in. Second, there is a real potential for degeneration over time as what gets taught can remain fixed in out-of-date materials and approaches. Third, we can view such processes as being nepotistic and intrinsically incestuous.

It is curious how careful we are with ex-clients and any future relationship with them but expect ex-trainees and ourselves to be able to move on easily from the training role. I wonder why? In fact this transition from student to colleague presents a number of dilemmas and creates a team with curious dynamics. One dynamic might be a reluctance to challenge the full-time tutor or the acting out of unresolved issues from the training process. At some level the dynamics might have an incestuous feel. Sometimes these teams will have team supervision, sometimes not, but it is a tall order for such supervision, especially as it is commonly less than monthly, to impact effectively on this complex situation.

Bringing outside tutors into such teams can mean both a breath of fresh air and conflict. Outsiders will not be privy to the training history and may find that when conflicts arise the explanation will be offered, 'Well of course, you are not one of us'. This may sound incredible but I have had it said to me.

Notice that it was a phrase used by Margaret Thatcher in the 1980s in relation to the so-called 'wets', the more liberal-minded Conservatives in her cabinet and party. It has echoes of a statement made by Jesus which is well known to Christians that 'he that is not with me is against me' (Luke 11: 23). This 'not one of us' saying implies a rather paranoid and primitive take on the world, the implication being that we are special and different, which is a fairly common view held by counselling trainers in relation to their institutions who of course 'don't understand us'. Such a phrase points to the entrenched view of the team and will be fed by the inevitable tensions between therapy teams and their institutions.

We can understand some of these relational dynamics in terms of allegiance to schools of therapy and subschools of therapy. Indeed, there may be complex feelings relating to other teams and practitioners of the same school but of a differing subschool. Such feelings may derive from shared original trainers – i.e. who trained the trainers. Tracing the lineage back can be enlightening. The niceties of these differences seem to be lost on, or albeit incomprehensible to, outsiders.

However, the implicit and at times explicit trashing of other programmes and hence other therapists is deeply troubling to me and shows a profound lack of respect. Bad practice is one thing and that needs challenging, but putting down other people because they don't subscribe to your own purist view of what it means to be a person-centred or psychodynamic therapist flies in the face of reason and research evidence.

I wonder if to be a trainer you have to have the faith that your approach to therapy does work and works better than other approaches? If so this is a faith position since we know that randomised controlled trials in which different therapeutic approaches are compared with carefully balanced groups of clients with the same problem result in little to choose between each therapy. When metanalyses are done the outcomes are flat (e.g. Wampold *et al.*, 2002). It is reckoned that the biggest factor in producing successful client outcomes is down to the therapeutic alliance. Indeed, such faith in the therapy is also important for the client to have (Frank, 1974). Perhaps this explains why trainers have to have faith too. Clarkson (1998) has argued that the logic from research would take us beyond what she refers to as 'schoolism'.

Even trainers who accept these research findings will argue that it is good for therapists in training to belong to a school and then they can develop more eclectic or integrative practice later. So person-centred trainers will focus on the importance of the core conditions of empathy, congruence and unconditional positive regard. Their psychodynamic colleagues will teach the value of our early childhood experiences and of the need to work with transference. The cognitive behavioural trainers will carefully focus on challenging faulty thinking and offering homework for their clients.

However, if we stay with the notion that therapist training is based on faith rather than research it might help us to understand the dynamics of training, the dynamics of the training team and the dynamics of the professional bodies. For all our understandings it is easy to see the same rivalries, factions and splittings in our therapeutic world as in the world of religion or politics. I find this truth very sobering but it could lead us to some much-needed humility. Maybe if we devoted a bit more time and energy to putting our own house in order we would have even more to offer our clients and students.

Jane Speedy (2000) did research into the story of counsellor trainers and educators at the University of Bristol. Jane identified three generations covering the previous two decades – pioneers, entrepreneurs and the established professionals. I find this an interesting way to think about therapy trainers. The pioneers, who have mostly retired now, had the vision and charisma to establish the courses, often in tension with the culture of the institutions. People becoming trainers now often see it as a career and themselves as professionals. They tend to be more accepting of the institutional framework they are in. Linked to this is another potential area for splitting since they are usually younger than their more established colleagues who may exhibit nostalgia for the 'good old days'. From my own observations of trainers there seems to be a gap or missing generation of trainers, aged about 40 to 50.

Add research to training and . . .

Some of the same dynamics can get played out in a somewhat similar way in the research side of therapy. It can become especially complex when the same tutors are both working as fellow trainers in the same team and also studying for doctorates and in supervision with a fellow tutor. In these situations we are not just facing dealing with an historic trainer/trainee relationship but a current academic supervisor/supervisee relationship that will typically last four or six years. If these commitments to research study have partially been undertaken to meet the needs of the institution or to preserve status or even employment, then an ambivalent attitude to research can develop within the supervisee.

Therapy training teams, especially in universities, but also increasingly elsewhere in FE and private training institutes, are under pressure to be research active – something that is also welcomed and encouraged by the professional bodies. However, many trainers still have an anti research stance, viewing it as largely statistical and irrelevant to practice. They will also feel that in a part-time course too much focus on research can get in the way of skills development. Add to this the facts that research has higher status than teaching/training, and that research traditionally is associated with men and therapy and training with women, and interesting dynamics result. There is often a split in the team between those more committed to training and those more committed to research. Typically also the more research-minded team members will be younger and they may well be viewed as 'not real practitioners'.

Case study

The following case study draws on a number of real experiences that I have brought into one story to highlight potential problems within therapy training teams. I have deliberately not chosen a too dramatic version of events:

> James has just joined the counselling team at his local FE college in the Midlands. The head of the team, Kathy, is a charismatic trainer who has trained many of the local counsellors over the previous 20 years. A number of these ex-trainees of Kathy's now manage many of the local counselling agencies that provide placement opportunities for Kathy's current trainees.
>
> James's appointment was partially an increase in resources for the team but also made up from the retirement of several part-time team members. This 'retirement' was not always welcomed by those involved, including the remaining team members. James's post had been created at the behest of the departmental head who was looking to the future and to Kathy's eventual retirement. It was the head of the department who strongly argued for James's appointment at his job interview.
>
> Like many formal appointments to therapy training teams James had recently completed a Masters research degree and was keen on further study for a doctorate and for research-informed training and practice. Kathy is openly critical of research and dismisses researchers as 'schizoid' characters.
>
> Although the job specification for James's post mentions research, it soon becomes clear to him that in Kathy's view his job is to teach 'all the hours God sends'. Kathy herself is a workaholic and she also runs courses at weekends for other training institutes. Her expectation is that James will do the same even though he has three young children.
>
> The team does not have team supervision. Kathy is convinced that things can always be sorted out within the team meetings – 'We are all grown up and professional aren't we?' – even though the whole team rarely if ever meets up. Instead, the members of the team delivering the certificates, diplomas, supervision and short courses meet in small course teams with Kathy.
>
> Things come to ahead when James asks for time and money for fees to pursue a PhD at the local university which has a thriving counselling programme but of a different school to Kathy's. Kathy turns down James's request so James goes over her head and consults the head of department. The head who is not

known for his tact insists that James be given time to pursue his PhD and that his fees are to be paid out of the counselling budget.

Kathy feels betrayed by James's behaviour in 'going over my head' to the head of department and then other members of the team back Kathy. There is a strained atmosphere in the team for several months before things are patched up somewhat. In discussing a hoped-for new appointment to the team, Jane, one of the part-time members of staff, said, laughing, in the presence of James, 'Well I hope we don't make the same mistake as we did with James'. Meanwhile James looks around for another job.

Questions to consider

In relation to the case study:

1 Notice who you most identify with, Kathy or James, and why?
2 How might the conflict have been handled differently, by Kathy, by James, by the head of department?
3 How might team supervision have helped?
4 Is this a disaster waiting to happen?

More generally:

1 Why take the risk of employing ex-trainees as colleagues? If it would be unfair to rule out employing ex-trainees, how can we minimise the impact of the potentially complex dynamics?
2 Why do many training teams make such poor use of team supervision?
3 How can we mitigate the worse aspects of the (blind?) faith of the trainers?
4 In what way in your experience of training have you noticed how the dynamics among the trainees played out within the training team and vice versa?
5 It seems to me that trainers have above average health problems and if so is this a consequence of demand on trainers currently? How might supervisors and others help trainers stay healthier (see Ballinger and Brooks, 2007)?

Conclusion

First, quality team and individual supervision of sufficient quantity is crucial, but supervision alone is not enough. There has to be a real commitment in the team to address these issues in an ongoing way, in fact a willingness to live with them. The more multiple relations there are in the team, the more the need for supervision and the more likely conflicts will occur.

Second, professional therapy bodies such as the British Association for Counselling and Psychotheraphy (BACP), the British Psychological Society (BPS) and the United Kingdom Council for Psychotherapy (UKCP) have a role to play in establishing guidelines for good practice and in funding the research of training which is not yet sufficiently evidence based. The issue of training and accreditation of trainers needs to be revisited. I am not aware of any robust scheme in operation and this seems extraordinary to me. If there are concerns about the quality of practice by therapists, then the issue of the quality and delivery of training becomes even more important.

Third, let us acknowledge that therapist training is difficult and demanding and needs proper resourcing to be carried out effectively. At my own institution a five-year review of the counselling programmes conducted in 1999 referred to the 'self-exploitation' of the staff involved. Such 'self-exploitation' is I believe endemic across therapist training and partially results from the underfunding and consequent under-resourcing of the training programmes.

Finally, it seems appropriate to end with some words from Dryden and Feltham (1996: 128): 'A great deal of successful training depends, in our experience, on flexibility, honesty and humour'.

Acknowledgements

It is impossible fully to acknowledge the role of colleagues, supervisors, my own trainers and my students that inform my understandings expressed in this chapter. However, it is important to mention the following: Liz Ballinger, Don Balmer, Mary Berry, Jim Davies, Em Edmondson, Colin Feltham, Adrian Foley, Elias Gikundi, Henry Hollanders, Nick Ladany, Clare Lennie, Ann Littlewood, John McLeod, George Manono, Jim Moorey, John Morris, Annie Murray, Lynn Myint-Maung, Cecilia Rachier, Boris Shapiro, John Southgate, Jane Speedy, Sandra Taylor, Nick Totton, Bill Walton and Ray Woolfe.

References

Ballinger, L. and Brooks, G. (2007) *The issues facing the contemporary counselling training professional.* Paper presented at the 13th BACP Annual Research Conference, York, May.

Clarkson, P. (1998) Beyond schoolism. *Changes* 16, 1, 1–11.

Dryden, D. and Feltham, C. (1996) *Developing Counsellor Training.* London: Sage.

Frank, J. D. (1974) Psychotherapy: the restoration of morale. *American Journal of Psychiatry* 131, 272–274.

Speedy, J. (2000) *The story of three generations: an exploration of the changing professional attitudes, cultures and self-descriptions of a group of counselling educators and trainers.* Paper presented to the BACP 6th Annual Counselling Research Conference, 20 May, Manchester.

Wampold, B. E., Minami, T., Baskin, T. W. and Callen Tierney, S. (2002) A meta-(re)analyis of the effects of cognitive therapy versus 'other therapies' for depression. *Journal of Affective Disorders* 68, 159–165.

West, W. (1998) Passionate research: heuristics and the use of self in counselling research. *Changes, an International Journal of Psychology and Psychotherapy* 16, 1, 60–66.

West, W. (2007) Kenyan students' expectations on beginning a Masters in Counselling Studies course. *British Journal of Guidance and Counselling* 35, 2, 237–245

Chapter 12

Relational ethics in small communities and organisations

Roger Casemore

Introduction

In this chapter I draw on my experiences of working in remote, isolated rural communities to show how those experiences have led me to revise my views on the strict application, in some settings, of some aspects of the Ethical Framework for Good Practice in Counselling and Psychotherapy (BACP, 2002). As a member of the British Association for Counselling and Psychotherapy (BACP) I was involved in the formulation of the original Code of Ethics for Counselling, and more recently I was one of a group convened to help formulate BACP's current Ethical Framework. One of our objectives in that later process was to get away from rigid prescriptive rules for ethical behaviour in order to develop an ethos in our profession in which therapists of whatever persuasion would take responsibility for becoming ethically mindful in their clinical practice. I firmly believe that counselling and psychotherapy are essentially professional relationships which need to be appropriately boundaried and managed, in order to provide a safe therapeutic space for the client and to protect both therapist and client from abuse of any kind. While boundaries need to be clear and explicitly agreed with the client, they should also take account of the social, emotional, psychological and cultural context of the client. Boundaries, while providing safety through being firm, clear and explicit, should not be so rigid that they hinder therapeutic practice and creativity on the part of the therapist. For me, regardless of the setting, the fundamental ethical principles have always applied in all areas of my clinical work. I also believe that the Ethical Framework (BACP, 2002) and the values and principles delineated in the framework apply to all counsellors and psychotherapists, whatever their theoretical orientation. The framework is about good therapeutic practice based on a commonly held set of values and principles irrespective of therapist modality. However, in recent years I have begun to recognise that there are some significant differences in the ways that some of these ethical principles need to be applied in different geographical and organisational settings.

I have practised as a person-centred therapist for over 40 years, predominantly in private practice. For the past 30 years I have also worked as a supervisor and trainer of counsellors and for more than 20 years as a consultant in organisational development and the management of cultural change in organisations across the public, private and not-for-profit sectors. In my time I have worked as a therapist and supervised other therapists working in private practice and in agencies, in a variety of urban and metropolitan settings. I have also worked in a number of small organisations and a range of small communities, a number of which are rural and isolated.

My experience of working in the Shetland Islands over the past six years doing consultancy, training, counselling and supervision has led me to reconsider my strongly held views on the need to always set and maintain strict boundaries in counselling and supervision, and the need to pay strict attention to firmly maintaining confidentiality. For example, I now believe that when working in small isolated communities and small organisations the stereotypical view of confidentiality in therapy cannot be so rigidly held in the same way that it can in larger organisations and urban settings. I am not suggesting that the principle of confidentiality should be ignored, as I believe that it is fundamental to the nature of the counselling relationship, in ensuring that clients feel safe to talk about anything that concerns them. What I am suggesting is that the rigidity with which we observe confidentiality may not be possible in certain rural and remote settings, or in some small organisations. Similarly, in isolated rural areas people often hold a number of interrelated roles and this may make it impossible to avoid dual or even multiple roles for therapists and for other health professionals.

In my private practice as a therapist in my usual work settings in urban areas, I would expect to keep a strict boundary of confidentiality about any client that I might be seeing. I would not even reveal to anyone, without the client's express permission, that an individual was coming to see me for therapy. In supervision, when describing my work with clients I would carefully anonymise their details. In social settings I would be very careful to preserve the anonymity of the clients I work with, taking care to avoid contacts with them socially and avoiding saying anything to anyone, including my family, which might indicate that an individual was my client. I have never found that discipline particularly hard to maintain in urban conurbations.

I do recall that earlier in my career when I lived with my family in a very small market town in a rural area that this was not so easy. My children were quite adept at recognising whose car was in my drive, if it belonged to the parents of one of their friends. As a family we had talked about the nature of my counselling work and how important it was not to talk to anyone about anyone who came to see me in my consulting room. Fortunately, my wife and children were prepared to keep these 'secrets' with me. It made for some interesting family dynamics around some 'secrets' being okay and some being inappropriate, particularly for two young adolescents. (However, that is another story!) What intrigues me is that after moving on to live and work in much more densely populated urban areas, I forgot about that issue for many years.

During the past six years I have been travelling regularly up to the Shetland Islands, where I have undertaken a wide variety of consultancy and training work with various departments in the Shetland Islands Council, the health authority, a number of voluntary organisations and the private sector. As a result of my involvement there, I was given the opportunity to support the development of counselling services and the counselling community in the Shetland Islands. This led to the opportunity to work in partnership with Shetland College of Further Education, a part of the Millennium Institute of the University of the Highlands and Islands, to develop a programme of counselling and supervision courses. This has led on to the certificate in person-centred counselling and the diploma in person-centred counselling and psychotherapy for which I am course director at the University of Warwick, now being run at Shetland College. It has also led to me developing a range of different social and professional relationships and roles in Shetland.

The remote rural context

Shetland, on the most northerly edge of the British Isles, is an archipelago of about 100 miles in length, comprising 100 islands, of which less than 20 are inhabited and the total population is just under 23,000. Lerwick is Shetland's only town, with a population of about 7500 – although about half of the islands' 23,000 people live within ten miles of the town (Shetland Islands Council, 2006). The majority of the population is indigenous to the islands and largely of Viking descent. There are also a reasonable proportion of 'incomers' who have chosen to live and work there. To get to Shetland from Worcester takes a one-and-a-half-hour flight from Birmingham to Aberdeen and then a one-hour flight from Aberdeen to Sumburgh at the southern tip of the islands. If the weather is bad, then a 12- to 14-hour boat trip from Aberdeen is the only means to get there. It is remote.

One of the consequences of the size and remoteness of Shetland is that the privacy and separateness we are able to expect in the most crowded urban areas is quite difficult to achieve. While it is not strictly true, it does begin to feel like everyone knows everyone else in the islands. It seems that there are just so many interconnecting relational networks that it can be very difficult to live in isolation and not to know what is going on in other people's lives. It is almost impossible for some people to avoid dual roles. Indeed, it is quite common for some people to have a plurality of roles and for this to be seen as the norm. On the positive side this brings with it a supportive culture of community which has a rare value for someone like me who is city born and bred. On the negative side it can lead to feelings of being exposed and watched, which can be quite inhibiting.

I would like to share some of the learning experiences I have had through my work in Shetland, which have given me significant cause to reflect on the application of the Ethical Framework in that and similar contexts.

The learning experiences

Managing confidentiality

One of my early learning experiences came through running a series of training workshops for staff from a number of local authority departments and voluntary agencies providing care services in the community. As with many such workshops, we would begin by agreeing some 'ground rules' for the day. As usual the ground rule of 'confidentiality' was brought up and following some discussion it was agreed that if people mentioned clients they were working with, they would try to anonymise them and nothing that was said would be repeated outside the training room. This seemed like pretty standard practice to me and to present no problems at the time. However, some six months later when I was up in Shetland for the third time, something happened to make me challenge my complacency.

During a workshop with a group of health professionals working in various care settings, one of the participants began to talk about some work she was doing with one of her clients. She was describing this work very carefully, avoiding giving too much detail about the client or their concerns. I suddenly realised that I thought I knew who this particular client was and found myself trying to check what I knew about them against what I was hearing to see if I was right. This seemed a very natural and human thing to do, to be curious. At the same time I realised that I was actively trying to breach the confidentiality boundary in order to satisfy my curiosity, and that this felt quite unethical. I also realised that probably everyone else in the room was doing exactly the same as me, without questioning it. When I asked if this was happening, everyone said that they were doing it and several had already worked out who the client was and that they now had new confidential information about the client that they were not entitled to.

One of the immediate reactions from the participants was, 'Well, this is Shetland, this is how it is up here'. My immediate intuitive response to that was, 'Shetlanditis does not give any one the right to be unethical'. We spent some time discussing this as an ethical dilemma within the social and cultural context of Shetland and recognised just how difficult it was to prevent this kind of thing happening. We agreed that we needed to add an additional clause to the contract of confidentiality. This was that each one of us would take personal responsibility to discipline ourselves not to try to work out who was being talked about when clients were being discussed. Furthermore, if one of us became aware that we did know who was being talked about, we would declare it at the time and check if it was appropriate for us to continue to take part in the discussion.

The process of identifying that constraint on maintaining confidentiality in that particular geographical location seemed to be really helpful, especially recognising the importance of being really explicit in managing the process. In all the training and consultancy work that I have done since then in Shetland, when agreeing ground rules for a workshop or training event, I have always raised the issue and sought agreement for those extensions to the rule of confidentiality. This has also proved to be a useful issue to raise and a good principle to work by in some of my consultancy work in small organisations, and even in teaching on the certificate and diploma courses. In reading students' personal journals, they will often disclose things about other students, or events which have happened, without sufficiently anonymising the details. Our teaching team has a commitment to that same discipline of not trying to work out who it is the student is describing, as well as encouraging them to be more circumspect in their writing.

Dual roles

Usually in my work as a therapist I seek to avoid the complications caused by dual roles. Lynne Gabriel has written extensively on the subject of dual roles (Gabriel, 2005) and gives a fresh perspective in Chapter Two of this book on the importance of avoiding dual roles where possible. The Ethical Framework states that dual roles are seldom neutral and should be avoided. So I would be unlikely to agree either to work as a therapist with a counsellor that I supervise, or to supervise the clinical practice of one of my students, or to see a family member or relative of one of my students as a client. I have not had any particular difficulty in maintaining that stance as there have always been other people around to undertake those roles. In places like Shetland and other remote areas it may be very difficult to find someone else who can take on a specific therapeutic role. In remote rural areas the avoidance of dual and often multiple roles can be quite difficult and can lead to ethical difficulties which are difficult to overcome. The particular context and the frequency of plurality of roles can result in a lack of questioning and consideration being given to whether particular roles should be entered into. It may be that dual roles cannot be avoided in some situations. However, they should not be entered into lightly and their appropriateness should always be reflected on in supervision and perhaps with the parties involved.

Some time ago I gave a presentation on ethical dilemmas at a training conference in Orkney that was also attended by a number of students from Shetland who were on one of the courses for which I am course consultant and on which I occasionally teach some sessions. In addition to teaching on the course, all the regular teaching team also work as counsellors in the area in which the course is run. At the end of the day, sitting in the bar with a small group of the students, one of them began to tell me that recently her partner had suffered a serious psychological breakdown as a result of a traumatic experience and was getting counselling to help him recover. This was putting a great deal of pressure on her and impacting on her capacity to manage the coursework. However, she said that she was really pleased with the support she was getting from one of her tutors on the course, who was also her partner's counsellor and really helping him. She wondered if this was actually ethical. I was quite surprised by this revelation. Though none of the other students actually knew about it, they did not seem surprised that this was happening. When I expressed my surprise and said that this would not be allowed to happen where I teach, she replied that there was no one else in the area who was suitably qualified or trained to provide the particular therapeutic help her partner needed. If her tutor did not see him he would get no help at all. I then recognised that I also had a dual relationship problem as the tutor/counsellor concerned was also a personal friend of mine for many years, as well as more recently becoming a teaching colleague.

It seemed impossible for the tutor to avoid a dual role in relation to her student and her student's partner in the remote area concerned. However, it should have been possible for that dual relationship to be declared to the rest of the teaching team and to the other students. This would then have given the opportunity to discuss ways to avoid that dual relationship causing problems, for example, in how it might be perceived by other students. It seems to me that as the dual relationship could not be avoided, the ethical thing to do was to be open and explicit about the relationship so that problems it might cause would be minimalised.

Supervision and client work

The rule of 'not trying to work out who is being talked about' to which I referred earlier is not without its difficulties, and on one occasion was actually unhelpful. In Shetland I had been supervising the clinical practice of an experienced counsellor, whom I will call John, for some time. At our supervision session he began to talk about one of his clients who wanted some guidance about a moral dilemma she was in, resulting from an extramarital relationship she was having with a married man. John felt that he had a dilemma as well, as he knew both of the people concerned and their families. Following our agreement around confidentiality in our work, I was trying hard to resist working out who the person was that his client was having a relationship with, when John revealed a piece of information that made it very clear who the other person was. I then had to reveal that not only did I know the person his client was having an affair with, but he was also a very recent counselling client of mine and additionally I knew his client's husband in a professional capacity.

We agreed that we would stop discussing anything to do with either John's client or mine, but that we would focus our supervision on how John would deal with his dilemma about continuing to work with this client when he knew all the parties involved. In the end John agreed that he would discuss the situation openly with his client and decide with her if they should continue to work together.

Once again, here was a situation which would be fairly unlikely to occur in an urban or less remote area, but which could happen quite frequently in Shetland and similar remote areas. It was important for us not to react to a rigid injunction to avoid dual relationships, but to reflect on the issue, carefully taking account of the particular geographical, social and cultural context in which it was occurring. Once again, the important thing to do was to be open and explicit about it. I know that if this had been happening in the urban area in which I live I would have been saying to John that he would have to take his work with this client to another supervisor. In this instance we agreed that I would continue to supervise John's work with this client, but that we would keep the focus on the way he was working with the client and avoid focusing on the client, her issues and her relationships. Although difficult to achieve, this proved to be an effective way to work for both of us.

A theoretical point

It is of course extremely difficult to manage one's curiosity and to resist trying to work out who is being talked about in this way and could of course lead to some incongruence in the therapist. I do not see this as insurmountable because my practice as a person-centred therapist is strongly rooted in the principles of phenomenology. Carl Rogers confirmed his belief in the importance of being phenomenological when he wrote: 'To be with another in this (empathic) way means that for the time being you lay aside your own views and values in order to enter another's world without prejudice' (Rogers, 1980).

In being truly phenomenological I set out to notice and pay attention to all the phenomena which I am experiencing in the therapeutic relationship, in my client and in myself. In addition to noticing these phenomena, I strive to put to one side any assumptions I may have resulting from my past experience and knowledge: a process in phenomenology known as 'bracketing off' (*Stanford Encyclopedia of Philosophy*, 2006). In working phenomenologically, I want to try to experience these phenomena as though I am experiencing them for the first time. The act of being explicit about the existence of dual or multiple relationships should help prevent incongruence from occurring, and of course sits well with the principle of fidelity in the Ethical Framework. For those wishing to gain a clearer understanding of the theory and practice of phenomenology, a good starting point is the *Stanford Encyclopaedia of Philosophy*, which can be accessed via the internet (see also Brazier, 1991).

Conclusion

These are just three examples of how the interconnecting circles of relationships in rural and remote communities have led me to consider that the rigid holding of boundaries and confidentiality is unhelpful. In such areas, therapists need to ensure that they are not cavalier in their work, totally disregarding boundary setting, management and maintenance and confidentiality. They do need to consider carefully what is in the best interests of the client, the community and the therapist and to maintain some measure of flexibility in managing dual and plural relationships. They also need to be clear and explicit and to seek agreement about the ways in which boundaries, relationships and aspects of confidentiality need to be varied within such a different cultural context.

I have focused in this chapter on the particular circumstances of remote rural communities. I have used some of the many examples from my work in such communities. I have also had a number of similar experiences in recent years in consultancy and counselling work in a variety of organisations This has led me to consider that those undertaking counselling and supervision in remote rural communities and perhaps in small organisations, need to give much more careful and explicit consideration to the management of confidentiality agreements and the appropriateness or otherwise of dual and multiple relationships. I think this has particular relevance for those working in remote or isolated communities and island communities such as Malta, Cyprus, the Hebrides, Channel Islands and Scilly Isles. It also has particular reference to working with employee access programmes (EAPs) in organisations which do not have their own counselling services, small voluntary organisations, organisations which form part of larger 'umbrella' organisations and small learning communities such as counselling courses.

What seems essential to me is that the values and principles described in the Ethical Framework should form the ethos of our work as therapists. Those principles need to be integrated as a part of our way of being which we are committed to, rather than trying to use them as rigid rules of behaviour.

References

Brazier, D. D. (1991) *Phenomenology in Counselling and Psychotherapy*. Amida Trust. http://www.amidatrust.com/article_phen.html (accessed 10 September 2008).

British Association for Counselling and Psychotherapy (BACP, 2002) *Ethical Framework for Good Practice in Counselling and Psychotherapy*. Rugby: BACP.

Gabriel, L. (2005) *Speaking the Unspeakable: The Ethics of Dual Relationships in Counselling and Psychotherapy*. London: Routledge.

Rogers, C. R. (1980) *A Way of Being*. Boston: Houghton Mifflin.

Shetland Islands Council (2006) *Shetland in Statistics*. Lerwick: Shetland Islands Council, Economic Development Unit (www.shetland.gov.uk/council/documents/sins2006.pdf).

Stanford Encyclopedia of Philosophy (2006). http://plato.stanford.edu/entries/phenomenology/ (accessed 10 September 2008).

Chapter 13

Exploring the researcher–contributor research alliance

Lynne Gabriel

Introduction

This chapter considers relational ethics in the context of qualitative research. The researcher–contributor alliance and the ethical challenges, tensions and conflicts that can arise when conducting in-depth qualitative research interviews are explored. The chapter discusses researcher–practitioner role conflict and offers a model for thinking about and supporting the research interview context.

Exploring ethics in researcher–participant relationships

Within counselling and psychotherapy, the relationship between therapist and client is often termed the *therapeutic alliance* and a substantial body of literature has arisen around the client–therapist relationship. Here, the term *research alliance* refers to the relationship and collaboration between researcher and research contributor, as shown in Figure 13.1. The term 'contributor' here denotes an individual who participates in or responds to a research inquiry.

The notion of a research alliance is derived from Bordin's (1979, 1994) concept of the *working alliance* and its three components: *bonds* (here, my relationship with the contributor), *goals* (here, my research aims and objectives) and *tasks* (here, the research processes required to achieve the research aims and objectives). Bordin's work provides a helpful base on which to construct a cognitive 'map' or conceptual tool through which to frame and 'manage' the researcher–contributor alliance. In a qualitative inquiry that explored clients' and practitioners' experiences and perceptions of being in dual or multiple role relationships (Gabriel, 2002, 2005), this model represents some of the ways in which I 'held' my researcher role.

Using an in-depth interview format holds potential to elicit rich narrative data. The researcher's capacity to develop a rapport with the research contributor influences the success of this method (McLeod, 1994). One way of

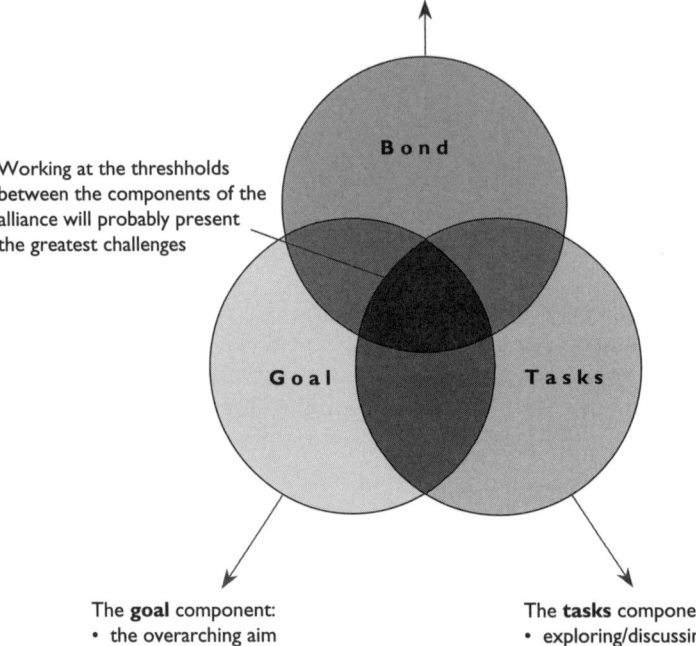

The **bond** component:
- the form, quality and processes of the relationship
- the attachment between researcher and participant (however brief the research alliance)
- the researcher's 'compassionate distance'

Working at the threshholds between the components of the alliance will probably present the greatest challenges

B o n d

G o a l   T a s k s

The **goal** component:
- the overarching aim of the research project: e.g. to further professional understanding of dual and multiple roles
- the research question(s)

The **tasks** component:
- exploring/discussing the research focus/interview question
- managing informed consent across the research relationship
- managing process ethics
- research contract: e.g. agreeing procedure if/for any future contact

Figure 13.1 The research alliance.

fostering a rapport with research contributors is to aim to create a 'safe base' (Bowlby, 1979) in the research interview context and offer the participant the opportunity to 'tell' their biographical account (Hollway and Jefferson, 1997, 2000). The creation of a safe space conducive to recounting potentially disturbing stories is important, especially so when researching sensitive topics (Lee, 1993; Schoener, 1999). As with forms of brief therapy, a brief research alliance (and in many instances it is likely to be a face-to-face meeting with some telephone or correspondence contact) can engender a respectful researcher–contributor bond that is conducive to the contributor telling their story and enables the overall goals and the myriad of tasks to be completed. That said, the research reality might differ, in which case the research alliance, as with any therapy approach and relationship, can be developed, repaired and managed through the researcher–practitioner invoking their helper skills and ability. In this respect, the researcher's helper skills can legitimately contribute to developing, maintaining and appropriately ending the research alliance.

Researcher–practitioner role conflict

Shame, guilt, taboo, predatory, exploitative, abusive, incestuous – these words have been associated with harmful dual and multiple role relationships (Gabriel, 2002, 2005). The words can be imbued with potent and negative interpretations and suggest that a research investigation exploring complex relationships or relational dynamics can enter unknown, perhaps dangerous territory – paradoxically, all the more reason to investigate the topic. Disclosing details of their relationships in the context of a research interview invites the contributors to enter into tricky terrain.

When researching dual and multiple role relationships, as a therapist researching a therapy related topic, I came to the research with experience of working with potent and conflicted material within therapy work. However, in the research interview setting I experienced conflict between my therapist and researcher roles and background. Maybe this is not surprising since, as Beauchamp and Childress (1994: 441) suggest, 'the dual roles of research scientist and clinical practitioner pull in different directions and present both conflicting obligations and conflicting interests'. While I did not see myself as a research scientist, I did experience a powerful tension between my research aims and my pull to invoke my practitioner skills and obligations. Mindful of the research topic and the potential for role conflict, I aimed to be present in research interviews in a position of 'researcher first'. Despite this aim, some interviews presented particular challenges and I chose to use my therapeutic skills to manage the situation.

The degree to which a researcher intervenes or collaborates with contributors to construct the research outcomes will vary according to the researcher's approach and project design – the degree of co-construction and collaboration will influence the nature and experience of the alliance, with subsequent implications for relational ethics in the context of the researcher–contributor relationship. Where a research alliance more closely resembles a therapy relationship, then researcher–practitioner role conflict may be greater.

Role conflict has been recognised by social psychologists as a source of stress for those involved in roles that carry different expectations and obligations (Kitchener, 1988), especially when the obligations of one role are incongruent with those of another. According to Kitchener, the potential for role conflict means that dual roles are inadvisable (Kitchener, 1988). Arguably, however, unavoidable role conflict could occur for the practitioner adopting in-depth qualitative research interviews to investigate counselling and psychotherapy, involving tension in the pull between the goals and focus of the researcher role and the obligations and responsibilities incumbent upon their practitioner role.

The literature on the practitioner–researcher role and challenges is developing. For example, the work of Thomas (1994), Hart and Crawford-Wright (1999) and Etherington (2001, 2007) offers resources for decision making in situations of researcher role conflict. Thomas (1994) defined her role as 'a counsellor first' when she undertook research work with her own clients and faced the challenge of reconciling her clinical practice with the demands of academic research. When researching experiences of adult male survivors of childhood sexual abuse, Etherington (2001) experienced the dilemma of competing role obligations in relation to what remains confidential to the research interview. Recent UK literature on role issues and conflicts in overlapping role relationships (Syme, 2003; Gabriel, 2005) offers welcome resources for practitioners.

In my own research on dual and multiple role relationships (Gabriel, 2002, 2005), while, on the one hand, I knew my research aims and focus were the priority in the research interview setting, on the other hand, I felt morally and ethically obligated to be prepared to respond to any distress a contributor might experience as a result of participating in the research interview. This role duality was challenging. On the occasions where a contributor became distressed or upset in the interview context, without seeking to transform the meeting into a therapy session, it was important to respond appropriately and reflexively by using helper skills to support the individual and move the situation on. In a researcher role, we can construe therapeutic skills as helpful research resources to draw on as and when necessary. At a minimum, they possess the potential to aid interviewing. By this, I do not mean that the research interview becomes a counselling interview. Rather, I am suggesting that it is a meeting in which my counselling skills can be used in a context-appropriate way. Nonetheless, this is easier to strive for than execute. What helped me to stay focused in my interviews was to aim for a researcher stance of 'compassionate distance' (Beauchamp and Childress, 1994) and hold in mind the purpose of the meeting. The notion of 'distance' implies a boundary, while 'compassionate' suggests an empathic presence – both of which can be invoked as necessary.

Arguably, failure to acknowledge a contributor's emotional distress constitutes a failure to uphold the moral principle of non-maleficence (do no harm) and raises questions about the researcher's capacity for fidelity (being faithful to the researcher–contributor contract and relationship). Coyle (1998: 57) argues a similar position: 'it verges on the unethical for a researcher to address sensitive issues with respondents, re-stimulate painful experiences, record them and then simply depart from the interview situation'.

How, then, could I as researcher respond to a participant's distress in a way that respected the individual, yet did not lose sight of the purpose of the research interview? I had to discover ways of holding the research alliance in a compassionate yet focused way. Given that the meeting focused on the contributor's experience of a dual relationship, I was mindful of wanting to hold a clear boundary between the researcher–contributor dynamic and other forms of relational interaction. By this, I mean that given the sensitive nature of the topic and the impact it had on some of the research contributors, appropriate boundary holding became important for both of us. Confidentiality was crucial, given that some of the interviews elicited highly sensitive material and intimate details of incidents and identities that could be identified if released into the public domain.

While the relational and ethical tensions or challenges might be evident for the researcher–practitioner in the context of an in-depth research interview, are they any different from the relational depth (Mearns and Cooper, 2006) of an intimate counselling conversation? Perhaps the difference is minimal and it is the intentionality of the parties concerned and the purpose of their meeting that matters most (Gabriel, 2008, Chapter 2 of this volume)? To make transparent our researcher intentions within the context of our research interviewing is crucial. To that end then, the contracting between researcher and contributor could closely resemble the process of therapy contracting. I interviewed in excess of 50 individuals and in the contact boundaries with contributors I chose not to enter into extended or non-research connections with them. After the research, requests from several contributors for me to become their therapist or supervisor endorsed my decision to hold a clear relational boundary around the research meeting and roles (for a full exploration of dual and multiple role relating, see Gabriel, 2002, 2005).

During the processes of preparing for and conducting the research interviews, I had not encountered texts that adequately captured the interviewing approach I had constructed, so I was delighted to come across Hollway and Jefferson's work (1997, 2000) and their accounts of struggling to construct an interview method. Their ideas resonated with my thinking and mirrored some of my concerns about seeking information from 'defended subjects' (Hollway and Jefferson, 1997). The notion of a 'defensive' contributor parallels analytical notions of a client's intrapsychic, psychological defences in the context of the therapy work and relationship and Hollway and Jefferson import this idea into the context of a research interview. Thus, they assume that the free-flowing biographical format for the interview will provide a context that encourages the contributor to be less defensive and more able to say what comes to mind about the topic under question – all the more reason to invoke a respectful and mindful relational ethic.

Given that the topic I was researching was a sensitive one, I anticipated some individuals might be reluctant to volunteer to contribute, or alternatively be anxious talking about their relationship in the research interview context. Some contributors might defend against the research question, despite the fact that it was delivered in the form of an invitation to 'tell me about your experience of a dual relationship'. In addition, some individuals might have had reservations about my presence, my researcher role or my research aims. It was partly for these reasons that I did not form extended contacts with contributors. Essentially, I wanted participants to be able to contribute their stories and move on with minimal fear or anxiety about future contact. Given the sensitive nature of the topic of investigation, this was a legitimate approach.

In their work, Hollway and Jefferson (1997, 2000) adopted the psycho-analytical notion of 'free association' to characterise and inform the type of research interview they sought. Thus, the free-flow format of the contributor's narrative is thought to bypass conscious psychological defences. In a similar way, I wanted to invite the contributor to talk about their own experience, with the flow and content of the interview largely contributor controlled, rather than set by me. By doing so, I hoped that the individuals would feel freer to talk about their dual relationship. However, while I share Hollway and Jefferson's argument that a contributor's defences are less rigid in an unstructured, free-flowing interview approach, I also see significant ethical considerations, not least of these being the contributor's fully informed consent to participate and willingly (or even unwittingly) disclose information. Although I believe ethical tensions are inevitable in any inquiry approach, nonetheless, my role and responsibility as researcher was to recognise and work with challenges unique to my research inquiry and the researcher–contributor relationships, rather than dismiss or ignore them.

When negotiating the researcher–contributor relationship, we cannot ignore power inequities. Arguably, in relation to power differentials in the researcher–contributor relationship, a good research alliance can militate against unhelpful power dynamics. At best, a biographical and narrative approach could encourage the storyteller to develop their own 'locus of control' (Mearns and Thorne, 2000) in the interview context, offering a contributor-centred research alliance. Prepared questions might only serve to reinforce defences (Hollway and Jefferson, 2000), whereas minimal and spontaneous comments are more likely to facilitate freer-flowing narrative contributions. While an opponent might argue that the narrator-contributor will be selective in their choice of storylines, equally, a biographical focus is less likely to make the narrator defensive and thus more inclined to 'loosen up' and share their uncensored (or certainly less censored) version of the events or experiences. In that interview setting, I regarded my role as that of an'ethically mindful' research-focused facilitator.

During the interviews I found that most contributors needed little prompting to aid their narration, aside from interpretive comments or questions to clarify or check out their meaning. While interpretive comments served as a focusing tool that at best facilitated the beginning of analysis, on the other hand, an interpretation can influence the contributor's response in an inappropriate direction, or distract them from their line of thought – these are key considerations that impact on the quality and integrity of the research. I found that aiming for a state of 'constant vigilance' helped me to check the motives and track the outcomes of my comments and interpretations. Fundamentally, however, the actual impact on the contributor of my researcher stance and presence can only be cautiously assumed. Essentially, qualitative research interviewing demands a great deal of the researcher's knowledge, skills, abilities and ethical literacy. Hence, they need to develop conceptual and practical 'tools' that are researcher, research and context specific – this is the *bricoleur* in action. As bricoleur, the researcher is a skilled craftsperson who can craft a research design that best fits their research focus and aims (Denzin and Lincoln, 1998).

The approach outlined in Box 13.1 shows some of the ways in which I aimed to support the interview process and participants. Of course, plans go awry. At times, revisiting the inquiry's aims and making good use of supervision helped to hold the research focus and manage the processes of ethical decision making. This example of *process ethics* demonstrates aspects of the research methodology, process and researcher–contributor relationships that inevitably change over time and circumstances. Hence, ethical decisions around, for instance, informed consent will need to be revisited within the changing context of the research project.

Box 13.1 *Minimising and containing researcher–practitioner role conflict*

1 Provide clear information for contributors

- Offer comprehensive details of the research project including its aims and objectives.
- Seek the contributor's informed consent.
- Inform the contributor of the need to revisit informed consent across the period of their involvement in the research project.
- Offer information on the possible consequences of participation.
- Offer the contributor the opportunity to withdraw their contribution at any time.
- Clearly outline the researcher role at interview; explain limits and role boundaries.

2 Form an effective research alliance

- Undertake clear initial contracting and boundary setting.
- Be compassionate in the researcher role – adopt a stance of 'compassionate distance' and strive to achieve a balance between an impassioned and impassive stance.

- Attend to maintaining a good enough balance in the research alliance between bond/task/goal elements of the alliance, as per Bordin's (1979, 1994) model of the working alliance.
- Consider any evidence/suggestion of parallel processes between research processes and research topic.
- Communicate clearly the type and limits of any post-interview contact.

3 Have a clear policy on confidentiality

- What is disclosed to a researcher within the context of the research interview, for instance, remains in confidence.
- Decide whether disclosures are treated as subject to the responsibilities and obligations that might be incumbent upon the researcher in any therapy-related role they fulfil, such as counsellor or supervisor.
- Be clear about the limits of confidentiality and when consultative support is required.
- Clarify the limits of disclosure.

4 Cultivate reflexivity

- Use research supervision to support thinking and practice.
- Regularly review researcher role/research process and practitioner–researcher dichotomy.
- Use self-reflection, supervisory meetings and peer/colleague meetings to develop reflexive approaches to the research process and researcher role.
- Use ethics codes and guidelines, moral principles, problem-solving models etc. as consultative resources to inform decision making and actions.

Source: adapted from Gabriel (1999)

In the research interview, I was creating a space in which contributors gifted their stories. Although my subsequent analyses and interpretations of the collective of contributors' stories would embody individual stories, ultimately I held authorship of the overarching narrative that contained their stories. Conversely, in a therapy interview context, ownership of the client's story remains firmly with the client.

In arguing for compassionate research interviewing, I am not recommending a 'laissez-faire' approach. What I am suggesting is the formation of a research alliance, however brief, that grows from ethically sound and compassionate foundations and is monitored through being a *process sentinel* (Gabriel, 2006, 2008, Chapter 2 of this volume) in the researcher role. Essentially, this means that the process, content and form of the interaction between researcher and contributor is constantly monitored. For example, in researching dual and multiple role relationships, I sought to hold my researcher and therapist knowledge and experience, aiming for a collaborative perception of both roles, rather than seeing them as conflicting. However, the ease with which I narrate this process belies the complexity and conflict that can arise, as the following story shows.

Recognising role conflict

As researcher-witness to a client-contributor's or therapist-contributor's story, I had to identify ways to deal with the more chaotic and conflicted stories. On several occasions, the stories I heard were especially poignant, but one in particular stands out. I found the woman's story profoundly moving and although I was able to hear it I found parts of it very disturbing, largely due to the evident distress she had experienced and my sense of frustration about what appeared to be an exploitative experience. When I left her home, I found myself crying for her. Fortunately, good supervision (both practitioner supervision and research supervision) was available to me, but nonetheless, hers was a story that will remain as a profound reminder of that research project. Although I was able to discuss some of my reactions in different supervisory and therapeutic contexts, what remained was that I knew of, and had to live with, the fact that an inept and harmful therapist continued to practice, albeit not with that research contributor. My relationship with this contributor was brief, extending to telephone and one face-to-face meeting, yet her impact was lasting and there were times when I was tempted to follow up on her story. To do this might have replicated some of the damaging intrusions she experienced in her multiple role relationship with a former therapist.

Although I did not research my own client group, I nevertheless encountered conflict during a number of research interviews, particularly in the early phases of the work when I was especially anxious about the quality and approach of my interviews and research activities. I found it challenging to mediate between my researcher-practitioner interests and conflicts and took these issues to supervision. I took some of my concerns to my therapy supervision and some of the research-related issues were discussed in research supervision. But there were no easy solutions and I felt I simply had to bear the conflict and find ways to hold the boundaries between my 'inner therapist' that might arise in the context of a research interview, say, and my research aims and purpose.

Whatever my personal or professional response to a contributor's story, I strove to put my immediate reactions to one side and hold them until they could be released in an appropriate context and way; such as, for example, personal supervision, academic supervision, research supervision or personal therapy. In my view, I simply had to find ways to deal with the conflicts and bear the knowledge that several individuals appeared to be in harmful dual or multiple role relationships. I was aware that, in order to facilitate the individual to share their story, I did not want to distort their telling of the story by my shock or disapproval. My anxiety about this type of conflict led to my original decision to interview only experienced therapists, irrespective of whether the contributor was to contribute from a client or a therapist perspective. As previously noted, my assumption was that these individuals would understand ethical implications and challenges implicit in researching a sensitive topic. This was not always the case and the need for clear boundaries and a well-held research alliance was no different from any other research relationship.

Conclusion

It is anxiety-invoking to accurately hold the essence of a contributor's story and respectively represent it in a more public domain. It is the concern of any researcher using qualitative approaches to explore human experience and perception – all the more reason why a good research alliance is essential. The approach to researcher–contributor relationships discussed above offers one representation of what I term the research alliance. As Denzin (2001) notes, however, any research approach can only ever be partial. I have given a glimpse of challenges I experienced in one research project when undertaking in-depth unstructured qualitative interviews. In the spirit of evolving a personal–professional relational ethic (as advocated by Gabriel in Chapter 2 of this volume), readers will form their own approach and this narrative might inform that approach.

Despite the personal, relational and ethical challenges described above, the overall experience of conducting in-depth research interviews was deeply rewarding. I lived to 'tell the tale' as they say and continue to research relational experiences and perceptions. In 'telling the tales' of the research contributors, the fidelity implicit to the research alliance must continue, thereby endorsing the value of process ethics and the importance of developing a good relational ethic.

References

Beauchamp, T. and Childress, J. (1994) *Principles of Biomedical Ethics*, 4th edn. New York: Oxford University Press.

Bordin, E. S. (1979) The generalizability of the psychoanalytic concept of the working alliance. *Psychotherapy: Theory, Research and Practice* 16, 252–260.

Bordin, E. S. (1994) Theory and research on the therapeutic working alliance: new directions. In A. O. Horvath and L. Greenberg (eds) *The Working Alliance: Theory, Research, and Practice*. New York: Wiley.

Bowlby, J. (1979) *The Making and Breaking of Affectional Bonds*. London: Tavistock.

Coyle, A. (1998) Qualitative research in counselling psychology: using the counselling interview as a research instrument. In P. Clarkson (ed.) *Counselling Psychology: Integrating Theory, Research and Supervised Practice*. London: Routledge.

Denzin, N. K. (2001) The reflexive interview and a performative social science. *Qualitative Research*, 1, 1, 23–46.

Denzin, N. K. and Lincoln, Y. S. (eds) (1998) *The Landscape of Qualitative Research: Theories and Issues*. Thousand Oaks, CA: Sage.

Etherington, K. (2001) Research with ex-clients: an extension and celebration of the therapeutic process. *British Journal of Guidance and Counselling* 29, 1, 5–19.

Etherington, K. (2007) Ethical research in reflexive relationships. *Qualitative Inquiry* 13, 5, 599–616.

Gabriel, L. (1999) *Practitioner–researcher role conflict*. Paper presented at BAC Research Conference, Leeds, UK.

Gabriel, L. (2002) *Speaking the unspeakable: dual relationships in counselling and psychotherapy*. Unpublished doctoral thesis. University of Leeds, UK.

Gabriel, L. (2005) *Speaking the Unspeakable: The Ethics of Dual Relationships in Counselling and Psychotherapy*. London: Brunner-Routledge.

Gabriel, L. (2006) *Boundary riders, process sentinels and ethics warriors: allies for ethical practice*. Seminar presented at the British Association for Counselling Annual Training Conference (BACP), London, October.

Gabriel, L. (2008) *Relational ethics, boundary riders, process sentinels: allies for ethical practice*. Presentation and seminar at the American Counseling Association's (ACA) Annual Conference and Exhibition, 26–30 March, Honolulu, Hawaii and published in ACA's VISTAS 2008.

Hart, N. and Crawford-Wright, A. (1999) Research as therapy, therapy as research: ethical dilemmas in new-paradigm research. *British Journal of Guidance and Counselling* 27, 2, 205–214.

Hollway, W. and Jefferson, T. (1997) Eliciting narrative through the in-depth interview. *Qualitative Inquiry* 3, 1, 53–70.

Hollway, W. and Jefferson, T. (2000) *Doing Qualitative Research Differently: Free Association, Narrative and the Interview Method*. London: Sage.

Kitchener, K. S. (1988) Dual role relationships: what makes them so problematic? *Journal of Counseling and Development* 67, 4, 217–221.

Lee, R. M. (1993) *Doing Research on Sensitive Topics*. London: Sage.

McLeod, J. (1994) *Doing Qualitative Research*. London: Sage.

Mearns, D. and Cooper, M. (2006) *Working at Relational Depth*. London: Sage.

Mearns, D. and Thorne, B. (2000) *Person-Centred Therapy Today: New Frontiers in Theory and Practice*. London: Sage.

Schoener, G. R. (1999) *Sexual abuse by psychotherapists and other helping professionals: victims, boundaries and our societal response*. Paper presented at POPAN (Prevention of Professional Abuse Network), London, 10 July.

Syme, G. (2003) *Dual Relationships in Counselling and Psychotherapy*. London: Sage.

Thomas, G. (1994) A counsellor first. *Counselling* 5, 1, 44–46.

Chapter 14

Relational ethics from a cognitive behavioural perspective

Jeremy Tudway

My background as a cognitive behavioural therapy (CBT) practitioner is intimately linked to my professional training as a clinical and forensic psychologist. While I work to the British Psychological Society's code of conduct and professional ethics, my own ethical perspective is fundamentally driven by a humanistic set of principles. These owe as much to Sartre's existentialism as they do to the philosophy of science which can at times be challenging and contradictory. In this chapter I endeavour to outline the philosophical and theoretical considerations that form the basis of my cognitive behavioural practice and approach to relational ethics in conjunction with a knowledge base that, by necessity, contains a considerable element of 'expertise'. These contradictions filter into my practice as I strive to be valuing of the humanity of clients and their experience while at the same time retaining a central theoretical basis that is avowedly directive.

Benke (2001) defines ethics as 'thinking about reasons in terms of values'. This presents a set of assumptions that clearly relate to the central model of the cognitive behavioural therapies and rational-emotive behaviour therapy (REBT) in particular. However, it also raises a set of very clear ethical dilemmas as this is also the basis of therapeutic change. Does this mean that, for CBT, therapy is about changing the ethics of clients? Consequently, is it necessary to begin to consider ethics from a new perspective, namely that of a relational one? It is my contention that for my practice it is necessary to do so and possibly to consider some of what has been written about CBT as part of the historical journey, as an evolution of theory and therapeutic practice.

Earlier writing about the relationship in the cognitive behavioural therapies and particularly REBT has suffered owing to the views of some of the earlier advocates of the model. For example, Young (1986b) delineates between two models of power to establish a therapeutic relationship, 'command' versus 'friendship' power. Command power relates to the use of authority, expertise and prestige with the consequence that the client is influenced by the competency and credibility of the therapist. Friendship power relates to the use of warmth, positive regard and empathy. Sadly, Young concluded that command power is particularly effective when approaching therapy with 'certain kinds' of client and I would contend that this fundamentally undermines the basic therapeutic principles of CBT and the ethical dimension of the client–therapist relationship. Indeed, Dryden (1995) writes about the therapeutic alliance in REBT and draws on Bordin's work concentrating on the three major components of therapeutic alliance: bonds, goals and tasks. In this chapter he highlights the need for REBT practitioners to concentrate on the 'fit' between the client and their therapeutic style and notes that clients who are very passive or reactive to interpersonal influence may not gain maximum benefit from REBT, or indeed CBT in general.

My understanding of the application of relational ethics to therapy is that this refers to the notion that decisions about therapy are guided by the benefits offered to the client and has been conceptualised as essentially intuitive in nature. This stands in opposition to organisational and statutory based ethical codes that are essentially rationalisations.

For an ethical code to be of use it has to have a meaning; consequently, it must be genuine. The result of this as applied to relational ethics is that it is extremely difficult to develop a set of relational ethics agreed by everyone in all cases. This highlights a strength of the agreed sets of ethical principles as these do not require any active participation. Rather, this process lends itself to a rigidity and dogmatism from which it is possible to avoid the personal consequences of dilemmas as these are simply 'the rules'.

McMahon (2003) notes four stages of values: the first refers to personally held subjective values; the second to purpose or intent; the third to acts that become habits or traditions; and the fourth to the establishment of general principles. McMahon continues on to cite examples of confusion between stages one and three; for example, wishing to engage in an activity owing to the relative value this is held in, yet being unable to do so owing to loyalty to a set of predetermined rules.

One clear ethical theme that emerges in practice is often associated with clients' expressed wish to have their problems 'cured' or thinking process 'put right' and, while this presenting problem may not necessarily be the exclusive province of CBT, it certainly poses a clear ethical challenge. Dryden (1995) notes that while authors have asserted that all psychotherapies can be conceptualised as a process of persuasion, this may be particularly so for REBT. The process of change in REBT involves the therapist challenging the irrational beliefs and inferences of the client. Dryden makes reference to the need for client autonomy to be maximised and emphasises that the client must remain in possession of their own thought processes and consequently the therapeutic bond is different for different clients.

Creating a positive therapeutic environment is as core to CBT as it is to any of the other modalities as this is the first and, according to research evidence (see, for example, Shapiro, 1995), the most central element in enabling clients to achieve some change. Consequently, the core of CBT in its many forms requires the client to become an active participant within the therapeutic model, understanding and owning the theory and consequently the personal implications of undertaking or avoiding change.

Unusually this involves initial sessions in which the client is 'schooled' in the model to use as a framework. Through this they can begin to understand what is often a bewildering morass of emotions and reactions, generally experienced with little recourse to the role that their own beliefs have in the process. As such, the initial role of the therapist in any of the cognitive behavioural therapies is to outline the nature of the theory and explain both the language and process of therapy towards an agreed set of goals that must be led and owned by the client.

This certainly poses an ethical dilemma as, at one level, it effectively means presenting a theoretical framework that is often in stark contrast to the value and belief system of the client. For this to be more than simply pointing out that the client's thinking is wrong, it should not be simply offering the message that changes within this framework are only possible if this new way of thinking is adopted. In many ways this process is particularly explicit in CBT owing to the active process of giving the theory to clients in order that they become the most active partner in their own process of change. However, as noted previously, it does not mean that CBT is the only form of psychological therapy that faces this dilemma.

The very nature of entering into psychological therapy with a therapist involves addressing a new and challenging way of considering the self, relationships, the world, the future and the ways in which these relate to each other. At one level maybe the cognitive behavioural therapies are very honest as these make a very clear statement about the nature of the link between ways of thinking and the consequent emotions that interfere with life goals. Consequently, addressing aspects of client thinking is central to effective change. Perhaps this is simply a way to justify a covert attempt to 'correct' the way that clients think, feel and behave?

An example of such a dilemma can be found when confronted by a client with a particularly strong set of fundamental religious beliefs in which their attention is focused on sin and damnation versus those who are more evangelical who place an emphasis on forgiveness and salvation (Young, 1986a). As such, while it may be possible to draw upon elements of divine intervention (i.e. the capacity for forgiveness and salvation inherent in developing personal responsibility for emotions and behaviours and acknowledgement of human fallibility), is this merely utilising the client's belief structure in a ruthless manner?

Although important to work within the client's belief system it cannot be considered ethical to simply utilise beliefs because they support the theoretical framework of the therapist. In my own practice I attempt to value the experience of the client and acknowledge that they hold beliefs very strongly and then make an explicit statement that it is neither my role nor intended practice to challenge or usurp these in the process of therapy. I am also very explicit in a statement that my own beliefs are not necessarily those of the client, but always decline to offer a declarative statement of exactly what my own beliefs are for two main reasons, one ethical and one practical.

The ethical reasoning underpinning my position not to declare my own beliefs about existence relates to the basis of the therapeutic relationship. Clients invest significant trust that I will work with them on their problems and this inevitably places me in a position of relative power. Consequently, there is an implicit contract that therapy is not only boundaried by the physical limits of space and time but by the differential in power and influence. Regardless of how devotedly the client may hold a religious belief, to hear a critical evaluation of this from a source of perceived greater power, and potentially greater wisdom, invariably invites greater critical evaluation of basic beliefs than was included in the initial contract. At times it may be necessary to discuss some elements of a religious belief system, for example, a devoutly Christian client who concludes that they are more evil than any other human because they have committed acts of considerable sin.

Inevitably, there are central notions of very strongly held beliefs that involve clear ethical and practical difficulties, for example, the notion of absolute evil or absolute good. An example of my attempts to be respectful about a client's belief system and not to challenge central tenets while enabling him to reduce the amount of distress he causes to himself is given in the following brief excerpt from a session. The client had become very distressed, believing himself to be thoroughly evil and bad, although in later sessions we discovered that his concept of self was riven with negative self-evaluation. Effectively nothing he could do would ever be good enough and consequently everything he did must, at some level, be bad.

Therapist:	Tell me more about what you mean, 'evil' . . . that you bring about evil without being aware of it.
Client:	I'm unsure about how this happens . . . I just have this awful dread. Truly awful dread that I am . . . I have.
Therapist:	And if you had done this, what would that make you?
Client:	You know, it's too horrific to say . . . I guess I must be the Devil, ultimately evil and this is horrible!
Therapist:	But you say that it feels horrible to think that you might be that evil . . . to be the Devil?
Client:	Yes.
Therapist:	Surely the Devil would not feel uncomfortable about being evil . . . How could it be the case that the Devil was anxious about being evil? It strikes me as unusual that this might be the case.
Client:	Well yes, I suppose but maybe I simply forgot who I was and have

been going around thinking I'm doing what I should and praying but really I'm evil.

Therapist: But, again, surely from that point of view the Devil is all bad, the worst and most evil that anything can be?

Client: Yes, and that's what is so dreadful about it!

Therapist: Again, I wonder if your conclusion is necessarily correct here. Surely the most evil of individuals would feel positive about the discovery that they were so evil, yet you experience this as dread and this is something that is clearly upsetting to you.

Client: I suppose . . . and it does feel so horrible.

Therapist: Then it certainly cannot be the case that you are the Devil as the Devil would not feel anxious about being evil and you clearly do.

Client: I suppose so.

Therapist: I wonder if your concern about who you are and how good a person you are invites this comparison?

Client: What, you mean bad things I've done?

Therapist: I am referring to things that you've done that you now consider to be bad, or might not do again. Does it necessarily follow that only bad people do bad things?

Client: No! People make mistakes but I worry about things I did before.

At this stage in the session we continued on to discover that the client recalled behaving in ways that were unacceptable to his currently held religious beliefs and therefore unacceptable to him. Further sessions uncovered that he had re-evaluated himself in a particularly unforgiving and harsh manner and that his original actions were not as definitive as he had reconstructed them as being. Consequently, these actions were not as sinful. Similarly, when we considered the reprehensibility of these actions in detail, his harsh self-judgement became more pronounced. We were then able to use this as an example of how he used extreme negative self-rating and that this prompted him to the falsely necessary conclusion that his actions were evil and therefore he was evil too.

A second direct ethical dilemma relates to working with clients that involves elements of their internal world that relate to an increased risk of harm to others. Clearly, any therapeutic work is bound by legislative and professional frameworks but also from a humanist position that preventable harm to others cannot be ignored. At times this involves a very complex relationship between the client and therapist. The core 'business' of therapeutic work with high-risk clients often requires discussion of exactly what emotions, thoughts and beliefs are associated with increased risk of harm. Similarly, as the therapeutic relationship deepens and clients develop greater trust, this will lead to them disclosing a more detailed and honest insight into the level of risk they might pose. Each of these is associated with a clear dilemma for the client. The nature of the relationship between the client and therapist inevitably becomes charged with power and subordination issues.

It would be an easy escape for me to announce that there are simply legislative requirements underpinning my practice and that consequently any discussion of risk-related information is governed by greater power dynamics than those operating in the therapeutic relationship. This does not, however, convey my genuineness in attempting to work on areas of such difficulty with clients and the need for me to be explicit in my initial assessment of whether this is an issue that I can offer help with.

At one stage I was working with a man who experienced a high degree of sexual desire towards young girls and a long history of sexual aggression against girls and women who were less powerful than himself. In approaching me for therapy he was, unusually, not subject to the constraints of a legal process and stated that it was his wish to address his sexual behaviour, in order to stop placing both himself and others at risk of harm. Consequently, we commenced therapeutic work, much of which involved the building of a trusting relationship, within which I strived to maintain a very clear message that in order for us to work effectively it was necessary for him to be honest and open with me. I also made it explicit that we would necessarily be considering elements of his thinking and behaviour that were closely associated with causing harm. I offered to him the very clear dilemma for both of us, encapsulated in a clear and an explicit statement that harm to others and avoidance of personal responsibility for harmful behaviour was contrary to the aims of therapy. Consequently, any description of an offence or illegal act committed by him must be reported to the relevant authorities. This was not only a basic legal requirement but was also driven by a humanistic principle in which victims could be enabled to access appropriate support and redress.

Despite this I was very clear with the client that we would need to understand how his thinking related to an increase in his desires and consequently the risk of acting on these. I was at pains to clarify that this was clearly not a necessary link but one that he had assumed as being 'powerless to control his urges' and therefore representing a pervasive risk to others. Much of the content of our early sessions was involved with defining the historical extent of his behaviour and thinking alongside his motivation to change this and therefore stop hurting people. Indeed, we dedicated a considerable amount of time to challenging whether he was, in fact, the passive recipient of his drives and thoughts or was active in his own phenomenology.

As therapy progressed, the client reported that the frequency of his thoughts and intensity of his desires was higher than he had previously stated. At which point he indicated that this was the result of an increase in his trust in our relationship and his investment in therapeutic change as opposed to an increase in the subjective experience. Consequently, this did not indicate an increase in the risk posed by him. At this stage it became necessary to consider how to enable the client to monitor his own risk and therefore develop his sense of autonomy and self-efficacy and the client agreed that this might be beneficial.

The client was unable to attend for the following session and arrived very late for the subsequent meeting at which it was agreed that we would review progress and consider what the issues were regarding his progress.

At our next meeting the client was more agitated than usual and presented as being angry with the notion of becoming active in the monitoring of the risk he posed. The client suggested that this was the role of 'professionals' or statutory services and not clients themselves. After considerable discussion about the source of his anger he indicated that he had attended late and missed the previous appointment owing to his decision that he did not wish to become involved in consideration of any risk. Furthermore that he had been actively engaged in high-risk behaviour and he finally acknowledged that he had coerced a woman who was intellectually less able than him and also very intoxicated at the time into having sex with him. The client was realistically concerned that this would have a consequence for him, although he avoided the consideration that it was his action (attacking the woman) and not his omission (failing to report) that could result in negative consequences. I acknowledged that his behaviour would have consequences and informed him that I would have to inform the police as this was potentially an illegal act. In addition, in choosing to continue with this way of behaving he had clearly undermined our explicit understanding and agreement. Although angry and agitated, the client accepted that this consequence would result.

In reflecting about the sequence with my supervisor at the time, it was possibly a naive expectation on both mine and the client's part regarding his motivation to address his desire to change versus his desire to meet his own needs at the expense of others. I have subsequently wondered about my explicit statement concerning the status of our work and the centrality of the aim to reduce harm with the inevitable consequences of this. Was such an explicit statement a truly negotiated statement of therapeutic aims? Did the client have an equal part in it or did it reflect demands placed upon our relationship by me? More importantly, did the process of renegotiating this so explicitly lead to a situation in which the client was less able to openly discuss just how close to offending he actually was? Some of these questions remain with me and I attempt to be mindful of these issues in my current practice.

I consider that my actions were certainly intended with the best interests of both the client and public safety. Furthermore that I remained true to my humanist principles of emotional responsibility and respect for the rights and values of others. The answers to such ethical difficulties, by virtue of the fact that they are difficult and complex, are likely to vary from one case to another.

Although I consider ethics to represent a set of moral decisions based around a set of frameworks, these decisions are constantly challenged and consequently the process of re-evaluation and redefinition is a dynamic one. My own personal journey in practice commenced with the development of my philosophical belief system which is existential and, consequently, humanistic. I initially trained in academic psychology and then in clinical and forensic psychology, where I continue to practise.

Although earlier in my career my initial conceptual framework for working with clients was person-centred, I became inspired by the work of Albert Ellis. I was privileged to receive training and supervision by Professor Peter Trower who brought the CBT model alive for me and particularly encouraged me to develop my interest in REBT. Inevitably as I have progressed and undertaken further training in REBT I have changed some of my practice as I have become more comfortable within the framework and particularly as my therapeutic skills have developed.

Initially I suspect that my practice was very bound by my, at times rigid, interpretation of the British Psychological Society's code of ethics and professional conduct and the challenges involved in working therapeutically with very complex clients. As I have grown as a practitioner and become more comfortable with the model, I believe that I have been able to see more of the shared ground between therapeutic schools and certainly become more tolerant of different forms of therapy. Perhaps this has developed in tandem with my capacity to reflect and perceive ethical practice as ultimately based in my own understanding of the general principles functioning within the relationship between myself and the client. Ultimately this involves my own and the client's understanding of their value system from the first to the third, and even fourth stage of McMahon's value stages and how these link into the habits and life patterns that they bind themselves into.

References

Benke, S. (2001) A question of values. *APA Monitor* October, 84.

Dryden, W. (ed.) (1995) *Rational Emotive Behaviour Therapy: A Reader*. London: Sage.

McMahon, J. (2003) Notes on self and values in REBT. In W. Dryden (ed.) *Rational Emotive Behaviour Therapy: Theoretical Developments*. London: Brunner-Routledge.

Shapiro, D. (1995) Finding out how psychotherapies help people change. *Psychotherapy Research* 5, 1, 1–21.

Young, H. S. (1986a) Practising RET with Bible-belt Christians. In W. Dryden and P. Trower (eds) *Rational-Emotive Therapy: Recent Developments in Theory and Practice*. Bristol: IRET.

Young, H. S. (1986b) Practising RET with lower class clients. In W. Dryden and P. Trower (eds) *Rational-Emotive Therapy: Recent Developments in Theory and Practice*. Bristol: IRET.

Chapter 15

Counselling survivors of abuse

Feminism, psychodynamic psychotherapy and ethics

Moira Walker

This chapter explores feminist therapy and considers it in the context of psychodynamic models and its significance to relational ethics when working with adult survivors of childhood abuse. (I have not attempted here to define abuse. See Walker, 2003: 1–5 for an exploration of definitions.) Finally, I will consider some of the many ethical questions and relationship challenges that arise in the course of this work. Throughout, I have used the terms therapy and counselling, therapist and counsellor interchangeably.

My own stance

I write as someone primarily informed by a psychodynamic perspective but not purely so. My interest in feminism and in working with survivors of childhood abuse has led me away from purism to pragmatism. Although key concepts core to psychodynamic thinking are integral to my work – transference, countertransference, splitting, projection, boundaries, defences and their causation, and recognising the significance of child development – my concern primarily is what works for whom and when? In that sense I am client led (a good feminist principle) and not simply model led; informed by psychodynamic theory and principles of practice, but not superglued to them. I could reasonably describe myself as having moved steadily to a more integrative stance with a psychodynamic foundation.

For instance, I recognise that cognitive interventions are helpful; that psychological education (that is, using my knowledge of child development, trauma and the impact of child abuse on the child victim and the adult survivor to explain and contextualise my clients' experiences and feelings) can demystify and help survivors understand and place truly horrendous experiences and effects; and that working with imagery and storytelling helps the apparently unmanageable and destructive become contained and containable. I also recognise that the real, in addition to the transferential, relationship is alive and kicking in therapy. Settling into a session where nothing seemingly happens other than 'chat' about shoes, the cat, the kids and holidays can be profoundly healing, significant and therapeutic.

Similarly, a client's concern when a counsellor returns from an absence due to illness does not always have to be interpreted but sometimes needs graceful acceptance as an expression of human kindness.

The trick and dilemma is to recognise when a response is therapeutically valid rather than being formulaic and merely technically correct. Moving into a different mode should be a genuine response to carefully considered therapeutic need; not a dangerous knee-jerk response to an unrecognised or unprocessed countertransference. I also know, because on occasions it has been powerfully communicated to me, that this flexibility is anathema to some colleagues who have been brought up and stayed with pure psychoanalytic thought and tradition.

What is feminist therapy?

Attempting to define and describe feminism and feminist therapy is fraught with difficulty even when the sole focus and purpose of a longer chapter than this. To attempt brevity is to risk slipping into oversimplification. Many writers have considered how there is no single definition of feminist therapy or counselling (Brown and Brodsky, 1992; Juntunen, 1994; Zerbe, 2004) and feminism has changed and developed hugely with time. It is arguable that its strength lies in its fluidity, flexibility and confidence and ability to incorporate change and difference. So the feminist perspective does not exist – there are many.

This is further emphasised by feminist counselling and therapy having no 'founding father' (and the gender-specific nature of this expression is pertinent) taking ownership, rather it was a grassroots response to systems and interventions perceived to be repressive to women, failing to understand the roots of their emotional distress. Much of significance has been written by many (Broverman et al., 1970; Mitchell, 1974; Dinnerstein, 1976; Chodorow, 1978, 1989; Gilligan, 1982; Eichenbaum and Orbach, 1983; Ernst and Maguire, 1987; Chesler, 1989) to name a few, but no one voice dominates. Additionally, as Marecek and Kravetz (1998: 3) point out, 'it was sometimes difficult to disentangle whether feminist therapy proceeds as it does merely because the therapist is a woman or because the therapist has self-consciously adopted a feminist model'.

Feminist therapy and counselling straddle different theoretical models and settings, assisting practitioners in varying contexts to understand women's experiences and difficulties: within the family (Rampage, 2002); balancing work and personal life (Zimmerman, 2001; Rhoden, 2003); eating disorders (Sesan and Katzman, 1998); depression (Sands and Howard-Hamilton, 1995); and violence (Burstow, 1992). There have been challenges to what some see as the white and western exclusivity of feminist therapy, emphasising that cultural diversity is essential to any discussion of women, their place in society and how they present in therapy (Williams, 1999; Malone, 2000; Worell and Remer, 2003; Remer and Oakley, 2005).

So this discussion is embedded in acknowledging diversity of definition; a fluidity in development and an inherent recognition that absolutes and false certainties have served distressed and unhappy women badly in the past (Broverman *et al.*, 1970; Showalter, 1987; Walker, 1990). This reflects the principle of justice outlined in the Ethical Framework for Good Practice (BACP, 2002). It is worth noting that although feminist therapies arose from concerns that women were badly served by traditional therapies, many feminist therapists work with both genders, either from choice – as I do – or because they work in generic services. I would argue that with its awareness of the impact of gender stereotyping, men can benefit from a feminist counsellor. Gender stereotypes are a disservice to all. Although feminist therapy is not unidimensional, key themes are evident. What follows is a brief synthesis of these, with particular reference to psychodynamic feminism.

Key themes in feminist therapy

Constructions of gender

The recognition and exploration of the roles of women and men in terms of social constructions of gender is of paramount significance. Chodorow (1996: 236) considers the complexities involved in understanding gender and the need to 'hold on to the clinical and theoretical truths that gender remains a useful category for psychological thinking, so that gender does not disappear completely into other aspects of subjectivity, identity, and self, while also holding on to the clinically observed personal uniqueness of the individual'. She also notes the importance of not falling into over-generalisations, not to universalise, and to recognise how cultural assumptions regarding gender infuse theory and practice. Attending to clinical uniqueness while simultaneously recognising the significance of societal constructs of gender is a difficult balance, but one that feminist therapy aims for.

Dinnerstein (1976) considers the impact for boys and girls and on men and women of being predominantly brought up by mothers and other women – the hand that rocks the cradle remains primarily female. She examines the significance of gender and childcare, suggesting that men 'fear the will of women, and employ such strategies to avoid facing their fears as the segregation of men and women . . . and the separation of physical and emotional love to avoid the "melting" experience of intense intimacy' (Dinnerstein, 1976: 236).

Other theorists (Eichenbaum and Orbach, 1983; Benjamin, 1988) have struggled to deconstruct object relations theory and, as Heenan describes, have 'sought to move debates within feminism beyond the theme of "oppressor-victim", through raising feminist consciousness about the tenacity of the gendered dynamics of unconscious process' (Heenan, 1998: 96). This demonstrates an inherent concern with fairness, justice and appreciating differences, while ensuring that difference does not equal discrimination, again in tune with the BACP Ethical Framework.

Emotional difficulties are not simply intrapsychic in causation

Recognising that emotional difficulties and problems can have external causes often stemming from cultural, political and social constructions also marks out feminist approaches. However, feminist therapy has also recognised that while theory is culturally and socially based it does not negate essential meaning:

> Psychoanalysis, as any other system of thought, was formed and developed within a certain time and place; that does not invalidate its claims to universal laws, it only means that these laws have to be extracted from their specific problematic – the particular material conditions of their formation.
>
> (Mitchell, 1974: xx)

Worell and Remer (2003: 68) state that 'the primary source of a client's "pathology" is not intrapyschic or personal, but rather, social and political'. There is recognition that the interaction of the external world with the internal psyche is complex and hard to unravel but that pathologising individual difficulties created by external factors is oppressive, repressive and essentially dishonest. Struggling with this interface can be messy and unclear but essentially reflects the client's reality.

It would be easier to focus on either external worlds or the internal psyche as the cause of human woe, but feminists believe this is essentially false. Assisting clients to unravel, identify, own and work with aspects of distress they can control, and recognising what is external and beyond the individual, is a vital tenet. For example, survivors need to understand the impact of the abuse they were subjected to and recognise how this may have been internalised. Some are content that change occurs in themselves and their personal world; for others the healing process extends beyond the individual to setting up self-help groups and services for survivors, or they are active in political lobbying. Feminist therapists acknowledge both as significant and valid therapeutic goals, recognising that individuals choose their route and journey.

Working with power relationships

Recognising the centrality of power relationships within society and all relationships and relational dynamics is also central although in the psychodynamic context this has not been straightforward:

The most significant difficulty in the encounter between feminism and psychoanalysis remains the refusal of the analytic world to recognise the role of power in male-female relations. Although gender and sexual identity are currently highly fashionable topics in psychoanalytic circles, I am often astonished to hear these discussed with barely any mention of the power differences between the sexes.

(Maguire, 1995: 226)

Marecek and Kravetz (1998: 21) suggest that 'power has been the central problematic in feminist social theory'. They note that in interviews with therapists a wariness and uncertainty is displayed when discussing power within the therapy relationship, but 'once the topic of conversation shifted away from feminist therapy and to the feminist movement, respondents spoke eloquently about injustice, domination and oppression noting that power and privilege were not distributed fairly in the world outside of therapy' (1988: 23).

How the issue of power within relationships is translated into the therapeutic process is many faceted. This is an ongoing debate and struggle but it does have a place, even if no conclusion – feminist therapy is a work in progress. However, there is an intention and objective to avoid re-creating the power imbalances so often seen in other relationships and in other structures. There is a dialogue within the self, with others and with clients in which acknowledging power and its impact on relationships is crucial. Feminist therapists value an egalitarian relationship in which 'counselors share power, avoid making decisions for the client, and communicate a confidence in the client's decision-making skills' (Enns, 1997: 16).

Significance to understanding abuse

Feminism from the 1960s onwards was significant in making the horribly private world of abuse to children and to women a very public issue. Child abuse struggled to find a place on political, social and policy-making agendas although its actual existence was becoming documented, particularly in the 1970s and 1980s (Middleton, 1971; DeMause, 1976; Herman, 1981; Hall and Lloyd, 1989). In spite of this it remained conveniently sidelined unless forced into public awareness by undeniable and dramatic tragedy storming unbidden and unwelcome into the nation's consciousness. The feminist movement of the 1970s and 1980s did not allow this sidelining and child abuse became a sociopolitical issue. In the 1970s, society struggled to face Maria Colwell's miserable life, suffering and finally death (DHSS, 1974) and this added further fuel to the fire of the feminist movement's determination to ensure that private, hidden horrors gave way to public gaze, political concern and action.

This concern to transform personal shame into public awareness was both reflected in, and reinforced by, powerful and moving accounts by individual survivors entering the public arena (McNaron and Morgan, 1982; Angelou, 1983; Spring, 1987). This time was characterised by considerable action organised for women by women, demonstrated in the massive growth of rape crisis centres, self-help groups and other organisations set up to work with women abuse survivors. The emphasis was therefore on helping one another, developing structures for care and support and essentially discovering both a political and personal voice. This move to challenging and dismantling the secrecy of abuse was momentous: 'when incest survivors break that circle of secrecy we begin to wield a great political power which has for centuries lain dormant' (Driver, 1989: 171).

The work of Herman on traumatic transference and traumatic countertransference remains invaluable to feminist psychodynamic therapists (Herman, 1994: 136–147). Understanding and working with transferential aspects is crucial because work with abuse survivors is demanding and complex for the counsellor (Walker, 1992, 2004). As Herman states:

> Re-enactment of the dynamics of victim and perpetrator in the therapy relationship can become extremely complicated. Sometimes the therapist ends up feeling like the patient's victim. Therapists often complain of feeling threatened, manipulated, exploited or duped.
>
> (1994: 147)

The work of feminists enabled abuse survivors to speak and also encouraged and gave a voice and a legitimacy to counsellors and psychotherapists working with them. Feminism validated the experience of the individual while at the same time not holding the individual responsible for the actions of others that had caused their distress. This was extremely important for abuse survivors. It challenged the message given by perpetrators – seemingly reinforced by some theories – that child abuse was fantasy, or the fault of the child or some sort of accident. As recently as 1983 a judge (Brian Gibbens) passed a two-year sentence on a man convicted of raping a seven year old with the comment:

> No force was used. It is one of the kind of accidents that can happen in life, although of a different kind, and could almost happen to anyone. This was a momentary lapse.
>
> (*The Times*, 20 December 1983)

A case example

Leila was a young woman who came from a culture where compliance and modesty were highly valued and girls and women viewed as less important. She was brought up to be quiet and appeasing but desperately wanted to study for a profession. She was clever and her uncle encouraged her studies, assuring her he would handle her father's objections. The price was 'accepting' her uncle's sexual abuse from the age of 14. She came for counselling in her late twenties, academically successful but struggling to cope in a gender- and culture-insensitive, male-dominated profession.

She presented with considerable shame about the abuse. She felt that she had complied to 'get her own way'; that she was therefore manipulative and devious. Work was difficult and she recognised a pattern of being pleasing and compliant to 'get her way' with 'powerful men' but wanted to make changes. The work focused on both issues. Psychodynamic concepts of projection and introjections informed the counselling, and the experience of being a girl of 14 in her culture was explored. She began to recognise that her uncle had been manipulative and devious, not her. He had blamed her for his actions and she had internalised the shame, guilt and responsibility that he should have experienced but did not. Counselling also involved looking at power relationships in her family and culture. It was important for Leila to explore her own actions and acknowledge her own part; she did feel that at 14 she had some agency and control over her actions. This led to further exploration of her own power, in relation to her personal and work worlds. This unravelling was complex; she thought carefully about this and how she could begin to deal with the power of others and claim some for herself.

Throughout, the relationship between the counsellor and client felt warm, negotiated and egalitarian. There was a point in the relationship of particular note. Leila arrived late and soaked having been caught in a storm with a broken-down car. The counsellor fetched her a towel and a hot drink, let her use her phone and the session went over time. Although apparently working in the real relationship and with external issues, this had transferential consequences. Leila was fulsome in her thanks and sessions returned to their usual length and shape but she seemed slightly withdrawn. It transpired that Leila had experienced the counsellor as like her mother – she would occasionally respond warmly if distress and need were obvious, but this would be withdrawn as rapidly as it had arrived. This was an unconscious transference until interpreted and intensified by a cultural layer. In Leila's culture you did not question or challenge those older or more knowledgeable than you. This injunction overrode for a while all the careful work on providing an egalitarian, negotiated relationship.

Leila also wanted to explore how she could effect change at work, recognising and disliking the sexist and racist attitudes. She wanted to change how she responded to colleagues, which she did after considerable struggle – in her cultural frame she felt 'very rude and unkind'. She also developed a women's group, hoping this would offer support and be a route to challenging the organisation.

Summary of feminist therapy

Feminist therapy is based essentially on dialogue and negotiation and a recognition that the client and therapist are equally important, albeit occupying different roles, and places an emphasis on the quality, dynamics and progress of the relationship. It avoids rigidity by recognising that choices are crucial, there are no panaceas. Feminist therapy challenges patriarchal based theories of human development. It recognises women's self-esteem as often low, tending to defer and comply to others and often caught in conflicts between caring for others and claiming their own place. There is transparency, explicitness and explanation that avoids patronising by oversimplicity, overwhelming with jargon, or mystifying by refusal to answer legitimate questions. Feminists view the world as larger than the individual, with gender and power as inevitable and prevailing elements. Working within the political and social context, while valuing and validating the individual's experience, is intrinsic.

Ethical issues

It is well recognised that abuse survivors are vulnerable to further abuse within the therapeutic relationship (Rutter, 1990; Russell, 1993; Cassidy, 1999; Moore, 1999) thus breaking the five ethical principles of fidelity, autonomy, beneficence, non-malificence and justice (BACP, 2002). I am aware that counsellors of any orientation can be abusive and abusers. However, I am also aware that the literature suggests abusers are generally male (Rutter, 1990) and have professional credibility (Stean, 1993). I have not attempted to debate whether feminist therapy is gender specific and whether men can be feminist, but their gender renders women less likely to abuse clients.

I would also suggest that key principles of feminist psychodynamic therapy – careful negotiation with clients, respect for their views, transparency and openness, awareness of power and gender relationships, recognising the real relationship while playing close attention to the transferential and the impact of external as well as internal worlds – are very much in tune with the philosophy of the BACP Ethical Framework for Good Practice.

However, dilemmas abound and it is crucial that those practising, supervising and training in this field are aware of them. Intrinsic to this is recognising that working with abuse brings the counsellor into contact with the worst horrors of human behaviour and hearing appalling details. One major ethical difficulty is clients who tell counsellors the identity and location of an abuser.

Working within the principles of beneficence and autonomy and the client's best interest may indicate that the counsellor maintains confidentiality, but this would disguise real conflicts.

Section 47 of the Children Act 1989 clearly states that those employed in police and social services have a statutory obligation to report when there is 'reasonable cause to believe that a child living or found in their area is suffering or likely to suffer significant harm', but this does not extend to counsellors working in other settings or privately. In the UK there is no mandatory reporting of child abuse, so there exists a moral dilemma between upholding privacy and confidentiality and potentially protecting children. Supervision is a first step in considering this, and in my experience a second is usually discussing the dilemma with the client. The client may have given this information consciously or unconsciously wanting a response. Only exceptionally have I taken action without consulting the client.

I have advised and assisted a supervisee to contact the police without consultation when her client was still in thrall to an abuse ring actively and currently involved in child abuse. In many other instances, clients have been supported and enabled to raise concerns with the appropriate authorities; once this led to the arrest and prosecution of a man working with children; in another case there was insufficient evidence but the client felt empowered by the respectful and helpful response of the police. This client felt that 'I acted as responsibly as I could to prevent other children suffering like I did'. There are not always happy endings. I worked with a client whom I actively encouraged to report concerns about his younger brother. He was promised confidentiality but this was broken. His abusing parents ceased contact with him, further isolating the younger sibling, and he abruptly ended therapy. The sibling was not helped and neither was my client. Retrospectively, I feel it was correct to have been proactive in this decision. His descriptions of abuse left me in no doubt that a child's life was at risk. Sometimes both acting or not acting will have equally negative consequences which cannot be predicted.

There are ethical dilemmas when working with a survivor who is also a perpetrator. As I have written elsewhere (Walker, 2003: 100), 'counsellors in agencies generally work in a context where this ethical issue has been considered, policies formulated and procedures specified', whereas those in private practice have to consider their own response, obviously taken with due cognisance of the BACP Ethical Framework. Resolving this type of dilemma is hugely complex and offering a simple formula would be misleading. Working with a perpetrator is unlike working with a survivor. The emphasis cannot just be on the individual; the well-being of vulnerable others has to be kept firmly in mind. Those working with perpetrators must be properly trained and adequately supervised (principle of beneficence). It is particularly complex for the counsellor who begins working with a survivor who then reveals they are also a perpetrator. Seeking advice rapidly is crucial and this may include looking beyond normal supervision arrangements and seeking out specialist advice and support.

As a supervisor and trainer I recognise many areas of potential difficulty that can create ethical issues. Being aware of traumatic countertransference is vital (Walker, 2004). The counsellor is traumatised by the work as the client was by the abuse and failure to recognise this may lead to the counsellor becoming unable to care for themselves (principle of respect in the Ethical Framework) and also failing to care appropriately for the client. The counsellor can become overwhelmed, resulting in unethical practice such as a premature ending of the counselling. The counsellor becomes caught in the split-off, projected child self of the survivor who feels that 'I've tried and tried, given all I've got, and I can't do any more', and ends without warning or preparation. Similarly, the counsellor can become exhausted, tries harder and harder, feels they are making no progress and feels trapped (just like the child victim) and may continue to work with the client in a way that ceases to be effective.

Counsellors and supervisors also need to know that the traumatising nature of the work can leave the counsellor unable to speak (mirroring the experience of the child victim who cannot tell). They may therefore be unable to use supervision, to talk with colleagues and to take support even when available. This is clearly dangerous both to the counsellor and to the client.

Many other dynamics exist and I would urge everyone working in this field to be very aware of the range of countertransferences that can come into play in this very demanding but very important work. It is crucial that ethical standards and relational ethics are of the highest in working with this very vulnerable group who have often been multiply abused as children and all too often reabused within the care and therapeutic systems as adults.

References

Angelou, M. (1983) *I Know Why the Caged Bird Sings*. London: Virago Press.

Benjamin, J. (1988) *The Bonds of Love: Psychoanalysis, Feminism and the Problem of Domination*. New York: Random House.

British Association for Counselling and Psychotherapy (BACP, 2002) *Ethical Framework for Good Practice in Counselling and Psychotherapy*. Rugby: BACP.

Broverman, I., Broverman, D., Clarkson, F., Rosenkrantz, P. and Vogel, S. (1970) Sex role stereotypes and clinical judgments of mental health. *Journal of Consulting and Clinical Psychology* 34, 1–7.

Brown, L. S. and Brodsky, A. M. (1992) The future of feminist therapy. *Psychotherapy* 29, 51–57.

Burstow, B. (1992) *Radical Feminist Therapy: Working in the Context of Violence*. Newbury Park, CA: Sage.

Cassidy, J. (1999) She was young, naïve – anorexic. Then she fell prey to a professor's 'caring' touch. *The Observer*, 13 June.

Chesler, P. (1989) *Women and Madness*, 2nd edn. San Diego, CA: Harcourt.

Chodorow, N. (1978) *The Reproduction of Mothering*. New Haven, CT: Yale University Press.

Chodorow, N. (1989) *Feminism and Psychoanalytic Theory*. New Haven, CT: Yale University Press.

Chodorow, N. (1996) Theoretical gender and clinical gender: epistemological reflections on the psychology of women. *Journal of the American Psychoanalytic Association* 44S, 215–238.

DeMause, L. (1976) The evolution of childhood. In L. DeMause (ed.) *The History of Childhood*. London: Souvenir Press.

Department of Health (1991) *Working Together Under the Children Act 1989: A Guide to Arrangements for Inter-Agency Co-operation for the Protection of Children from Abuse*. London: HMSO.

Department of Health and Social Security (DHSS, 1974) *Report of the Committee of Inquiry into the Care and Supervision Provided in Relation to Maria Colwell*. London: HMSO.

Dinnerstein, D. (1976) *The Mermaid and the Minotaur: Sexual Arrangements and Human Malaise*. New York: Harper and Row.

Driver, E. (1989) Positive action. In E. Driver (ed.) *Child Sexual Abuse: Feminist Perspectives*. London: Macmillan.

Eichenbaum, L. and Orbach, S. (1983) *Understanding Women: A Basic Feminist Psychoanalytic View*. New York: Basic Books.

Enns, C. Z. (1997) *Feminist Theories and Feminist Psychotherapies*. New York: Harrington Park Press.

Ernst, S. and Maguire, M. (eds) (1987) *Living with the Sphinx: Papers from the Women's Therapy Centre*. London: Women's Press.

Gilligan, C. (1982) *In a Different Voice*. Cambridge, MA: Harvard University Press.

Hall, L. and Lloyd, S. (1989) *Surviving Childhood Abuse*. Lewes: Falmer Press.

Heenan, M. C. (1998) Feminist object relations theory and therapy. In I. B. Seu and M. C. Heenan (eds) *Feminism and Psychotherapy: Reflections on Contemporary Theories and Practice*. London: Sage

Herman, J. L. (1981) *Father–Daughter Incest*. Cambridge, MA: Harvard University Press.

Herman, J. (1994) *Trauma and Recovery*. London: Pandora.

Juntunen, C. L., Atkinson, D. R., Reyes, C. and Gutierrez, M. (1994) Feminist identity and feminist therapy behaviours of women psychotherapists. *Psychotherapy* 31, 327–333.

McNaron, T. and Morgan, Y. (1982) *I Never Told Anyone*. London: Harper and Row.

Maguire, M. (1995) *Men, Women, Passion and Power: Gender Issues in Psychotherapy*. London: Routledge.

Malone J. L. (2000) Working with Aboriginal women: applying feminist therapy in a multicultural counselling context. *Canadian Journal of Counselling* 34, 1, 33–42

Marecek, J. and Kravetz, D. (1998) Power and agency in feminist therapy. In B. Seu and C. Heenan (eds) *Feminism and Psychotherapy*. London: Sage.

Middleton, N. (1971) *When Family Failed: The Treatment of Children in the Care of the Community During the First Half of the Twentieth Century*. London: Gollancz.

Mitchell, J. (1974) *Psychoanalysis and Feminism*. Harmondsworth: Penguin.

Moore, A. (1999) I was seduced by my counsellor. *You*, 9 May.

Rampage, C. (2002) Marriage in the 20th century: a feminist perspective. *Family Perspective* 41, 261–268.

Remer, P. and Oakley, D. (2005) Practice talk: working with multicultural clients' traditional gender-role attitudes and beliefs, part two. *The Feminist Psychologist* 32, 4, 12, 21.

Rhoden, J. L. (2003) Marital cohesion, flexibility and communication in the marriages of nontraditional and traditional women. *Family Journal: Counseling and Therapy for Couples and Families* 11, 3, 248–256.

Russell, J. (1993) *Out of Bounds: Sexual Exploitation in Counselling and Therapy*. London: Sage.

Rutter, P. (1990) *Sex in the Forbidden Zone*. London: Aquarius Press.

Sands, T. and Howard-Hamilton, M. (1995) Understanding depression among gifted adolescent females: feminist therapy strategies. *Roeper Review* 17, 3, 192–195.

Sesan, R. and Katzman, M. (1998) Empowerment and the eating-disordered client. In I. B. Seu and M. C. Heenan (eds) *Feminism and Psychotherapy: Reflections on Contemporary Theories and Practice*. London: Sage.

Showalter, E. (1987) *The Female Malady: Women, Madness and English Culture, 1830–1980*. London: Virago.

Spring, J. (1987) *Cry Hard and Swim*. London: Virago.

Strean, H. S. (1993) *Therapists Who Have Sex with their Patients: Treatment and Recovery*. New York: Brunner–Mazel.

The Times (1983) Report from the trial of Watson-Sweeney, Old Bailey, London, 19 December.

Walker, M. (1990) *Women in Therapy and Counselling: Out of the Shadows*. Maidenhead: Open University Press.

Walker, M. (1992) *Surviving Secrets: The Experience of Abuse for the Child, the Family and the Helper*. Maidenhead: Open University Press.

Walker, M. (2003) *Abuse: Questions and Answers for Counsellors and Therapists*. London: Whurr.

Walker, M. (2004) Supervising practitioners working with survivors of childhood abuse: counter transference, secondary traumatization and terror. *Psychodynamic Practice* 10, 2.

Williams, C. B. (1999) African American women, Afrocentrism and feminism: implications for therapy. *Women and Therapy* 22, 4, 1–16.

Worell, J. and Remer, P. (2003) *Feminist Perspectives in Therapy: Empowering Diverse Women*. New York: Wiley.

Zerbe, C. (2004) *Feminist Theories and Feminist Psychotherapies: Origins, Themes, and Diversity*. Philadelphia: Haworth Press.

Zimmerman, T. S. (2001) Introduction: barriers to and possibilities in balancing family and work. *Journal of Feminist Family Therapy* 13, 2/3, 1–2.

Chapter 16

Experiencing the edge

Ethical and unethical relationships with self and others in times of intense or enduring trauma

Lynne Gabriel

Introduction

This chapter considers the impact of personal and situational trauma on a practitioner's capacity for ethical relations with self and others. The author's personal experience of traumatic loss forms the basis for an exploration of self-harm and self-care. The chapter considers challenges, tensions and conflicts that can arise when working through intense emotional and psychological trauma. Different domains of experience – physical, relational, contextual, professional, ethical and spiritual – are introduced. Personal faith and beliefs and their potential to aid recovery are noted. Theory, practice and personal experience are interwoven to form a personal-professional narrative that highlights the complex and multidimensional nature of relational ethics and the challenges which helping practitioners face in relation to care of self in order that we might care for and facilitate others.

I became deeply disturbed after the sudden death of my 22-year-old son and found myself contemplating suicide – what some regard as the ultimate act of self-harm. That period of my life led me to discover the ways in which I denied myself adequate self-care and self-respect. With the love of a good therapist I was eventually able to develop a different relationship with myself. This evolved in a therapeutic relationship that was sustained over more than eight years and which increasingly brought my self-harming behaviours and relational patterns more clearly into my awareness. The work enabled me to understand the deeper emotional and psychological processes that can lead to self-harming and self-limiting patterns of behaving and relating. Now I live a full life and experience my robustness and warm personality in many good relationships with family, friends and colleagues, as well as in relationships with clients and supervisees. I have wondered about the impact on past and present clients of sharing my story and have chosen to do so in the knowledge that my process of recovery from traumatic loss has paradoxically strengthened and reshaped my personality and led to me becoming a more skilful and self-aware practitioner.

While today I am aware of my robustness and relational capacity, I recognise that in disclosing these personal details I am opening parts of my life and relationships that have until recently (Gabriel, 2007) remained in a private domain. In the spirit of generating debate on self-care and self-respect as factors central to one's capacity to develop an appropriate relational ethic, I chose to share some of my story. As well as recounting my personal experience, the chapter considers wider social and cultural aspects of harm that can be hidden from both self and others. In this context, self-harm, self-care and the notion of the *wounded healer* are regarded as existing on a continuum (Turp, 2003) that includes visible and hidden dimensions.

The wounded healer concept is noted in Wosket's chapter in this volume (Chapter 5) and issues of personal well-being are discussed in Dunnett's chapter (Chapter 10 of this volume) on practitioner self-care – these matters are central to explorations of one's capacity to work as a practitioner. Here, the notion of one's emotional wounds and how they might or do impact on well-being and relationships with self and others is significant in two key ways: if I am aware of my wounds, then I am more able to do something to address them; if I am not aware, then the potential exists for unintentional and unacknowledged harm to self and others. I recognise that there have been, and continue to be, debates on practitioner well-being and counsellor/therapist competence and how these can be demonstrated (for instance, through training and personal development, including personal therapy). While these are significant debates, my intention here is to focus more on personal experience of loss as a heuristic route through which to consider relational ethics and self-care. For a detailed exploration of predisposing factors and the impact of self-harm see Turp (2003). I begin with my near-death experience.

On the edge

My son, Simon, died on 8 November 1996. The morning after he died, I found myself looking out over the sea. I felt compelled to jump over the edge of the cliff beneath my feet, not wanting to stay in a world without my son. I stood for several minutes, perched on the edge of reason, the edge of the cliff, no part of me desiring to stay in this world. A voice – Simon? Someone else? – said, 'It's not your time, you must stay'. I reeled back from the edge.

After Simon's death, I paid little attention to my physical or emotional well-being and my body and mind faded. I peered into a black hole and entered an unfathomable void. My body became thin and my psyche and soul struggled. My capacity for self-care was damaged and the traumatic loss of Simon tapped into archaic and primitive defence measures. Prior to his death I had been a therapist for several years and had experienced being a client in person-centred therapy. My own practice was small as I had been studying for an MEd in counselling and human resource management and I had to withdraw from work. For a while, I was not capable of forming a good relational ethic with myself or with others. It is only in retrospect that I can appreciate that this period in my life and the associated processes of dissembling and reassembling of my psyche and myself played a central part in my development of a deeper capacity for self-care and self-love – thus ultimately making me fit to practise with others.

Retreating into self: the abyss

Manson and O'Neill (2007) claim that some concepts and experiences defy generic definition, requiring instead a specific description which differs according to context or situation. This notion of the generic and the specific can be applied to traumatic loss and self-harm. Arguably, there is a unique and individual nature to how one's self-harm may be described or understood. For example, in relation to my experience of Simon's sudden death, what I would call *situational self-harm* developed, whereby I was unable to provide myself with thoughtful care. What compounded this difficult situation was the tendency of others to 'tip-toe' around me, thus generating a relational vacuum out of which I found it difficult to exit. This and the relational experiences with self and others influence the dimensions set out below. In addition, they are informed by the work of Maggie Turp (2003), who has written insightfully about hidden self-harm.

Defining self-harm

An accessible description of self-harm is offered by Turp (2003). She suggests that self-harm exists on a continuum from 'normal' culturally acceptable forms of self-harming acts to 'abnormal' acts of harm to oneself. She sees *self-harm* as an umbrella term for behaviour:

- that results, whether by commission or omission, in avoidable physical harm to self
- that breaches the limits of acceptable behaviour, as they apply at the place and time of enactment, and hence elicits a strong emotional response.

Dimensions of harm: physiological

Most often the term 'self-harm' is used to denote actual bodily harm including: cutting, head-banging, burning, scratching or picking at flesh. These are visible forms of self-harm. Trauma (sexual, physical, psychological) can result in later physical self-harm (Turp, 2003). My own experience of traumatic loss led to 'hidden' self-harming behaviours including not eating and withdrawing from contact with others.

There are other hidden ways in which we might damage ourselves. For example, I used smoking as a means both to liberate myself from anxiety and to mediate between conflicting intrapsychic dynamics. Overworking was another way of dampening anxiety and distress and dulling my capacity to relate to self and others. While these might seem less harmful than more obvious physical and visible forms of self-harm, their impact is nonetheless invidious and insidious, spreading into all aspects of life and undermining relationships with self and others.

Dimensions of harm: relational

Key issues
- Disturbed self-concept and low self-esteem (including self-loathing).
- Disturbances in capacity for 'appropriate' attunement with and attachment to significant others.
- Difficulty in developing and maintaining psychological contact with self and others.
- Processess of dissembling and reassembling self.

(Source: derived from Shneidman, 1993)

Attachment theory suggests that an individual's self-concept and capacity to sustain meaningful, reciprocal and intimate relating can be impaired through difficult formative relationships with significant caregivers. Self-harming tendencies might develop from these early attachment disorders or relational disruptions. Whatever the type of self-harm, whether hidden or visible, the impetus for self-harming behaviour can be explored within the context of the 'good enough' (Winnicott, 1960) therapy relationship that provides a 'safe space' (Bowlby, 1983, 1989) for intricate and intimate exploring of the self and of one's capacity for relationships with others. A sound working alliance (Bordin, 1979, 1994) is essential, as destructive intrapsychic forces can generate dissonance, difficulty in mediating relational conflict (both internal and external) and ongoing self-harming behaviour – all of which can impinge on the client–therapist relationship and work and the therapist's capacity to facilitate the development of a good relational ethic. The working relationship can be long, as recovering from self-destructive tendencies and discovering ways of being that are self-caring can be a long-term venture. Certainly, profound change can occur through the relational space created in the client–therapist relationship. That said, reparative work can be undertaken by the client in a range of settings other than the one-to-one contracted therapy context.

Different therapy approaches offer alternative perspectives on the sources or root of the disturbances to the individual and their relationships with self and others. The psychoanalytical paradigm offers a rich spectrum of therapeutic theory and practice. For example, Freud, Winnicott, Klein, Jung and Bowlby provide theories that can offer resources on healthy and harmful relating to self and other. In addition, Shneidman's (1993) notion of *dissembling and reassembling self*, resonant with Winnicott's (1960) notion of *continuity of being*, provides rich material from the psychoanalytical and psychodynamic domain. The metaphor of the fragmented self and the reformulation of self as a surviving and sentient being are potent ideas that appear in life, arts and literature, so it is no surprise that they feature in therapy literature.

Dimensions of harm: ethical and professional practice

Depending upon our professional role and affiliated professional body, as a practitioner we will work to a set of ethical principles to inform our helping role and practice. For example, the British Association for Counselling and Psychotherapy's Ethical Framework for Good Practice (2002) is a comprehensive set of values, principles and pointers for ethical practice. These pointers, however, need to be embedded and embodied in the relational domain occupied by the client and therapist.

So, each practitioner must develop their own *relational ethic* for helping work and relationships (see Gabriel, Chapter 2, for further reading). By this, I am not suggesting it is strictly within the therapist's remit to develop a relational ethic – at best it becomes a collaborative and reciprocal venture involving both therapist and client. It goes without saying that in a therapist role the ways in which we perceive a client and the origins of their self-harm will depend upon our theoretical approach, as will the ways in which we work and the degree to which we work collaboratively with a client towards changing self-harming attitudes and actions. My own approach draws on person-centred principles that value congruence, respect and acceptance and is resourced by ideas from a range of psychodynamic (particularly attachment theory), feminist and constructionist concepts (influenced in particular by Kenneth Gergen). As someone also trained in Egan's solution-focused 'skilled helper model', I value the capacity to flex my approach to fit the client's needs. However, this capacity to 'flex' within the context of client work and relationships demands a good degree of fitness to practise. For example, where my capacity to work ethically and effectively is impaired, then relationships with clients will be compromised. My relational ethic leads me to maintain access to good personal therapy, as well as contact with colleagues interested in relationship ethics – all of which supports keeping a 'watchful eye' on oneself.

Dimensions of harm: cultural and social harbingers of healing

When considering the issue of self-harm and capacity for self-care, we cannot ignore the contexts in which we live, relate and work. Nor can we ignore the wider social, cultural mores and norms that influence and sometimes impinge upon our ability to care for self and others. Not only do we have the mores of our social and familial groupings, we also have those of our professional bodies and affiliated groups. As practitioners, we might harbour unrealistic self-expectations and deny our limitations. In addition, actual and perceived expectations of our professional associations and wider social and cultural groups may render us silent. To acknowledge oneself in a public domain as a 'wounded healer' can intimidate and silence, thus sadly perpetuating an unhelpful myth that those who offer themselves as facilitators of others' healing or development are themselves fully and forever 'healed'.

Finding faith

Wary of sharing information about my deep distress and spiritual searching that took place after the death of my son, I erred on the side of caution and kept counsel to contexts that I saw as 'appropriate' and 'safe' (including personal therapy and supervision). Although I am a deeply spiritual person, I do not follow a Christian path and am more attuned to the notion of honouring the earth and our cosmos, without necessarily following a deity or god. For several years prior to my son's death I was interested in early forms of personal and communal faith, including pagan and shamanic practices of indigenous Europeans. These explorations and developing beliefs were a lifeline in the immediate aftermath of Simon's death. My sense of faith and spiritual beliefs continue to evolve and I am thankful that I live in a country and community that recognises and encourages diverse life and faith positions.

Returning from the edge

I gradually became aware of ways of not just surviving Simon but of being in the world in a way that respected my relationship with him and enabled me to move on in life. The narrative flow of this chapter belies the deeply disturbing, fragmented and distressing journey it took to reach a point of wanting to be alive in the world. That journey included crossing the dimensions identified in the chapter.

The process of healing from traumatic loss and moving from self-harming to self-caring occurred over a number of years. Reflecting on those years, I recognise phases of varying degrees of emotional and relational intensity and of a developing capacity for proximity to self and others. The rebuilding of my soul and psyche and my return to self and others signalled a new phase in my life – one that truly symbolised a return from the edge.

Returning from the edge

Coming back
            to self and others
                        reaching in, reaching out
                                    struggling, flying
                pity, pain, passion
            damaged wings
desparate dives
      searing hopes
            soaring pyches
                  new pathways in the soul
                              bitter-sweet breaths of life . . . breathe on . . .

References

Bordin, E. S. (1979) The generalizability of the psychoanalytic concept of the working alliance. *Psychotherapy: Theory, Research and Practice* 16, 252–260.

Bordin, E. S. (1994) Theory and research on the therapeutic working alliance: new directions. In A. O. Horvath and L. Greenberg (eds) *The Working Alliance: Theory, Research, and Practice*. New York: Wiley.

Bowlby, J. (1983) *A Secure Base: Clinical Applications of Attachment Theory*. London: Routledge.

Bowlby, J. (1989) *The Making and Breaking of Affectional Bonds*. London: Routledge.

British Association for Counselling and Psychotherapy (BACP, 2002) *Ethical Framework for Good Practice in Counselling and Psychotherapy*. Rugby: BACP.

Gabriel, L. (2007). *Boundary riders, process sentinels and ethics warriors.* Keynote and workshop materials presented at a conference on self-harm at Warwick University, May.

Manson, N. C. and O'Neill, O. (2007) *Rethinking Informed Consent in Bioethics*. Cambridge: Cambridge University Press.

Shneidman, E. (1993) *Suicide as Psychache*. Northvale, NJ: Jason Aronson.

Turp, M. (2003) *Hidden Self-Harm: Narratives from Psychotherapy*. London: Jessica Kingsley Publishers.

Winnicott, D. W. (1960) Ego distortion in terms of true and false self. In D. W. Winnicott *The Maturational Processes and the Facilitating Environment*. London: Hogarth Press.

Endnote

We hope that you have enjoyed reading this text and that you find it has a variety of uses to inform and encourage others to broaden their thinking on relational ethics. Contrary to popular opinion, rather than occupying a dry and dusty spot on the shelves, ethics is actually a creative, engaging and enlivening field. We anticipate that readers will find themselves prompted to further explore ethics and to formulate their own relational ethic.

Finally, we want to acknowledge the excellent contributions of our chapter authors, whose work brings this text alive for a diverse audience of practitioners from across the helping professions and psychological therapies.

Lynne Gabriel and Roger Casemore
October 2008

Index